Multi Agent Systems - Strategies and Applications

Edited by Ricardo López - Ruiz

Published in London, United Kingdom

IntechOpen

Supporting open minds since 2005

Multi Agent Systems - Strategies and Applications
http://dx.doi.org/10.5772/intechopen.81766
Edited by Ricardo López - Ruiz

Contributors
Punnarumol Temdee, Adesegun Titus, Satheeshkumar G S, Tamil Selvi S, Muhammad Waseem Khan, Jie Wang, Linyun Xiong, Sunhua Huang, Chengzhi Yuan, Xiaonan Dong, Paolo Stegagno, Wei Zeng, Leo Raju, Antony Amalraj Morais, Alexandre Zamberlan, Rafael Bordini, Solange Fagan, Guilherme Kurtz, Mehmet Serdar Guzel, Ümit Ulusoy, Erkan Bostanci, Nadia Kanwal, Metehan Aydın

First published in London, United Kingdom, 2020 by IntechOpen
IntechOpen is the global imprint of INTECHOPEN LIMITED, registered in England and Wales, registration number: 11086078, 7th floor, 10 Lower Thames Street, London, EC3R 6AF, United Kingdom
Printed in Croatia

British Library Cataloguing-in-Publication Data
A catalogue record for this book is available from the British Library

Additional hard and PDF copies can be obtained from orders@intechopen.com

Multi Agent Systems - Strategies and Applications
Edited by Ricardo López - Ruiz
p. cm.
Print ISBN 978-1-78984-488-7
Online ISBN 978-1-78984-489-4
eBook (PDF) ISBN 978-1-78985-394-0

An electronic version of this book is freely available, thanks to the support of libraries working with Knowledge Unlatched. KU is a collaborative initiative designed to make high quality books Open Access for the public good. More information about the initiative and links to the Open Access version can be found at www.knowledgeunlatched.org

For EU product safety concerns:
IN TECH d.o.o., Prolaz Marije Krucifikse Kozulić 3, 51000 Rijeka, Croatia, info@intechopen.com or visit our website at intechopen.com.

Meet the editor

Ricardo López-Ruiz, M.S., Ph.D., works as an Associate Professor in the Department of Computer Science and Systems Engineering, Faculty of Science, University of Zaragoza, Spain. He also serves as an associate researcher in Complex Systems at the School of Mathematics, University of Zaragoza. He also worked as a Lecturer at the University of Navarra, the Public University of Navarra and the UNED of Calatayud. He completed his postdoctorate sturdies with Prof. Yves Pomeau at the École Normale Supérieure of Paris and with Prof. Gabriel Mindlin at the University of Buenos Aires. His areas of interest include statistical complexity and nonlinear models, chaotic maps and applications, multi-agent systems, and econo-physics.

Contents

Preface

Research on multi-agent systems is enlarging our technical future capabilities as humans and as an intelligent society. During recent years many effective applications have been implemented and are part of our daily life. These applications have agent-based models and methods as an important ingredient. Markets, finance world, robotics, medical technology, social negotiation, video games, big-data science, etc. are some of the branches where the knowledge gained through multi-agent simulations is necessary and where new software engineering tools are continuously created and tested in order to reach an effective technology transfer to impact our lives.

This book brings together researchers working in several fields that cover the techniques, the challenges and the applications of multi-agent systems in a wide variety of aspects related to learning algorithms for different devices such as vehicles, robots and drones, computational optimization to reach a more efficient energy distribution in power grids and the use of social networks and decision strategies applied to the smart learning and education environments in emergent countries. We hope that this book can be useful and become a guide or reference to an audience interested in the developments and applications of multi-agent systems.

The first section of the book presents different techniques and algorithms applied to multi-agent systems formed by vehicles, drones, robots and nano-objects. In Chapter 1, Dong et al. propose a control algorithm to estimate the nonlinear dynamics of a group of homogeneous unicycle-type vehicles. In Chapter 2, Bostanciet al. explain how 3D data acquisition can be handled using a multi-agent drone system. In Chapter 3, Guzel et al. study some popular machine-learning algorithms applied to sets of robots competing in a 2D simulator. The last chapter of this first section, Chapter 4 by Zamberlan et al., presents how multi-agent systems techniques can be useful to simulate moving objects in nanoscience.

The second section of the book addresses the question of improvement and optimization of grid systems for the electric energy distribution. In Chapter 5, Satheesh Kumar and Tamil Selvi study the effective demand-side management in the smart grid operating the power system. In Chapter 6, Khan et al. discuss optimal procedures of the microgrid energy supervision and power distribution system. The last chapter of this second section, Chapter 7 by Raju and Morais, presents a method of using a multi-agent system to control the microgrid operation in a smart microgrid for effective energy administration.

The last section of the book highlights the use of social networks and decision strategies for the smart learning and to enhance the education methodology in emergent countries. In Chapter 8, Temdee uncovers some machine-learning techniques to be used in smart learning environments. In Chapter 9, Adesegun suggests the adoption of new technologies as a significant contribution to the educational development and social transformation of emergent countries.

As the editor of this book, I would like to thank all the authors who have contributed to this volume as well as the reviewers for their assessment. Also, I must express my gratitude to the IntechOpen Editorial Staff for their invitation to be editor for this fourth time and that, with the particular help of Ms. Jasna Bozic, the Author Service Manager, we have arrived to convert in this new IntechOpen/Knowledge Unlatched book. Finally, at this moment where the human life is imprisoned by the coronavirus around the whole world, I want to thank my family members, especially my siblings, uncles, cousins and nephews for their support. Of course, all my friends and advisors are not forgotten in this dedicatory final paragraph.

Ricardo López-Ruiz
University of Zaragoza,
Spain

Section 1

Multi-Agent Systems Applied to Devices

Chapter 1

Cooperative Adaptive Learning Control for a Group of Nonholonomic UGVs by Output Feedback

Xiaonan Dong, Paolo Stegagno, Chengzhi Yuan and Wei Zeng

Abstract

A high-gain observer-based cooperative deterministic learning (CDL) control algorithm is proposed in this chapter for a group of identical unicycle-type unmanned ground vehicles (UGVs) to track over desired reference trajectories. For the vehicle states, the positions of the vehicles can be measured, while the velocities are estimated using the high-gain observer. For the trajectory tracking controller, the radial basis function (RBF) neural network (NN) is used to online estimate the unknown dynamics of the vehicle, and the NN weight convergence and estimation accuracy is guaranteed by CDL. The major challenge and novelty of this chapter is to track the reference trajectory using this observer-based CDL algorithm without the full knowledge of the vehicle state and vehicle model. In addition, any vehicle in the system is able to learn the knowledge of unmodeled dynamics along the union of trajectories experienced by all vehicle agents, such that the learned knowledge can be re-used to follow any reference trajectory defined in the learning phase. The learning-based tracking convergence and consensus learning results, as well as using learned knowledge for tracking experienced trajectories, are shown using the Lyapunov method. Simulation is given to show the effectiveness of this algorithm.

Keywords: cooperative control, deterministic learning, neural network, multi-agent systems, distributed adaptive learning and control, unmanned ground vehicles

1. Introduction

The two-wheel-driven, unicycle-type vehicle is one of the most common mobile robot platforms, and many research results have been published regarding this system [1–4]. There are two major challenges for controlling this system: the knowledge of all state variables, and the actuate modeling of the system. For the unicycle-type vehicle that we use in this chapter, the vehicle position and velocity are both required for the trajectory tracking control. The position of the vehicle can be obtained using cameras or GPS signals, while direct measurement of the vehicle velocity is difficult. State observer has been proposed to estimate the full state of the system using the measured signals [5, 6], however, traditional observers require the knowledge of the system model for accurate state estimations. High-gain observer has been proposed to estimate the unmeasured state variables in case that the system model is not fully known to the observer, and the estimated states can be used for control purposes [7–10]. In this chapter, we follow the standard high-gain observer design method [8] to obtain the estimation of vehicle velocity using the measured vehicle position.

For the second challenge, adaptive control has been introduced to deal with system uncertainties [11, 12], in which neural network (NN) based control is able to further deal with nonlinear system uncertainties [13, 11]. Though tracking control can be achieved by NN-based adaptive control, however, traditional NN-based control methods failed to achieve parameter (NN weight) convergence. This shortage requires the controller to update the system parameter (NN weight) all the time when the controller is operating, which is time consuming and computational demanding. To overcome this deficiency, a deterministic learning (DL) method has been proposed to model the system uncertainties under the partial persistency of excitation (PE) condition [14]. To be more specific, it has been shown that the system uncertainties can be accurately modeled with a sufficient large number of radial basis function (RBF) NNs, and local NN weights online updated by DL will converge to their optimal values, provided that the input signal of the RBFNNs is recurrent.

Since the RBFNN estimation is locally accurate around the recurrent trajectory, this becomes a disadvantage when there exists multiple tracking tasks. The learned knowledge of the system uncertainties, presented by the RBFNNs, cannot be directly applied on a different control task, and it will need a significant amount of storage space for a large number of different tasks. In recent years, distributed control is a rising topic regarding the control of multiple coordinated agents [15–20]. In this chapter, we took the idea of communicating inside the multi-agent system (MAS) and apply it on DL, such that in the learning phase, any vehicle in the MAS is able to learn the unmodeled dynamics not only along its own trajectory, but along the trajectories of all other vehicle agents in this MAS as well. In other words, the NN weight of any vehicle in this MAS will converge to a common constant, which presents the unmodeled dynamics along the union trajectory of all vehicles, and any vehicle in the MAS is able to use this knowledge to achieve trajectory tracking for any control task learned in the learning phase.

The main contributions of this chapter are summarized as follows.

i. A high-gain observer is introduced to estimate the vehicle velocities using the measurement of vehicle position.

ii. An observer and RBFNN-based adaptive learning control algorithm is developed for a multi-vehicle system, such that each vehicle agent will be able to follow the desired reference trajectory.

iii. An online cooperative adaptive NN learning law is proposed, such that the RBFNN weight of all vehicle agents will converge to one common value, which represents the unmodeled dynamics of the vehicle along the union trajectories experienced by all vehicle agents.

iv. An observer and experience-based controller is developed using the common NN model obtained from the learning phase, such that vehicles are able to follow the reference trajectory experienced by any vehicle before with improved control performance.

In the following sections, we briefly describe some preliminaries on graph theory and RBFNNs based DL method, then present the vehicle dynamics and the problem statement, all in Section 2. The main results of this chapter, including the high-gain observer design, CDL-based trajectory tracking control, accurate cooperative learning using RBF NNs, and experience-based trajectory tracking control, are provided in Section 3, respectively. Simulation results of an example with four vehicles running three different tasks are provided in Section 4. The conclusions are drawn in Section 5.

Notations. $\mathbb{R}$, $\mathbb{R}_+$ and $\mathbb{Z}_+$ denote, respectively, the set of real numbers, the set of positive real numbers and the set of positive integers; $\mathbb{R}^{m\times n}$ denotes the set of $m \times n$ real matrices; $\mathbb{R}^n$ denotes the set of $n \times 1$ real column vectors; I_n denotes the $n \times n$ identity matrix; $O_{m\times n}$ denotes the zero matrix with dimension of $m \times n$; Subscript $(\cdot)_k$ denotes the kth column vector of a matrix; $|\cdot|$ is the absolute value of a real number, and $\|\cdot\|$ is the 2-norm of a vector or a matrix, i.e., $\|x\| = (x^T x)^{\frac{1}{2}}$; $\dot{z}$ denotes the total derivative of z with respect to the time; $\partial/\partial\mathbf{z}$ denotes the Jacobian matrix as $\frac{\partial}{\partial\mathbf{z}} = \left[\frac{\partial}{\partial z_1} \cdots \frac{\partial}{\partial z_n}\right]$.

2. Preliminaries and problem statement

2.1 Graph theory

In a graph defined as $\mathcal{G} = (\mathcal{V}, \varepsilon, \mathcal{A})$, the elements of $\mathcal{V} = \{1, 2, ..., n\}$ are called vertices, the elements of ε are pairs (i,j) with $i, j \in \mathcal{V}, i \neq j$ called edges, and the matrix $\mathcal{A}$ is called the adjacency matrix. If $(i,j) \in \varepsilon$, then agent i is able to receive information from agent j, and agent i and j are called adjacent. The adjacency matrix is thus defined as $\mathcal{A} = [a_{ij}]_{n\times n}$, in which $a_{ij}>0$ if and only if $(i,j) \in \varepsilon$, and $a_{ij} = 0$ otherwise. For any two nodes $v_i, v_j \in \mathcal{V}$, if there exists a path between them, then the graph $\mathcal{G}$ is called connected. Furthermore, the graph $\mathcal{G}$ is called fixed if ε and $\mathcal{A}$ do not change over time, and called undirected if $\forall(i,j) \in \varepsilon$, pair (j, i) is also in ε. According to [21], for the Laplacian matrix $L = [l_{ij}]_{n\times n}$ associated with the undirected graph $\mathcal{G}$, in which $l_{ij} = \begin{pmatrix} \sum_{j=1, j\neq i}^{n} a_{ij} & i = j \\ -a_{ij} & i \neq j \end{pmatrix}$. If the graph is connected, then L is a positive semi-definite symmetric matrix, with one zero eigenvalue and all other eigenvalues being positive and hence, $\text{rank}(L) \leq n - 1$.

2.2 Localized RBF neural networks and deterministic learning

The RBF networks can be described by $f_{nn}(Z) = \sum_{i=1}^{Nn} w_i s_i(Z) = W^T S(Z)$ [22], where $Z \in \Omega_Z \subset \mathbb{R}^q$ is the input vector, $W = [w_1, \cdots, w_{N_n}]^T \in \mathbb{R}^{N_n}$ is the weight vector, N_n is the NN node number, and $S(Z) = [s_1(\|Z - \mu_1\|), \cdots, s_{N_n}(\|Z - \mu_{N_n}\|)]^T$, with $s_i(\cdot)$ being a radial basis function, and μ_i $(i = 1, 2, \cdots, N_n)$ being distinct points in state space. The Gaussian function $s_i(\|Z - \mu_i\|) = \exp\left[\frac{-(Z-\mu_i)^T(Z-\mu_i)}{\sigma^2}\right]$ is one of the most commonly used radial basis functions, where $\mu_i = [\mu_{i1}, \mu_{i2}, \cdots, \mu_{iq}]^T$ is the center of the receptive field and σ_i is the width of the receptive field. The Gaussian function belongs to the class of localized RBFs in the sense that $s_i(\|Z - \mu_i\|) \to 0$ as $\|Z\| \to \infty$. It is easily seen that $S(Z)$ is bounded and there exists a real constant $S_M \in \mathbb{R}_+$ such that $\|S(Z)\| \leq S_M$ [14].

It has been shown in [22, 23] that for any continuous function $f(Z) : \Omega_Z \to \mathbb{R}$ where $\Omega_Z \subset \mathbb{R}^q$ is a compact set, and for the NN approximator, where the node number N_n is sufficiently large, there exists an ideal constant weight vector W^*, such that for any $\epsilon^*>0, f(Z) = W^{*T}S(Z) + \epsilon, \forall Z \in \Omega_Z$, where $|\epsilon| < \epsilon^*$ is the ideal approximation error. The ideal weight vector W^* is an "artificial" quantity required for analysis, and is defined as the value of W that minimizes $|\epsilon|$ for all $Z \in \Omega_Z \subset \mathbb{R}^q$, i.e., $W^* := \text{argmin}_{W \in \mathbb{R}^{N_n}} \left\{ \sup_{Z \in \Omega_Z} |f(Z) - W^T S(Z)| \right\}$. Moreover, based on the localization property of RBF NNs [14], for any bounded trajectory $Z(t)$ within the compact set $\Omega_Z, f(Z)$ can be approximated by using a limited number of neurons located in a local region along the trajectory: $f(Z) = W_\zeta^{*T} S_\zeta(Z) + \epsilon_\zeta$, where ϵ_ζ is the approximation error, with $\epsilon_\zeta = O(\epsilon) = O(\epsilon^*)$, $S_\zeta(Z) = \left[s_{j1}(Z), \cdots, s_{j\zeta}(Z)\right]^T \in \mathbb{R}^{N_\zeta}$, $W_\zeta^* = \left[w_{j1}^*, \cdots, w_{j\zeta}^*\right]^T \in \mathbb{R}^{N_\zeta}$, $N_\zeta < N_n$, and the integers $j_i = j_1, \cdots, j_\zeta$ are defined by $|s_{j_i}(Z_p)| > \theta$ ($\theta > 0$ is a small positive constant) for some $Z_p \in Z(k)$.

It is shown in [14] that for a localized RBF network $W^T S(Z)$ whose centers are placed on a regular lattice, almost any recurrent trajectory $Z(k)$ (see [14] for detailed definition of "recurrent" trajectories) can lead to the satisfaction of the PE condition of the regressor subvector $S_\zeta(Z)$. This result is recalled in the following Lemma.

Lemma 1 [14, 24]. *Consider any recurrent trajectory $Z(k)$: $\mathbb{Z}_+ \rightarrow \mathbb{R}^q$. $Z(k)$ remains in a bounded compact set $\Omega_Z \subset \mathbb{R}^q$, then for RBF network $W^T S(Z)$ with centers placed on a regular lattice (large enough to cover compact set Ω_Z), the regressor subvector $S_\zeta(Z)$ consisting of RBFs with centers located in a small neighborhood of $Z(k)$ is persistently exciting.*

2.3 Vehicle model and problem statement

As shown in **Figure 1**, this unicycle-type vehicle is a nonholonomic system, with the constraint force preventing the vehicle from sliding along the axis of the actuated wheels. The nonholonomic constraint can be presented as follows

$$A^T(\mathbf{q}_i)\dot{\mathbf{q}}_i = 0 \tag{1}$$

in which $A(\mathbf{q}_i) = [\sin\theta_i \quad -\cos\theta_i \quad 0]^T$, and $\mathbf{q}_i = [x_i \quad y_i \quad \theta_i]^T$ is the general coordinates of the ith vehicle ($i = 1, 2, \ldots, n$, with n being the number of vehicles in

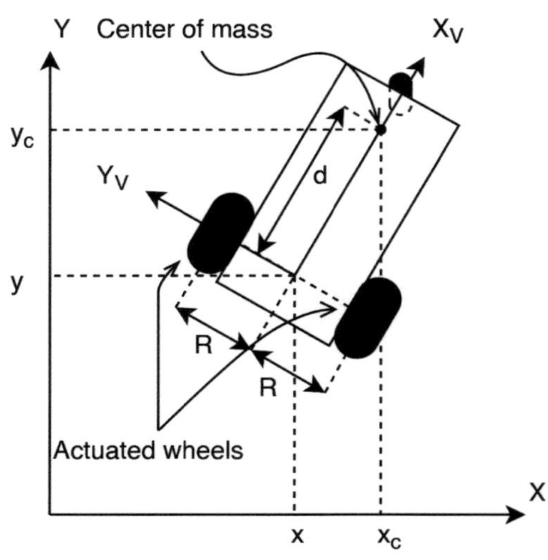

Figure 1.
A unicycle-type vehicle.

the MAS). (x_i, y_i) and θ_i denote the position and orientation of the vehicle with respect to the ground coordinate, respectively.

With this constraint, the degree of freedom of the system is reduced to two. Independently driven by the two actuated wheels on each side of the vehicle, the non-slippery kinematics of the ith vehicle is

$$\dot{\mathbf{q}}_i = \begin{bmatrix} \dot{x}_i \\ \dot{y}_i \\ \dot{\theta}_i \end{bmatrix} = \begin{bmatrix} \cos\theta_i & 0 \\ \sin\theta_i & 0 \\ 0 & 1 \end{bmatrix} \begin{bmatrix} v_i \\ \omega_i \end{bmatrix} \stackrel{\text{def}}{=} J(\mathbf{q}_i)\mathbf{u}_i \tag{2}$$

where v_i and ω_i are the linear and angular velocities measured at the center between the driving wheels, respectively. The dynamics of the ith vehicle can be described by [25].

$$M(\mathbf{q}_i)\ddot{\mathbf{q}}_i + C(\mathbf{q}_i, \dot{\mathbf{q}}_i)\dot{\mathbf{q}}_i + F(\mathbf{q}_i, \dot{\mathbf{q}}_i) + G(\mathbf{q}_i) = B(\mathbf{q}_i)\tau_i + A(\mathbf{q}_i)\lambda_i, \tag{3}$$

in which $M \in \mathbb{R}^{3\times3}$ is a positive definite matrix that denotes the inertia, $C \in \mathbb{R}^{3\times3}$ is the centripetal and Coriolis matrix, $F \in \mathbb{R}^{3\times1}$ is the friction vector, $G \in \mathbb{R}^{3\times1}$ is the gravity vector. $\tau_i \in \mathbb{R}^{2\times1}$ is a vector of system input, i.e., the torque applied on each driving wheel, $B = \frac{1}{r}\begin{bmatrix} \cos\theta_i & \cos\theta_i \\ \sin\theta_i & \sin\theta_i \\ R & -R \end{bmatrix} \in \mathbb{R}^{3\times2}$ is the input transformation matrix, projecting the system input τ onto the space spanned by (x, y, θ), in which $D = 2R$ is the distance between two actuation wheels, and r is the radius of the wheel. λ_i is a Lagrange multiplier, and $A\lambda_i \in \mathbb{R}^{3\times1}$ denotes the constraint force.

Matrices M and C in Eq. (3) can be derived using the Lagrangian equation with the follow steps. First we calculate the kinetic energy for the ith vehicle agent

$$T_i = \frac{m\left(\dot{x}_{ic}^2 + \dot{y}_{ic}^2\right)}{2} + \frac{I\dot{\theta}_{ic}^2}{2} \tag{4}$$

where m is the mass of the vehicle, I is the moment of inertia measured at the center of mass, x_{ic}, y_{ic}, and θ_{ic} are the position and orientation of the vehicle at the center of mass, respectively. The following relation can be obtained from **Figure 1**:

$$\begin{cases} x_{ic} = x_i + d\cos\theta_i \\ y_{ic} = y_i + d\sin\theta_i \\ \theta_{ic} = \theta_i \end{cases}, \begin{cases} \dot{x}_{ic} = \dot{x}_i - d\dot{\theta}\sin\theta_i \\ \dot{y}_{ic} = \dot{y}_i + d\dot{\theta}\cos\theta_i \\ \dot{\theta}_{ic} == \dot{\theta}_i \end{cases} \tag{5}$$

Then Eq. (4) can be rewritten into

$$\begin{aligned} T(\mathbf{q}_i, \dot{\mathbf{q}}_i) &= \frac{m\left[\left(\dot{x}_i - d\dot{\theta}\sin\theta_i\right)^2 + \left(\dot{y}_i + d\dot{\theta}\cos\theta_i\right)^2\right]}{2} + \frac{I\dot{\theta}_i^2}{2} \\ &= \frac{1}{2}\left[m\dot{x}_i^2 + m\dot{y}_i^2 + \left(md^2 + I\right)\dot{\theta}^2 - 2md\sin\theta\dot{x}_i\dot{\theta}_i + 2md\cos\theta\dot{y}_i\dot{\theta}_i\right] \\ &= \frac{\dot{\mathbf{q}}_i^T M(\mathbf{q}_i)\dot{\mathbf{q}}_i}{2} \end{aligned} \tag{6}$$

in which $M = \begin{bmatrix} m & 0 & -md\sin\theta_i \\ 0 & m & md\cos\theta_i \\ -md\sin\theta_i & md\cos\theta_i & md^2 + I \end{bmatrix}$. It will be shown later that the inertia matrix M shown above is identical to that in Eq. (3). Then the dynamics equation of the system is given by the following Lagrangian equation [26],

$$\frac{\mathrm{d}}{\mathrm{d}t}\left(\frac{\partial L}{\partial \dot{\mathbf{q}}_i}\right)^T - \left(\frac{\partial L}{\partial \mathbf{q}_i}\right)^T = A(\mathbf{q}_i)\lambda_i + \mathbf{Q}_i \tag{7}$$

in which $L(\mathbf{q}_i, \dot{\mathbf{q}}_i) = T(\mathbf{q}_i, \dot{\mathbf{q}}_i) - U(\mathbf{q}_i)$ is the Lagrangian of the ith vehicle, $U(\mathbf{q}_i)$ is the potential energy of the vehicle agent, $\lambda \in \mathbb{R}^{k\times 1}$ is the Lagrangian multiplier, and $A^T\lambda$ is the constraint force. $\mathbf{Q}_i = B(\mathbf{q}_i)[\tau_i - \mathbf{f}(\mathbf{u}_i)]$ denotes the external force, where τ_i is the force generated by the actuator, and $\mathbf{f}(\mathbf{u}_i)$ is the friction on the actuator. Then Eq. (7) can be rewritten into

$$M(\mathbf{q}_i)\ddot{\mathbf{q}}_i + \dot{M}\dot{\mathbf{q}}_i - \left(\frac{\partial T_i}{\partial \mathbf{q}_i}\right)^T + \left(\frac{\partial U_i}{\partial \mathbf{q}_i}\right)^T + B(\mathbf{q}_i)\mathbf{f}(\dot{\mathbf{q}}_i) = A(\mathbf{q}_i)\lambda_i + B(\mathbf{q}_i)\tau_i \tag{8}$$

By setting $C(\mathbf{q}_i, \dot{\mathbf{q}}_i)\dot{\mathbf{q}}_i = \dot{M}\dot{\mathbf{q}}_i - \left(\frac{\partial T_i}{\partial \mathbf{q}_i}\right)^T$, $F(\mathbf{q}_i, \dot{\mathbf{q}}_i) = B(\mathbf{q}_i)\mathbf{f}(\dot{\mathbf{q}}_i)$, and $G(\mathbf{q}_i) = \left(\frac{\partial U_i}{\partial \mathbf{q}_i}\right)^T$, Eq. (8) can be thereby transferred into Eq. (3). Notice that the form of $C_{n\times n}$ is not unique, however, with a proper definition of the matrix C, we will have $\dot{M} - 2C$ to be skew-symmetric. The $(i,j)^{\text{th}}$ entry of C is defined as follows [26].

$$c_{ij} = \sum_{k=1}^{n} c_{ijk}\dot{q}_k \tag{9}$$

where $\dot{q}_k$ is the kth entry of $\dot{\mathbf{q}}$, and $c_{ijk} = \frac{1}{2}\left(\frac{\partial m_{ij}}{\partial q_k} + \frac{\partial m_{ik}}{\partial q_j} - \frac{\partial m_{jk}}{\partial q_i}\right)$ is defined using the Christoffel symbols of the first kind. Then we have the centripetal and Coriolis matrix calculated as $C = \begin{bmatrix} 0 & 0 & -md\dot{\theta}_i\cos\theta_i \\ 0 & 0 & -md\dot{\theta}_i\sin\theta_i \\ 0 & 0 & 0 \end{bmatrix}$. Since the vehicle is operating on the ground, the gravity vector G is equal to zero. The friction vector F is assumed to be a nonlinear function of the general velocity $\mathbf{u}_i$, and is unknown to the controller.

To eliminate the nonholonomic constraint force $A(\mathbf{q}_i)\lambda_i$ from Eq. (3), we left multiplying $J^T(\mathbf{q}_i)$ to the equation, it yields:

$$J^TMJ\dot{\mathbf{u}}_i + J^T(M\dot{J} + CJ)\mathbf{u}_i + J^TF + J^TG = J^TB\tau_i + J^TA\lambda_i \tag{10}$$

From Eqs. (1) and (2), we have $J^TA = \mathbf{0}_{2\times 1}$, then the dynamic equation of $\mathbf{u}_i$ is simplified as

$$\overline{M}(\mathbf{q}_i)\dot{\mathbf{u}}_i + \overline{C}(\mathbf{u}_i)\mathbf{u}_i + \overline{F}(\mathbf{u}_i) + \overline{G}(\mathbf{q}_i) = \overline{\tau}_i, \tag{11}$$

where

$$\overline{M} = J^T M J = \begin{bmatrix} m & 0 \\ 0 & md^2 + I \end{bmatrix}, \quad \overline{C} = J^T (M\dot{J} + CJ) = \begin{bmatrix} 0 & -md\dot{\theta}_i \\ md\dot{\theta}_i & 0 \end{bmatrix},$$

$$\overline{F} = J^T F, \quad \overline{G} = J^T G = \mathbf{0}_{2\times1}, \quad \overline{\tau}_i = \begin{bmatrix} \overline{\tau}_{vi} \\ \overline{\tau}_{\omega i} \end{bmatrix} = J^T B \tau_i = \begin{bmatrix} 1/r & 1/r \\ R/r & -R/r \end{bmatrix} \tau_i.$$

The degree of freedom of the vehicle dynamics is now reduced to two. Since $J^T B$ is of full rank, then for any transformed torque input $\overline{\tau}_i$, there exists a unique corresponding actual torque input $\tau_i \in \mathbb{R}^2$ that applied on each wheel.

The main challenge for controlling the system includes (i) the direct measurement of the linear and angular velocities is not feasible, and (ii) system parameter matrices $\overline{C}$ and $\overline{F}$ are unknown to the controller.

Based on the above system setup, we are ready to formulate our objective of this chapter. Consider a group of n homogeneous unicycle-type vehicles, the kinematics and dynamics of each vehicle agent are described by Eqs. (2) and (11), respectively. The communication graph of such n vehicles is denoted as $\mathcal{G}$. Regarding this MAS, we have the following assumption.

Assumption 1. The graph $\mathcal{G}$ *is undirected and connected.*

The objective of this chapter is to design an output-feedback adaptive learning control law for each vehicle agent in the MAS, such that

i. *State estimation:* The immeasurable general velocities $\mathbf{u}_i = [v_i \quad \omega_i]^T$ can be estimated by a high-gain observer using the measurement of the general coordinates $\mathbf{q}_i = [x_i \quad y_i \quad \theta_i]^T$.

ii. *Trajectory tracking:* Each vehicle in the MAS will track its desired reference trajectory, which will be quantified by $(x_{ri}(t), y_{ri}(t), \theta_{ri}(t))$; i.e., $\lim_{t\to\infty}(x_i(t) - x_{ri}(t)) = 0$, $\lim_{t\to\infty}(y_i(t) - y_{ri}(t)) = 0$, $\lim_{t\to\infty}(\theta_i(t) - \theta_{ri}(t)) = 0$.

iii. *Cooperative Learning:* The unknown homogeneous dynamics of all the vehicles can be locally accurately identified along the union of the trajectories experienced by all vehicle agents in the MAS.

iv. *Experience based control:* The identified/learned knowledge from the cooperative learning phase can be re-utilized by each local vehicle to perform stable trajectory tracking with improved control performance.

In order to apply the deterministic learning theory, we have the following assumption on the reference trajectories.

Assumption 2. The reference *trajectories $x_{ri}(t)$, $y_{ri}(t)$, $\theta_{ri}(t)$ for all $i = 1, \cdots, n$ are recurrent.*

3. Main results

3.1 High-gain observer design

In mobile robotics control, the position of the vehicle can be easily obtained in real time using GPS signals or camera positioning, while the direct measurement of the velocities is much more difficult. For the control and system estimation purposes, the velocities of the vehicle are required for the controller. To this end, we follow the high-gain observer design method in [8, 9], and introduce a high-gain observer to estimate the velocities using robot positions. First, we define two new variables as follows

$$\begin{aligned} p_{x_i} &= x_i \cos\theta_i + y_i \sin\theta_i \\ p_{y_i} &= y_i \cos\theta_i - x_i \sin\theta_i \end{aligned} \tag{12}$$

Notice that the operation above can be considered as a projecting the vehicle position onto the a frame whose origin is fixed to the origin of ground coordinates, and the axes are parallel to the body-fixed frame of the vehicle. The coordinates of the vehicle in this rotational frame is $\left(p_{x_i}, p_{y_i}\right)$ and hence, p_{x_i} and p_{y_i} can be calculated based on the measurement of the position and the orientation. The rotation rate of this frame equals to the angular velocity of the vehicle $\dot{\theta}_i = \omega_i$. Based on this, we design the high-gain observer for ω as

$$\begin{aligned} \dot{\hat{\theta}}_i &= \hat{\omega}_i + \frac{l_1}{\delta}\left(\theta_i - \hat{\theta}_i\right) \\ \dot{\hat{\omega}}_i &= \frac{l_2}{\delta^2}\left(\theta_i - \hat{\theta}_i\right) \end{aligned} \tag{13}$$

in which δ is a small positive scalar to be designed, and l_1 and l_2 are parameters to be chosen, such that $\begin{bmatrix} -l_1 & 1 \\ -l_2 & 0 \end{bmatrix}$ is Hurwitz stable. The time derivative of this coordinates defined in Eq. (12) is given by $\dot{p}_{x_i} = v_i + p_{y_i}\omega_i$, and $\dot{p}_{y_i} = -p_{x_i}\omega_i$, then we design the high-gain observer for v as

$$\begin{aligned} \dot{\hat{p}}_{x_i} &= \hat{v}_i + p_{y_i}\hat{\omega}_i + \frac{l_1}{\delta}\left(p_{x_i} - \hat{p}_{x_i}\right) \\ \dot{\hat{v}}_i &= \frac{l_2}{\delta^2}\left(p_{x_i} - \hat{p}_{x_i}\right) \end{aligned} \tag{14}$$

To prevent peaking while using this high-gain observer and in turn improving the transient response, parameter δ cannot be too small [9]. Due to the use of a globally bounded control, decreasing δ does not induce peaking phenomenon of the state variables of the system, while the ability to decrease δ will be limited by practical factors such as measurement noise and sampling rates [7, 27]. According to [8], it is easy to show that the estimation error between the actual and estimated velocities of the ith vehicle $\mathbf{z}_i = \mathbf{u}_i - \hat{\mathbf{u}}_i$ will converge to zero, detailed proof is omitted here due to space limitation.

3.2 Controller design and tracking convergence analysis

After obtaining the linear and angular velocities from the high-gain observer, we now proceed to the trajectory tracking. First, we define the tracking error $\tilde{\mathbf{q}}_i$ by projecting $\mathbf{q}_{ri} - \mathbf{q}_i$ onto the body coordinate of the ith vehicle, with the x axis set to be the front and y to be the left of the vehicle, as shown in **Figure 2**.

$$\tilde{\mathbf{q}}_i = \begin{bmatrix} \tilde{x}_i \\ \tilde{y}_i \\ \tilde{\theta}_i \end{bmatrix} = \begin{bmatrix} \cos\theta_i & \sin\theta_i & 0 \\ -\sin\theta_i & \cos\theta_i & 0 \\ 0 & 0 & 1 \end{bmatrix} \begin{bmatrix} x_{ri} - x_i \\ y_{ri} - y_i \\ \theta_{ri} - \theta_i \end{bmatrix}, \tag{15}$$

using the constraint Eq. (1) and kinematics Eq. (2), we have the derivative of the tracking error as follows

$$\begin{aligned} \dot{\tilde{x}}_i &= v_{ri} \cos\tilde{\theta}_i + \omega_i \tilde{y}_i - v_i \\ \dot{\tilde{y}}_i &= v_{ri} \sin\tilde{\theta}_i - \omega_i \tilde{x}_i \\ \dot{\tilde{\theta}}_i &= \omega_{ri} - \omega_i \end{aligned} \tag{16}$$

where v_i and ω_i are the linear and angular velocities of the ith vehicle, respectively.

In order to utilize the backstepping control theory, we treat v_i and ω_i in Eq. (16) as virtual inputs, then following the methodology from [28], we can design a stabilizing virtual controller as

$$\mathbf{u}_{c_i} = \begin{bmatrix} v_{c_i} \\ \omega_{c_i} \end{bmatrix} = \begin{bmatrix} v_{r_i} \cos\tilde{\theta}_i + K_x \tilde{x}_i \\ \omega_{r_i} + v_{r_i} K_y \tilde{y}_i + K_\theta \sin\tilde{\theta}_i \end{bmatrix}, \tag{17}$$

in which K_x, K_y, and K_θ are all positive constants. It can be shown that this virtual velocity controller is able to stabilize the closed-loop system Eq. (16) kinematically by replacing v_i and ω_i with v_{c_i} and ω_{c_i}, respectively. To this end, we define the following Lyapunov function for the ith vehicle

$$V_{1_i} = \frac{\tilde{x}_i^2}{2} + \frac{\tilde{y}_i^2}{2} + \frac{(1 - \cos\tilde{\theta}_i)}{K_y} \tag{18}$$

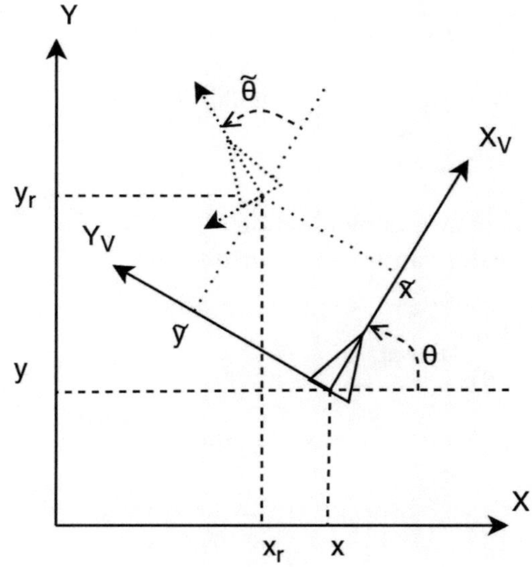

Figure 2.
Projecting tracking error onto the body-fixed frame.

and the derivative of V_{1_i} is

$$\begin{aligned}
\dot{V}_{1_i} &= \tilde{x}_i\dot{\tilde{x}}_i + \tilde{y}_i\dot{\tilde{y}}_i + \frac{\sin\tilde{\theta}_i}{K_y}\dot{\tilde{\theta}}_i \\
&= \tilde{x}_i\left(v_{r_i}\cos\tilde{\theta}_i + \omega_i\tilde{y}_i - v_{c_i}\right) + \tilde{y}_i\left(v_{r_i}\sin\tilde{\theta}_i - \omega_i\tilde{x}_i\right) + \frac{\sin\tilde{\theta}_i}{K_y}\left(\omega_{r_i} - \omega_{c_i}\right) \\
&= \tilde{x}_i\left(\omega_i\tilde{y}_i - K_x\tilde{x}_i\right) + \tilde{y}_i\left(v_{r_i}\sin\tilde{\theta}_i - \omega_i\tilde{x}_i\right) + \frac{\sin\tilde{\theta}_i}{K_y}\left(-v_{r_i}K_y\tilde{y}_i - K_\theta\sin\tilde{\theta}_i\right) \\
&= -K_x\tilde{x}_i^2 - \frac{K_\theta}{K_y}\sin^2\tilde{\theta}_i \leq 0
\end{aligned} \tag{19}$$

Since $\dot{V}_{1i}$ is negative semi-definite, then we can conclude that this closed-loop system is stable, i.e., the tracking error $\tilde{\mathbf{q}}_i$ for the ith vehicle will be bounded.

Remark 1. *In addition to the stable conclusion above, we could also conclude the asymptotic stability by finding the invariant set of* $\dot{V}_{1_i} = 0$. *By setting* $\dot{V}_{1_i} = 0$, *we have* $\tilde{x}_i = 0$ *and* $\sin\tilde{\theta} = 0$. *Applying this result into Eqs. (16) and (17), we have the invariant set equals to* $\{\tilde{x}_i = 0, \tilde{y}_i = 0, \sin\tilde{\theta} = 0\} \cup \{\tilde{x}_i = 0, \sin\tilde{\theta} = 0, \tilde{y}_i \neq 0, v_{r_i} = 0, \omega_{ri} = 0\}$. *With the assumption 2, the velocity of the reference cannot be constant over time, then we can conclude that the only invariant subset of* $\dot{V}_{1_i} = 0$ *is the origin* $\tilde{\mathbf{q}}_i = \mathbf{0}$. *Therefore, we can conclude that the closed-loop system Eqs. (16) and (17) is asymptotically stable [29].*

With the idea of backstepping control, we then derive the transformed torque input $\overline{\tau}_i$ for the ith vehicle with the following steps. By defining the error between the virtual controller $\mathbf{u}_{c_i}$ and the actual velocity $\mathbf{u}_i$ as $\tilde{\mathbf{u}}_i = [\tilde{v}_i\ \tilde{\omega}_i]^T = \mathbf{u}_{c_i} - \mathbf{u}_i$, we can rewrite Eq. (16) in terms of $\tilde{v}_i$ and $\tilde{\omega}_i$ as

$$\begin{aligned}
\dot{\tilde{x}}_i &= v_{r_i}\cos\tilde{\theta}_i + \omega_i\tilde{y}_i - v_{c_i} + \tilde{v}_i = -K_x\tilde{x}_i + \omega_i\tilde{y}_i + \tilde{v}_i \\
\dot{\tilde{y}}_i &= -\omega_i\tilde{x}_i + v_{r_i}\sin\tilde{\theta}_i \\
\dot{\tilde{\theta}}_i &= \omega_{r_i} - \omega_{c_i} + \tilde{\omega}_i = -v_{r_i}K_y\tilde{y}_i - K_\theta\sin\tilde{\theta}_i + \tilde{\omega}_i
\end{aligned} \tag{20}$$

Then we define a new Lyapunov function $V_{2_i} = V_{1_i} + \frac{\tilde{\mathbf{u}}_i^T\overline{M}\tilde{\mathbf{u}}_i}{2}$ for the closed-loop system Eq. (20), whose derivative can be written as

$$\begin{aligned}
\dot{V}_{2_i} &= \tilde{x}_i\dot{\tilde{x}}_i + \tilde{y}_i\dot{\tilde{y}}_i + \frac{\sin\tilde{\theta}_i}{K_y}\dot{\tilde{\theta}}_i + \tilde{\mathbf{u}}_i^T\overline{M}\dot{\tilde{\mathbf{u}}}_i \\
&= \tilde{x}_i\left(-K_x\tilde{x}_i + \omega_i\tilde{y}_i + \tilde{v}_i\right) + \tilde{y}_i\left(-\omega_i\tilde{x}_i + v_{r_i}\sin\tilde{\theta}_i\right) + \frac{\sin\tilde{\theta}_i}{K_y}\left(-v_{r_i}K_y\tilde{y}_i - K_\theta\sin\tilde{\theta}_i + \tilde{\omega}_i\right) \\
&\quad + \tilde{\mathbf{u}}_i^T\overline{M}\dot{\tilde{\mathbf{u}}}_i \\
&= -K_x\tilde{x}_i^2 - \frac{K_\theta}{K_y}\sin^2\tilde{\theta}_i + \tilde{\mathbf{u}}_i^T\left(\begin{bmatrix}\tilde{x}_i \\ \dfrac{\sin\tilde{\theta}_i}{K_y}\end{bmatrix} + \overline{M}\dot{\tilde{\mathbf{u}}}_i\right)
\end{aligned} \tag{21}$$

To make the system stable, the term $\tilde{\mathbf{u}}_i^T \left(\begin{bmatrix} \tilde{x}_i \\ \frac{\sin \tilde{\theta}_i}{K_y} \end{bmatrix} + \overline{M}\dot{\tilde{\mathbf{u}}}_i \right)$ needs to be negative definite. From the definition of $\tilde{\mathbf{u}}_i$ and Eq. (11), we have

$$\overline{M}\dot{\tilde{\mathbf{u}}}_i = \overline{M}\dot{\tilde{\mathbf{u}}}_{c_i} - \overline{M}\dot{\mathbf{u}}_i = \overline{M}\dot{\tilde{\mathbf{u}}}_{c_i} + \overline{C}\mathbf{u}_i + \overline{F} - \overline{\tau}_i \tag{22}$$

Motivated from the results of [9], it is easy to show that this term is negative definite if $\overline{\tau}_i$ is designed to be

$$\overline{\tau}_i = \overline{M}\dot{\mathbf{u}}_{c_i} + \overline{C}\mathbf{u}_i + \overline{F} + K_u\tilde{\mathbf{u}}_i + \begin{bmatrix} \tilde{x}_i \\ \frac{\sin \tilde{\theta}_i}{K_y} \end{bmatrix}, \tag{23}$$

where K_u is a positive constant. Since the actual linear and angular velocity of the vehicle is unknown, we use $\hat{v}_i$ and $\hat{\omega}_i$ generated by the high-gain observer Eqs. (13) and (14) to replace v_i and ω_i in Eq. (23). From the discussion in previous subsection, the convergence of velocities estimation is guaranteed.

In Eq. (23), $\overline{C}(\mathbf{u}_i)$ and $\overline{F}(\mathbf{u}_i)$ are unknown to the controller. To overcome this issue, RBFNN will be used to approximate this nonlinear uncertain term, i.e.,

$$H(X_i) = \overline{C}(\mathbf{u}_i)\mathbf{u}_i + \overline{F}(\mathbf{u}_i) = W^{*T}S(X_i) + \epsilon_i, \tag{24}$$

in which $S(X_i)$ is the vector of RBF, with the variable (RBFNN input) $X_i = \mathbf{u}_i$, W^* is the common ideal estimation weight of this RBFNN, and ϵ_i is the ideal estimation error, which can be made arbitrarily small given sufficiently large number of neurons. Consequently, we proposed the implementable controller for the ith vehicle as follows

$$\overline{\tau}_i = \overline{M}\dot{\mathbf{u}}_{c_i} + \hat{W}_i^T S(X_i) + K_u \begin{bmatrix} v_{c_i} - \hat{v}_i \\ \omega_{c_i} - \hat{\omega}_i \end{bmatrix} + \begin{bmatrix} \tilde{x}_i \\ \frac{\sin \tilde{\theta}_i}{K_y} \end{bmatrix}, \tag{25}$$

For the NN weights used in Eq. (25), we propose an online NN weight updating law as follows

$$\dot{\hat{W}}_i = \Gamma S(X_i)\tilde{\mathbf{u}}_i^T - \gamma \hat{W}_i - \beta \sum_{j=1}^{n} a_{ij}\left(\hat{W}_i - \hat{W}_j\right), \tag{26}$$

where Γ, γ, and β are positive constants.

Theorem 1. Consider *the closed-loop system consisting of the n vehicles in the MAS described by Eqs. (2) and (11), reference trajectory* $\mathbf{q}_{r_i}(t)$*, high-gain observer Eqs. (13) and (14), adaptive NN controller Eq. (25) with the virtual velocity Eq. (17), and the online weight updating law (26), under the Assumptions 1 and 2, then for any bounded initial condition of all the vehicles and* $\hat{W}_i = 0$*, the tracking error* $\tilde{\mathbf{q}}_i$ *converges asymptotically to a small neighborhood around zero for all vehicle agents in the MAS.*

Proof: We first derive the error dynamics of velocity between $\mathbf{u}_{c_i}$ and $\mathbf{u}_i$ using Eqs. (22) and (25)

$$\dot{\tilde{\mathbf{u}}}_i = \overline{M}^{-1}\left[\tilde{W}_i^T S(X_i) + \varepsilon_i - K_u \begin{bmatrix} v_{c_i} - \hat{v}_i \\ \omega_{c_i} - \hat{\omega}_i \end{bmatrix} - \begin{bmatrix} \tilde{x}_i \\ \frac{\sin\tilde{\theta}_i}{K_y} \end{bmatrix}\right] \tag{27}$$

where $\epsilon_i = [\epsilon_{v_i} \quad \epsilon_{\omega_i}]^T$ and $\tilde{W}_i = W^* - \hat{W}_i$. Notice that the convergence of $\hat{\mathbf{u}}_i$ to $\mathbf{u}_i$ is guaranteed by the high-gain observer. Then we derive the error dynamics of NN weight as follows

$$\dot{\tilde{W}}_i = -\dot{\hat{W}}_i = -\Gamma S(X_i)\tilde{\mathbf{u}}_i^T + \gamma\hat{W}_i + \beta\sum_{j=1}^{n} a_{ij}(\hat{W}_i - \hat{W}_j)) \tag{28}$$

For the closed-loop system given by Eqs. (20), (27), and (28), we can build a positive definite function V as

$$V = \sum_{i=1}^{n}\left[\frac{\tilde{x}_i^2}{2} + \frac{\tilde{y}_i^2}{2} + \frac{(1 - \cos\tilde{\theta}_i)}{K_y} + \frac{\tilde{\mathbf{u}}_i^T\overline{M}\tilde{\mathbf{u}}_i}{2} + \frac{\text{trace}\left(\tilde{W}_i^T\tilde{W}_i\right)}{2\Gamma}\right] \tag{29}$$

whose derivative is equal to

$$\dot{V} = \sum_{i=1}^{n}\left[\tilde{x}_i\dot{\tilde{x}}_i + \tilde{y}_i\dot{\tilde{y}}_i + \frac{\sin\tilde{\theta}_i}{K_y}\dot{\tilde{\theta}}_i + \tilde{\mathbf{u}}_i^T\overline{M}\dot{\tilde{\mathbf{u}}}_i + \frac{\text{trace}\left(\tilde{W}_i^T\dot{\tilde{W}}_i\right)}{\Gamma}\right] \tag{30}$$

By using Eqs. (27) and (28), the equation above is equivalent to

$$\begin{aligned}
\dot{V} = \sum_{i=1}^{n}\Bigg\{ &\tilde{x}_i(\tilde{v}_i + \omega_i\tilde{y}_i - K_x\tilde{x}_i) + \tilde{y}_i(v_{r_i}\sin\tilde{\theta}_i - \omega_i\tilde{x}_i) + \frac{\sin\tilde{\theta}_i}{K_y}(\tilde{\omega}_i - v_{r_i}K_y\tilde{y}_i - K_\theta\sin\tilde{\theta}_i) \\
&+ \tilde{\mathbf{u}}_i^T\left[\tilde{W}_i^T S(X_i) + \varepsilon_i - K_u\tilde{\mathbf{u}}_i - \begin{bmatrix} \tilde{x}_i \\ \frac{\sin\tilde{\theta}_i}{K_y} \end{bmatrix}\right] \\
&+ trace\left(\tilde{W}_i^T\left[-S(X_i)\tilde{\mathbf{u}}_i^T + \frac{\gamma\hat{W}_i}{\Gamma} + \frac{\beta}{\Gamma}\sum_{j=1}^{n}a_{ij}(\hat{W}_i - \hat{W}_j)\right]\right)\Bigg\} \\
= \sum_{i=1}^{n}\Bigg\{ &-K_x\tilde{x}_i^2 - \frac{K_\theta}{K_y}\sin^2\tilde{\theta}_i - K_u\tilde{\mathbf{u}}_i^T\tilde{\mathbf{u}}_i + \tilde{\mathbf{u}}_i^T\varepsilon_i + \tilde{\mathbf{u}}_i^T\left[\tilde{W}_i^T S(X_i)\right] \\
&- \text{trace}\left(\left[\tilde{W}_i^T S(X_i)\right]\tilde{\mathbf{u}}_i^T\right) + \text{trace}\left(\frac{\gamma\tilde{W}_i^T\hat{W}_i}{\Gamma}\right)\Bigg\} - \text{trace}\left(\sum_{i=1}^{n}\frac{\beta}{\Gamma}\tilde{W}_i^T\sum_{j=1}^{n}a_{ij}(\hat{W}_i - \hat{W}_j)\right) \\
= \sum_{i=1}^{n}\Bigg\{ &-K_x\tilde{x}_i^2 - \frac{K_\theta}{K_y}\sin^2\tilde{\theta}_i - K_u\tilde{\mathbf{u}}_i^T\tilde{\mathbf{u}}_i + \tilde{\mathbf{u}}_i^T\varepsilon_i + \frac{\gamma}{\Gamma}\text{trace}\left(\tilde{W}_i^T\hat{W}_i\right)\Bigg\} - \frac{\beta}{\Gamma}\text{trace}(\tilde{W}T(L\otimes I)\tilde{W})
\end{aligned} \tag{31}$$

where L is the Laplacian matrix of $\mathcal{G}$, and $\tilde{W} = \left[\tilde{W}_1^T \cdots \tilde{W}_n^T\right]^T$. Since β and Γ are all positive, and L is positive semi-definite, then we have $\frac{\beta}{\Gamma}\text{trace}\left(\tilde{W}^T(L\otimes I)\tilde{W}\right) \geq 0$. Notice that the estimation error can be made arbitrary small with a sufficient large number of neurons, and γ is the leakage term chosen as a small positive constant. Therefore, we can conclude that the closed-loop system Eqs. (20), (27), and (28) is stable, i.e., $\dot{V} \leq 0$, if the following condition stands

$$K_x\tilde{x}_i^2 + \frac{K_\theta}{K_y}\sin^2\tilde{\theta}_i + K_u\tilde{\mathbf{u}}_i^T\tilde{\mathbf{u}}_i \geq \tilde{\mathbf{u}}_i^T\epsilon_i + \frac{\gamma}{\Gamma}\text{trace}\left(\tilde{W}_i^T\hat{W}_i\right) \tag{32}$$

Hence, the closed-loop system is stable, and all tracking error are bounded. Since all variables in Eq. (31) are continuous (i.e., $\ddot{V}$ is bounded), then with the application of Barbalat's Lemma [30], we have $\lim_{t\to\infty}\dot{V} = 0$, which implies that the tracking error $\tilde{\mathbf{q}}_i$ for all agents will converge to a small neighborhood of zero, whose size depends on the norm of $\tilde{\mathbf{u}}_i^T\epsilon_i + \frac{\gamma}{\Gamma}\text{trace}\left(\tilde{W}_i^T\hat{W}_i\right)$. *Q.E.D.*

3.3 Consensus convergence of NN weights

In addition to the tracking convergence shown in the previous subsection, we will show that all vehicles in the system is able to learn the unknown vehicle dynamics along the union trajectory (denoted as $\cup_{i=1}^n\zeta_i[X_i(t)]$) experienced by all vehicles in this subsection.

By defining $\tilde{v} = \left[\tilde{v}_1 ... \tilde{v}_n\right]^T$, $\tilde{\omega} = \left[\tilde{\omega}_1 ... \tilde{\omega}_n\right]^T$, $\tilde{W}_v = \left[\tilde{W}_{1,1} ... \tilde{W}_{n,1}\right]^T$, and $\tilde{W}_\omega = \left[\tilde{W}_{1,2} ... \tilde{W}_{n,2}\right]^T$, we combine the error dynamics in Eqs. (27) and (28) for all vehicles into the following form:

$$\begin{bmatrix} \dot{\tilde{v}} \\ \dot{\tilde{\omega}} \\ \dot{\tilde{W}}_v \\ \dot{\tilde{W}}_\omega \end{bmatrix} = \begin{bmatrix} A & B \\ C & D \end{bmatrix} \begin{bmatrix} \tilde{v} \\ \tilde{\omega} \\ \tilde{W}_v \\ \tilde{W}_\omega \end{bmatrix} + E \tag{33}$$

in which

$$A_{2n\times 2n} = \begin{bmatrix} -\frac{K_u}{m}I_n & 0 \\ 0 & -\frac{K_u}{I}I_n \end{bmatrix}, B_{2nN\times 2n} = \begin{bmatrix} \frac{\mathbf{S}^T}{m} & 0 \\ 0 & \frac{\mathbf{S}^T}{I} \end{bmatrix},$$

$$C_{2n\times 2nN} = \begin{bmatrix} -\Gamma\mathbf{S} & 0 \\ 0 & -\Gamma\mathbf{S} \end{bmatrix}, D_{2nN\times 2nN} = \begin{bmatrix} -\beta(L\otimes I_N) & 0 \\ 0 & -\beta(L\otimes I_N) \end{bmatrix},$$

where $\mathbf{S} = \text{diag}(S(X_1), S(X_2), ..., S(X_n))$, and

$$E_{(2nN+2nN)\times 1} = \begin{bmatrix} E_1 \\ E_2 \\ E_3 \\ E_4 \end{bmatrix}, \quad E_1 = \frac{1}{m}\begin{bmatrix} \epsilon_{v_1} - \tilde{x}_1 \\ \vdots \\ \epsilon_{v_n} - \tilde{x}_n \end{bmatrix}, \quad E_2 = \frac{1}{I}\begin{bmatrix} \epsilon_{\omega_1} - \frac{\sin\tilde{\theta}_1}{K_y} \\ \vdots \\ \epsilon_{\omega_n} - \frac{\sin\tilde{\theta}_n}{K_y} \end{bmatrix},$$

$$E_3 = \frac{\gamma}{m}\begin{bmatrix} \hat{W}_{1,1} \\ \vdots \\ \hat{W}_{n,1} \end{bmatrix}, \quad E_4 = \frac{\gamma}{m}\begin{bmatrix} \hat{W}_{1,2} \\ \vdots \\ \hat{W}_{n,2} \end{bmatrix}.$$

As is shown in Theorem 1, the tracking error $\tilde{\mathbf{q}}_i$ will converge to a small neighborhood of zero for all vehicle agents in the MAS. Furthermore, the ideal estimation errors ϵ_{vi} and $\epsilon_{\omega i}$ can be made arbitrarily small given sufficient number of RBF neurons, and γ is chosen to be a small positive constant, therefore, we can conclude that the norm of E in Eq. (33) is a small value. In the following theorem, we will show that $W_i = [\,W_{i,1} \quad W_{i,2}\,]$ converges to a small neighborhood of the common ideal weight W^* for all $i = 1, \ldots, n$ under Assumptions 1 and 2.

Before proceeding further, we denote the system trajectory of the ith vehicle as ζ_i for all $i = 1, \cdots, n$. Using the same notation from [14], $(\cdot)_\zeta$ and $(\cdot)\overline{\zeta}$ represent the parts of $(\cdot)$ related to the region close to and away from the trajectory ζ, respectively.

Theorem 2. Consider *the error dynamics Eq. (33), under the Assumptions 1 and 2, then for any bounded initial condition of all the vehicles and $\hat{W}_i = 0$, along the union of the system trajectories $\cup_{i=1}^n \zeta_i[X_i(t)]$, all local estimated neural weights $\hat{W}_{\zeta_i}$ used in Eqs. (25) and (26) converge to a small neighborhood of their common ideal value W_ζ^*, and locally accurate identification of nonlinear uncertain dynamics $H(X(t))$ can be obtained by $\hat{W}_i^T S(X)$ as well as $\overline{W}_i^T S(X)$ for all $X \in \cup_{i=1}^n \zeta_i[X_i(t)]$, where*

$$\overline{W}_i = \underset{t_{a_i} \le t \le t_{b_i}}{\text{mean}} \hat{W}_i(t) \tag{34}$$

with $[t_{a_i}, t_{b_i}]$ $(t_{b_i} > t_{a_i} > T_i)$ being a time segment after the transient period of tracking control.

Proof: According to [14], if the nominal part of closed loop system shown in Eq. (33) is uniformly locally exponentially stable (ULES), then $\tilde{v}$, $\tilde{\omega}$, $\tilde{W}_v$, and $\tilde{W}_\omega$ will converge to a small neighborhood of the origin, whose size depends on the value of $\|E\|$.

Now the problem boils down to proving ULES of the nominal part of system Eq. (33). To this end, we need to resort to the results of Lemma 4 in [31]. It is stated that if the Assumptions 1 and 2 therein are satisfied, and the associated vector $S_\zeta(X_i)$ is PE for all $i = 1, \cdots, n$, then the nominal part of Eq. (33) is ULES. The assumption 1 therein is automatically verified since $\mathbf{S}$ is bounded, and Assumption 2 therein also holds, if we set the counterparts $P = \Gamma\begin{bmatrix} m & 0 \\ 0 & I \end{bmatrix}$ and $Q = -2\Gamma\begin{bmatrix} K_u I_n & 0 \\ 0 & K_u I_n \end{bmatrix}$. Furthermore, the PE condition of $S_\zeta(X_i)$ will also be met, if X_i of the learning task is recurrent [14], which is guaranteed by Assumption 2 and results from Theorem 1. Therefore, we can obtain the conclusion that $\tilde{v}$, $\tilde{\omega}$, $\tilde{W}_v$, and $\tilde{W}_\omega$ will converge to a small neighborhood of the origin, whose size depends on the small value of $\|E\|$.

Similar to [24], the convergence of $\hat{W}_{\zeta i}$ to a small neighborhood of W_ζ^* implies that for all $X \in \cup_{i=1}^n \zeta_i[X_i(t)]$, we have

$$H(X) = W_\zeta^{*T} + \epsilon_\zeta = \hat{W}_{\zeta_i}^T S_\zeta(X) + \tilde{W}_{\zeta_i}^T S_\zeta(X) + \epsilon_{\zeta i} = \hat{W}_{\zeta_i}^T S_\zeta(X) + \epsilon_{1\zeta_i} \tag{35}$$

where $\epsilon_{1\zeta i} = \tilde{W}_{\zeta i}^T S_\zeta(X) + \epsilon_{\zeta i}$ is close to $\epsilon_{\zeta i}$ due to the convergence of $\tilde{W}_{\zeta i}$. With the $\overline{W}_i$ defined in Eq. (34), then Eq. (35) can be rewritten into

$$H(X) = \hat{W}_{\zeta_i}^T S_\zeta(X) + \epsilon_{1\zeta_i} = \overline{W}_{\zeta_i}^T S_\zeta(X) + \epsilon_{2\zeta_i} \tag{36}$$

where $\overline{W}_{\zeta_i}^T = [\,w_{1_\zeta} \quad \cdots \quad w_{k_\zeta}\,]^T$ is a subvector of $\overline{W}_i$ and $\epsilon_{2\zeta_i}$ is the error using $\overline{W}_{\zeta i}^T S_\zeta(X)$ as the system approximation. After the transient process, $\|\epsilon_{1\zeta_i}\| - \|\epsilon_{2\zeta_i}\|$ is small for all $i = 1, \cdots, n$.

On the other hand, due to the localization property of Gaussian RBFs, both $S\bar{\zeta}$ and $\frac{W}{\bar{\zeta}}S\bar{\zeta}(X)$ are very small. Hence, along the union trajectory $\cup_{i=1}^{n}\zeta_i[X_i(t)]$, the entire constant RBF network $\overline{W}^T S(X)$ can be used to approximate the nonlinear uncertain dynamics, demonstrated by the following equivalent equations

$$\begin{aligned} H(X) &= W_{\zeta}^{*T} S_{\zeta}(X) + \epsilon_{\zeta} \\ H(X) &= \hat{W}_{\zeta_i}^{T} S_{\zeta}(X) + \hat{W}_{\bar{\zeta}_i}^{T} S\bar{\zeta}(X) + \epsilon_{1_i} = \hat{W}_i^T S(X) + \epsilon_{1_i} \\ H(X) &= \overline{W}_{\zeta_i}^{T} S_{\zeta}(X) + \overline{W}_{\bar{\zeta}_i}^{T} S\bar{\zeta}(X) + \epsilon_{2_i} = \overline{W}_i^T S(X) + \epsilon_{2_i} \end{aligned} \tag{37}$$

where $\|\epsilon_{1_i}\| - \|\epsilon_{1\zeta_i}\|$ and $\|\epsilon_{2_i}\| - \|\epsilon_{2\zeta_i}\|$ are all small for all $i = 1, \cdots, n$. Therefore, the conclusion of Theorem 2 can be drawn. *Q.E.D.*

3.4 Experience-based trajectory tracking control

In this section, based on the learning results from the previous subsections, we further propose an experience-based trajectory tracking control method using the knowledge learned in the previous subsection, such that the experience-based controller is able to drive each vehicle to follow any reference trajectory experienced by any vehicle on the learning stage.

To this end, we replace the NN weight $\hat{W}_i$ in Eq. (25) by the converged constant NN weight $\overline{W}_i$ for the ith vehicle. Therefore, the experience-based controller for the ith vehicle is constructed as follows

$$\overline{\tau}_i = \overline{M}\dot{\mathbf{u}}_{c_i} + \overline{W}_i^T S(X_i) + K_u \begin{bmatrix} v_{c_i} - \hat{v}_i \\ \omega_{c_i} - \hat{\omega}_i \end{bmatrix} + \begin{bmatrix} \tilde{x}_i \\ \frac{\sin\tilde{\theta}_i}{K_y} \end{bmatrix}, \tag{38}$$

in which $\dot{\mathbf{u}}_{ci}$ is the derivative of the virtual velocity controller from Eq. (17), and $\overline{W}_i$ is obtained from Eq. (34) for the ith vehicle. The system model Eqs. (2) and (11), and the high-gain observer design Eqs. (14) and (13) remain unchanged.

Theorem 3. Consider *the closed-loop system consisting of Eqs. (2) and (11), reference trajectory $\mathbf{q}_{ri} \in \cup_{j=1}^{n}\mathbf{q}_j(t)$, high-gain observer Eqs. (14) and (13), and the experience-based controller Eq. (38) with virtual velocity Eq. (17). For any bounded initial condition, the tracking error $\tilde{\mathbf{q}}_i$ converges asymptotically to a small neighborhood around zero.*

Proof: Similar to the proof of Theorem 1, by defining $\tilde{\mathbf{q}}_i$ and $\tilde{\mathbf{u}}_i$ to be the error between the position and velocity of the ith vehicle and its associated reference trajectory, we have the error dynamics of the ith vehicle as

$$\begin{aligned} \dot{\tilde{x}}_i &= v_{r_i}\cos\tilde{\theta}_i + \omega_i\tilde{y}_i - v_i = \tilde{v}_i + \omega_i\tilde{y}_i - K_x\tilde{x}_i \\ \dot{\tilde{y}}_i &= v_{r_i}\sin\tilde{\theta}_i - \omega_i\tilde{x}_i \\ \dot{\tilde{\theta}}_i &= \omega_{r_i} - \omega_i = \tilde{\omega}_i - v_{r_i}K_y\tilde{y}_i - K_\theta\sin\tilde{\theta}_i \\ \dot{\tilde{\mathbf{u}}}_i &= \overline{M}^{-1}\left[H(X_i) - \overline{W}_i^T S(X_i) - K_u \begin{bmatrix} v_{c_i} - \hat{v}_i \\ \omega_{c_i} - \hat{\omega}_i \end{bmatrix} - \begin{bmatrix} \tilde{x}_i \\ \frac{\sin\tilde{\theta}_i}{K_y} \end{bmatrix}\right] \end{aligned} \tag{39}$$

With the same high-gain observer design used in the learning-based tracking, the convergence of $\hat{\mathbf{u}}_i$ to $\mathbf{u}_i$ is also guaranteed. For the closed-loop system shown above, we can build a positive definite function as

$$V_i = \frac{\tilde{x}_i^2}{2} + \frac{\tilde{y}_i^2}{2} + \frac{1 - \cos\tilde{\theta}_i}{K_y} + \frac{\tilde{\mathbf{u}}_i^T \overline{M} \tilde{\mathbf{u}}_i}{2} \tag{40}$$

and the derivative of V_i is

$$\begin{aligned}
\dot{V}_i &= \tilde{x}_i \dot{\tilde{x}}_i + \tilde{y}_i \dot{\tilde{y}}_i + \sin\frac{\tilde{\theta}_i}{K_y} \dot{\tilde{\theta}}_i + \tilde{\mathbf{u}}_i^T \overline{M} \dot{\tilde{\mathbf{u}}}_i \\
&= \tilde{x}_i \left(\tilde{v}_i + \omega_i \tilde{y}_i - K_x \tilde{x}_i\right) + \tilde{y}_i \left(v_{r_i} \sin\tilde{\theta}_i - \omega_i \tilde{x}_i\right) + \frac{\sin\tilde{\theta} i}{K_y} \left(\tilde{\omega}_i - v_{r_i} K_y \tilde{y}_i - K_\theta \sin\tilde{\theta}_i\right) \\
&\quad + \tilde{\mathbf{u}}_i^T \left(\epsilon_{2i} - K_u \tilde{\mathbf{u}}_i - \begin{bmatrix} \tilde{x}_i \\ \dfrac{\sin\tilde{\theta}_i}{K_y} \end{bmatrix} \right) \\
&= -K_x \tilde{x}_i^2 - \frac{K_\theta}{K_y} \sin^2\tilde{\theta}_i - K_u \tilde{\mathbf{u}}_i^T \tilde{\mathbf{u}}_i + \tilde{\mathbf{u}}_i^T \epsilon_{2i}
\end{aligned} \tag{41}$$

where $\epsilon_{2i} = H(X_i) - \overline{W}_i^T S(X_i)$. Then following the similar arguments in the proof of Theorem 1, given positive K_x, K_y, K_θ, and K_u, then we can conclude that the Lyapunov function V_i is positive definite and $\dot{V}_i$ is negative semi-definite in the region $K_x \tilde{x}_i^2 + \frac{K_\theta}{K_y} \sin^2\tilde{\theta}_i + K_u \tilde{\mathbf{u}}_i^T \tilde{\mathbf{u}}_i \geq \tilde{\mathbf{u}}_i^T \overline{\epsilon}_i$. Similar to the proof of Theorem 1, it can be shown that $\lim_{t\to\infty} \dot{V}_i = 0$ with Barbalat's Lemma, and the tracking errors will converge to a small neighborhood of zero. *Q.E.D.*

4. Simulation studies

Consider four identical vehicles, whose unknown friction vector is assumed to be a nonlinear function of v and ω as follows $\overline{F} = \begin{bmatrix} 0.1mv_i + 0.05mv_i^2 \\ 0.2I\omega_i + 0.1I\omega_i^2 \end{bmatrix}$, and since we assume the vehicles are operating on the horizontal plane, the gravitational vector $\overline{G}$ is equal to zero. The physical parameters of the vehicles are given as $m = 2\,\text{kg}$, $I = 0.2\,\text{kg} \cdot \text{m}^2$; $R = 0.15\,\text{m}$, $r = 0.05\,\text{m}$ and $d = 0.1\,\text{m}$. The reference trajectories of the three vehicles are given by

$$\begin{cases} x_{r_1} = -\sin t \\ y_{r_1} = 2\cos t \end{cases} \begin{cases} x_{r_2} = 2\cos t \\ y_{r_2} = \sin t \end{cases} \begin{cases} x_{r_3} = -2\sin t \\ y_{r_3} = 3\cos t \end{cases} \begin{cases} x_{r_4} = 3\cos t \\ y_{r_4} = 2\sin t \end{cases} \tag{42}$$

and for all vehicles, the orientations of reference trajectories and vehicle velocities satisfy the following equations

$$\tan\theta_{ri} = \frac{\dot{y}_{ri}}{\dot{x}_{ri}}, v_{ri} = \sqrt{\dot{x}_{ri}^2 + \dot{y}_{ri}^2}, \omega_{ri} = \frac{\dot{x}_{ri} \ddot{y}_{ri} - \ddot{x}_{ri} \dot{y}_{ri}}{\dot{x}_{ri}^2 + \dot{y}_{ri}^2}. \tag{43}$$

The parameters of the observer Eqs. (13) and (14) are given as $\delta = 0.01$, and $l_1 = l_2 = 1$. The parameters of the controller Eq. (25) with Eq. (17) are given as $K_x = K_y = K_\theta = 1$, and $K_u = 2$. The parameters of Eq. (26) are given as $\Gamma = 10$, $\gamma = 0.001$, and $\beta = 10$. For each $i = 1, 2, 3, 4$, since $X_i = [v_i \quad \omega_i]^T$, we construct the

Gaussian RBFNN $\hat{W}_i S(X_i)$ using $N = 5 \times 5 = 25$ neuron nodes with the centers evenly placed over the state space $[0, 4] \times [0, 4]$ and the standard deviation of the Gaussian function equal to 0.7. The initial position of the vehicles are set at the origin, with the velocities set to be zero, and the initial weights of RBFNNs are also set to be zero. The connection between three vehicles is shown in **Figure 3**, and the Laplacian matrix L associated with the graph $\mathcal{G}$ is

$$L = \begin{bmatrix} 2 & -1 & 0 & -1 \\ -1 & 2 & -1 & 0 \\ 0 & -1 & 2 & -1 \\ -1 & 0 & -1 & 2 \end{bmatrix}. \tag{44}$$

Simulation results are shown as following. **Figure 4a** shows that the observer error will converge to a close neighborhood around zero in a very short time period, and **Figure 4b** shows that all tracking errors $\tilde{x}_i$ and $\tilde{y}_i$ will converge to zero, and **Figures 5a–f** show that all vehicles (blue triangles) will track its own reference trajectory (red solid circles) on the 2-D frame. **Figure 6b** shows that the NN weights of all vehicle agents converge to the same constant, and **Figure 6a** shows that all RBFNNs of three vehicles are able to accurately estimate the unknown dynamics, as the estimation errors converging to a small neighborhood around zero.

To demonstrate the results of Theorem 3, which states that after the learning process, each vehicle is able to use the learned knowledge to follow any reference trajectory experienced by any vehicle on the learning stage. In this part of our simulation, the experience-based controller Eq. (38) will be implemented with the

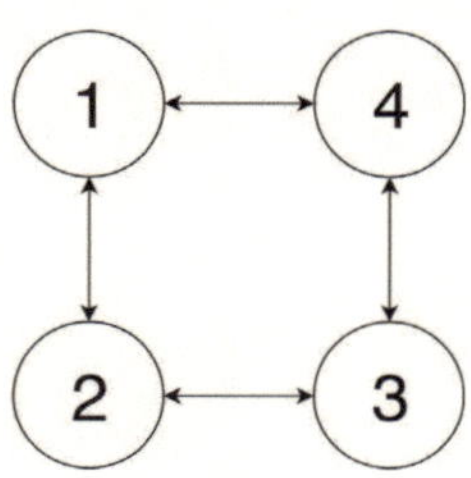

Figure 3.
Connection between four vehicles.

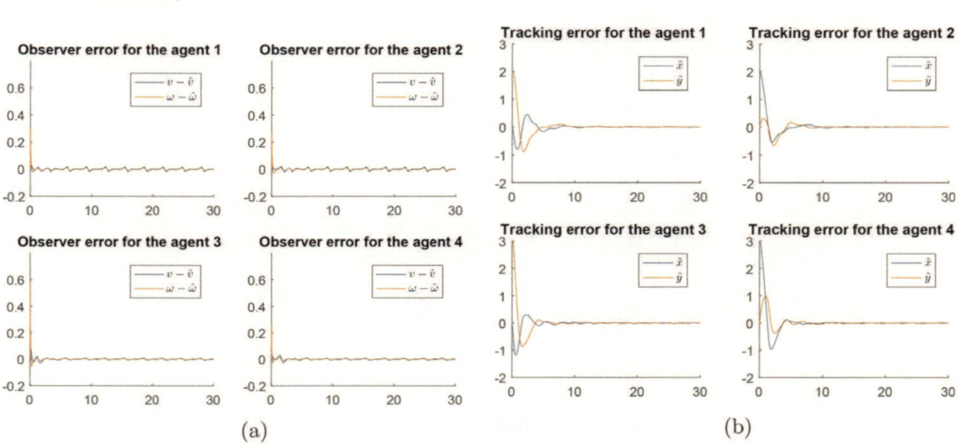

Figure 4.
Observer errors and tracking errors using observer-based controller. (a) Observer errors using observer (13) and (14). (b) Tracking errors using controller (25) with (17) and (26).

same parameters as those of the previous subsection, such that vehicle 1 will follow the reference trajectory of vehicle 3, vehicle 2 will follow the reference trajectory of vehicle 1, and vehicle 3 will follow the reference trajectory of vehicle 2. The initial position of the vehicles are set at the origin, with all velocities equal to zero.

Simulation results are shown as following. **Figure 7a** shows that the observer error will converge to a close neighborhood around zero in a very short time period. **Figures 8a–c** show that all vehicles (blue triangles) will track its own reference trajectory (red solid circles), and **Figure 7b** shows that all tracking errors $\tilde{x}_i$ and $\tilde{y}_i$ will converge to zero.

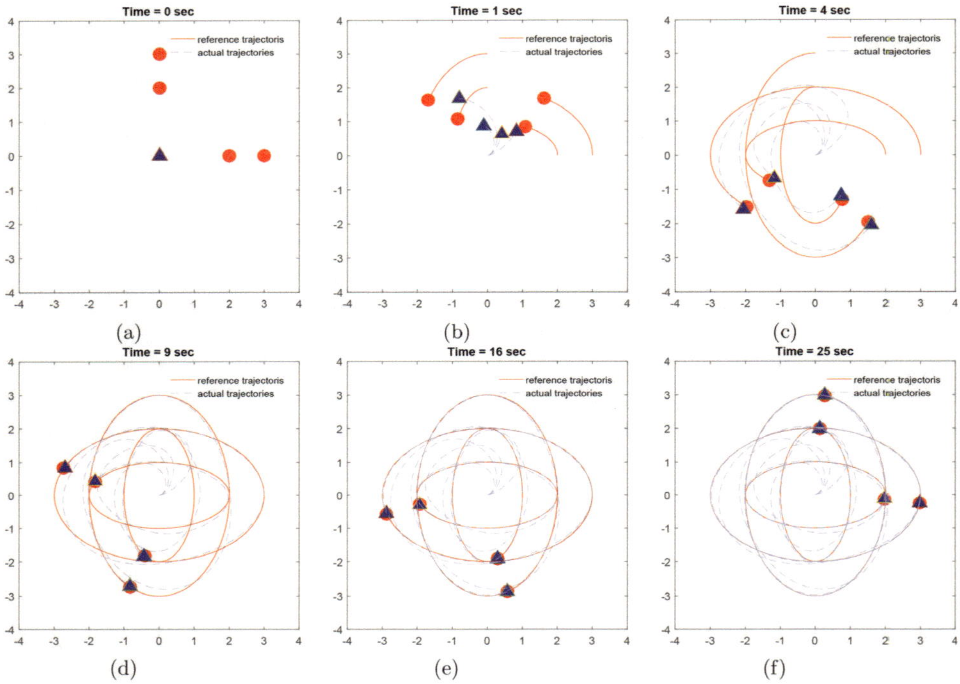

Figure 5.
Snapshot of trajectory tracking using controller Eq. (25) with Eqs. (17) and (26). (a) time at 0 seconds. (b) time at 1 seconds. (c) time at 4 seconds. (d) time at 9 seconds. (e) time at 16 seconds. (f) time at 25 seconds.

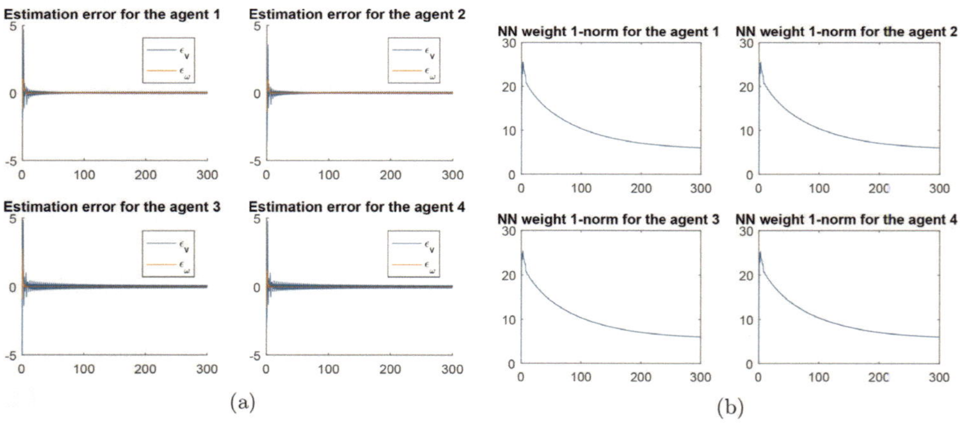

Figure 6.
Estimation errors and NN weight convergence. (a) Estimation errors using controller (25) with(17) and (26). (b) Weight vector 1-norm of Wv and Ww.

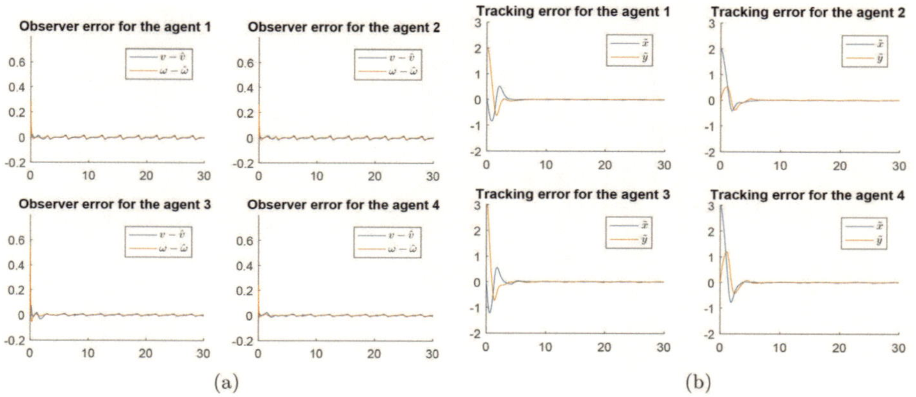

Figure 7.
Observer errors and tracking errors using observer-based controller. (a) Observer errors using observer (13) and (14). (b) Tracking errors using controller (38) with (17).

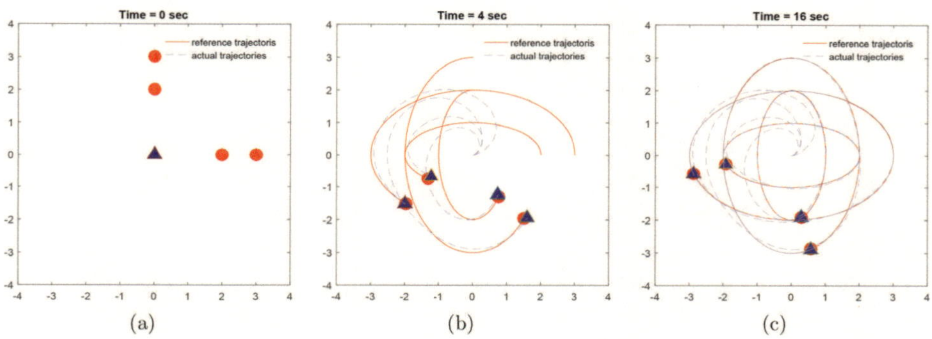

Figure 8.
Snapshot of trajectory tracking using controller Eqs. (38) with Eq. (17). (a) time at 0 seconds. (b) time at 4 seconds. (c) time at 16 seconds.

5. Conclusion

In this chapter, a high-gain observer-based CDL control algorithm has been proposed to estimate the unmodeled nonlinear dynamics of a group of homogeneous unicycle-type vehicles while tracking their reference trajectories. It has been shown in this chapter that the state estimation, trajectory tracking, and consensus learning are all achieved using the proposed algorithm. To be more specific, any vehicle in the system is able to learn the unmodeled dynamics along the union of trajectories experienced by all vehicles with the state variables provided by measurements and observer estimations. In addition, we have also shown that with the converged NN weight, this knowledge can be applied on the vehicle to track any experienced trajectory with reduced computational complexity. Simulation results have been provided to demonstrate the effectiveness of this proposed algorithm.

Author details

Xiaonan Dong[1*], Paolo Stegagno[2], Chengzhi Yuan[1*] and Wei Zeng[3]

1 Department of Mechanical, Industrial and Systems Engineering, University of Rhode Island, Kingston, RI, USA

2 Department of Electrical, Computer, and Biomedical Engineering, University of Rhode Island, Kingston, RI, USA

3 School of Mechanical and Electrical Engineering, Longyan University, Longyan, China

*Address all correspondence to: dong xn@uri.edu; cyuan@uri.edu

References

[1] Yu X, Liu L, Feng G. Trajectory tracking for nonholonomic vehicles with velocity constraints. In: IFAC-Papers Online. Vol. 48, No. 11. 2015. pp. 918-923

[2] Chen X, Jia Y. Simple tracking controller for unicycle-type mobile robots with velocity and torque constraints. Transactions of the Institute of Measurement and Control. 2015; **37**(2):211-218

[3] Seyboth GS, Wu J, Qin J, Yu C, Allgöwer F. Collective circular motion of unicycle type vehicles with nonidentical constant velocities. IEEE Transactions on control of Network Systems. 2014;**1**(2):167-176

[4] Dong X, Yuan C, Wu F. Cooperative deterministic learning-based trajectory tracking for a group of unicycle-type vehicles. In: ASME 2018 Dynamic Systems and Control Conference. 1em plus 0.5em minus 0.4em; American Society of Mechanical Engineers. 2018. p. V003T30A006

[5] Luenberger DG. Observing the state of a linear system. IEEE transactions on military electronics. 1964;**8**(2):74-80

[6] Luenberger D. An introduction to observers. IEEE Transactions on Automatic Control. 1971;**16**(6):596-602

[7] Lee KW, Khalil HK. Adaptive output feedback control of robot manipulators using high-gain observer. International Journal of Control. 1997;**67**(6):869-886

[8] Khalil HK. High-gain observers in nonlinear feedback control. In: 2008 International Conference on Control, Automation and Systems. 1em plus 0.5em minus 0.4em; IEEE. 2008. pp. xlvii-xlvii

[9] Zeng W, Wang Q, Liu F, Wang Y. Learning from adaptive neural network output feedback control of a unicycle-type mobile robot. ISA Transactions. 2016;**61**:337-347

[10] Boker A, Yuan C. High-gain observer-based distributed tracking control of heterogeneous nonlinear multi-agent systems. In: 2018 37th Chinese Control Conference (CCC). 1em plus 0.5em minus 0.4em; IEEE. 2018. pp. 6639-6644

[11] Rossomando FG, Soria CM. Identification and control of nonlinear dynamics of a mobile robot in discrete time using an adaptive technique based on neural pid. Neural Computing and Applications. 2015;**26**(5):1179-1191

[12] Miao Z, Wang Y. Adaptive control for simultaneous stabilization and tracking of unicycle mobile robots. Asian Journal of Control. 2015;**17**(6): 2277-2288

[13] Fierro R, Lewis FL. Control of a nonholonomic mobile robot using neural networks. IEEE Transactions on Neural Networks. 1998;**9**(4):589-600

[14] Wang C, Hill DJ. Deterministic Learning Theory for Identification, Recognition, and Control. Vol. 32. Boca Ration, FL: CRC Press Taylor & Francis Group; 2009

[15] Cai X, de Queiroz M. Adaptive rigidity-based formation control for multirobotic vehicles with dynamics. IEEE Transactions on Control Systems Technology. 2015;**23**(1):389-396

[16] Yuan C. Distributed adaptive switching consensus control of heterogeneous multi-agent systems with switched leader dynamics. Nonlinear Analysis: Hybrid Systems. 2017;**26**: 274-283

[17] Yuan C, Licht S, He H. Formation learning control of multiple autonomous

underwater vehicles with heterogeneous nonlinear uncertain dynamics. IEEE transactions on cybernetics. 2017;**99**: 1-15

[18] Yuan C, Zeng W, Dai S. Distributed model reference adaptive containment control of heterogeneous uncertain multi-agent systems. ISA Transactions. 2019;**86**:73-86

[19] Yuan C, He H, Wang C. Cooperative deterministic learning-based formation control for a group of nonlinear uncertain mechanical systems. IEEE Transactions on Industrial Informatics. 2019;**15**(1):319-333

[20] Stegagno P, Yuan C. Distributed cooperative adaptive state estimation and system identification for multi-agent systems. IET Control Theory and Applications. 2019;**13**(1):815-822

[21] Agaev R, Chebotarev P. The matrix of maximum out forests of a digraph and its applications. arXiv preprint math/0602059; 2006

[22] Park J, Sandberg IW. Universal approximation using radial-basis-function networks. Neural Computation. 1991;**3**(2):246-257

[23] Buhmann MD. Radial Basis Functions: Theory and Implementations. Vol. 12. Cambridge, UK: Cambridge University Press; 2003

[24] Wang C, Hill DJ. Learning from neural control. IEEE Transactions on Neural Networks. 2006;**17**(1):130-146

[25] Fierro R, Lewis FL. Control of a nonholonomic mobile robot: Backstepping kinematics into dynamics. In: Proceedings of the 34th IEEE Conference on Decision and Control. Vol. 4; IEEE. 1995. pp. 3805-3810

[26] Siciliano B, Sciavicco L, Villani L, Oriolo G. Robotics: Modelling, Planning and Control. London, United Kingdom: Springer Science and Business Media; 2009

[27] Oh S, Khalil HK. Nonlinear output-feedback tracking using high-gain observer and variable structure control. Automatica. 1997;**33**(10):1845-1856

[28] Kanayama Y, Kimura Y, Miyazaki F, Noguchi T. A stable tracking control method for an autonomous mobile robot. In: Proceedings 1990 IEEE International Conference on Robotics and Automation; IEEE. 1990. pp. 384-389

[29] Ioannou PA, Sun J. Robust Adaptive Control. 1em plus 0.5em minus 0.4em; Courier Corporation; 2012

[30] Barbalat I. Systemes d'équations différentielles d'oscillations non linéaires. Reviews Mathematics Pures Applied. 1959;**4**(2):267-270

[31] Chen W, Wen C, Hua S, Sun C. Distributed cooperative adaptive identification and control for a group of continuous-time systems with a cooperative pe condition via consensus. IEEE Transactions on Automatic Control. 2014;**59**(1):91-106

Chapter 2

Multiagent Systems for 3D Reconstruction Applications

Metehan Aydın, Erkan Bostancı, Mehmet Serdar Güzel and Nadia Kanwal

Abstract

3D models of scenes are used in many areas ranging from cultural heritage to video games. In order to model a scene, there are several techniques. One of the well-known and well-used techniques is image-based reconstruction. An image-based reconstruction starts with data acquisition step and ends with 3D model of the scene. Data are collected from the scene using various ways. The chapter explains how data acquisition step can be handled using a multiagent system. The explanation is provided by literature reviews and a study whose purpose is reconstructing an area in 3D using a multiagent UAV system.

Keywords: multiagent systems, concepts, architecture, control, communication, 3D reconstruction, image-based reconstruction

1. Introduction

Multiagent systems concern with the coordination of multiple interacting agents in order to complete a single task. Its objective is coordinating relatively simple agents instead of using a complex agent. The coordination of agents gives some abilities to these systems. These abilities are flexibility, robustness and scalability [1, 2].

Flexibility gives the ability of generating an effective solution to different problems. A single agent system can have flexibility but a multiagent system results a more flexible system because using multiple agents can solve and it can be adapted problems which are beyond of capabilities of a single agent. Robustness gives multiagent systems to complete the task despite of failures on the environment and the agents. A single agent system can be robust but it can never be robust as much as a multiagent system because whenever the agent in a single agent system is damaged, the task cannot be completed. However, when an agent in a multiagent system is damaged, the other agents can complete the task. Scalability gives the ability of adding new agents or new groups to the system and working properly with these new elements. This can be provided in a single agent system by changing the elements of the agent but this is not a good solution because this solution has many disadvantages such as cost, re-design and integration. On the other hand, this process can be handled just adding a new agent to the system in a multiagent system.

These abilities give multiagent systems some advantages [3] against a single agent system. These advantages are listed below.

- Multiagent systems are cheaper and consume less energy. Because, its agents are simpler than the agent of a single agent system. Even in the case of having so many agents, it will be cheaper because of complexity of the agent in the single agent system.

- Multiagent systems are faster. Because, the task is shared among agents. This gives the power of parallel processing and results a faster system.

- Multiagent systems are more reliable. If the agent in a single agent system is damaged, the task cannot be completed. But, if any agent in a multiagent system is damaged, the system can still complete the task. This makes multiagent systems more reliable.

However, the coordination of the agents has some challenges. In this chapter, these challenges are addressed and they are explained with a study whose purpose is reconstructing an area in 3D using a multiagent system. The rest of chapter addresses the challenges which are facing while constructing a multiagent system. These challenges are selection of architecture, control techniques and communication mechanism in multiagent systems. The rest of the chapter is structured as follows. Applications areas are addressed in Section 2. An overview to the study is addressed in Section 3. In Section 4, architecture is addressed. Control techniques are explained in Section 5. How multiagent systems communicate is explained in Section 6. The results are presented in Section 7. Finally, the chapter is concluded in Section 8.

2. Application areas

There are many applications of multiagent systems ranging from networking to robotics [4]. But, the advantages and abilities of these systems make them more suitable for some problems [1, 2].

One of the problems is area coverage. This problem can be solved using a single agent system but a multiagent system can be a better solution for this problem. The characteristics of the problem and multiagent systems is the reason for this because when an area is wanted to be covered, it is required that this process should be as fast as and as reliable as possible. These requirements make multiagent systems more suitable for this problem.

The other problem type is dynamic problems. These types of problems are not fixed sized. Their size can change according the time or some other parameters. Using a single agent system cannot fulfill the requirements when the problem size differs. The agent can be either an overhead or not capable enough for the problem. These problems can be easily solved using a multiagent system because it allows us to add or remove agents. In this way, there can be no overheads or capacity issues.

The other problem type is searching. In order to search for an object in an area, a scalable and faster system is needed. A single agent system can provide these properties but when it is constructed once, it will be hard to reconstruct it again. This yields a system which is not fully scalable and fast. However, these types of problems can easily be solved by a multiagent system. When a larger scene must be searched, adding more agents to the system can solve scalability problem and the system will be faster because there are more than one agent in the system, this approach allows searching faster in a given time interval.

3. An overview of the study

There are different 3D reconstruction techniques. An image based 3D reconstruction technique is used in the study. Image based 3D reconstruction generally has a reconstruction pipeline in which there are several steps. The pipeline generally starts with data acquisition. In data acquisition, the study uses a multiagent UAV system. The reason of using a multiagent system is that their advantages and strengths are well suitable for the requirement of image based 3D reconstruction.

In order to reconstruct a scene in 3D with an image-based 3D reconstruction, the objects in the scene must be photographed in all the viewpoints. **Figure 1** shows how the scene must be photographed.

The multiagent system is started with a command which gives an order to one of the agents in the system. The command is given by giving the positions of the area. This command can be given to any agent. The control mechanism of the system is designed to provide that any agent can get a mission and can share it among other agents. This control mechanism is designed for the study. There are some known and used control mechanisms but we want to benefit from the advantages of two known and used control mechanisms. These mechanisms are distributed control and centralized control. The designed control mechanism is a hybrid version of these two mechanisms. It takes the advantages of master-slave side of centralized control and the advantages of distributed mission sharing of distributed control and results a system in which any agent can be a master and any agent can give order to other agents. The control mechanism works with communication mechanism and it can even be said that the control mechanism works above communication mechanism because the most suitable communication mechanism is selected for the designed control mechanism. The selected communication mechanism is direct communication. All the agents can send and get messages with it. The messages determined when the system is designed and there can be different types of agents in the system, in other words, the architecture of the system provides heterogeneous agents. The communication mechanism is selected for this property, too. Any agent which implements it can easily join the system and be part of the mission.

When an area is selected using any of the agent, the agent shares the mission among the other agents equally. Then, the agents start the rotate around the area. They rotate as long as their mission, for example, if 60° are given for an agent, it rotates only 60°. While they are rotating, they capture the video of the scene. The master agents check if all the agents complete their mission. When all of them complete it, they all go to a location which is determined in advance. Then, the videos transferred to a computer and 3D reconstruction pipeline is started.

The 3D reconstruction pipeline includes tree main steps which is similar but its purpose and the steps not same with the work [5]. These steps are summarization of the videos as frames, extracting camera positions and creating point cloud,

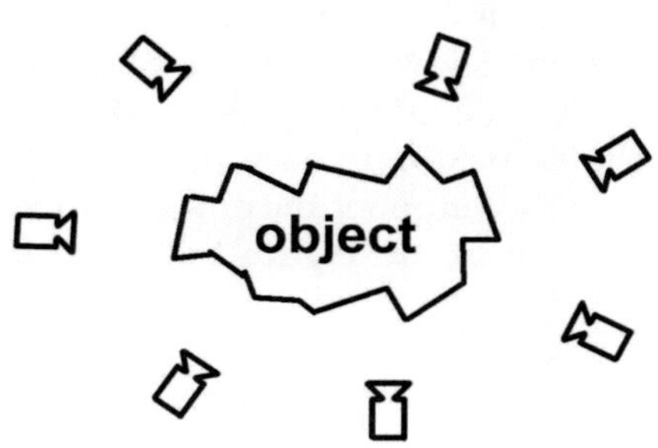

Figure 1.
Photographing an object.

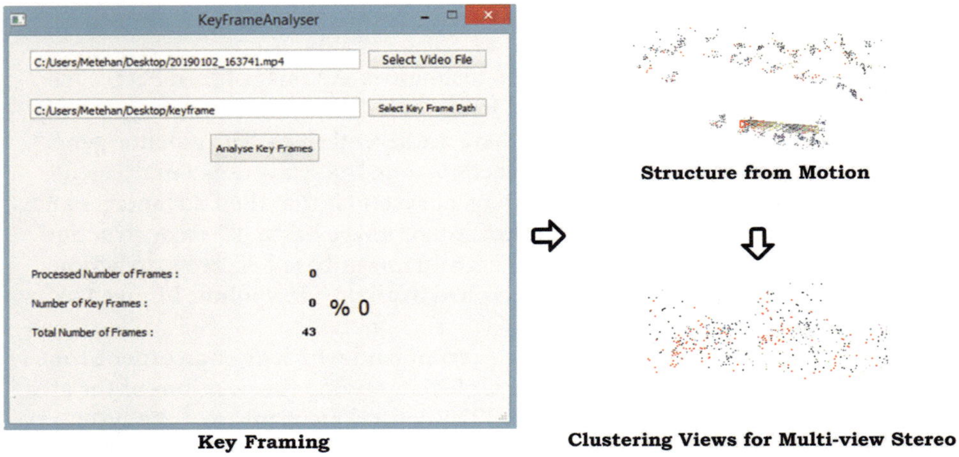

Figure 2.
Overview of the pipeline.

dense reconstruction. The summarization of the video is handled using a technique known as key framing. They are summarized because there are lots of frames in the video which sees the scene with similar view angle. These similar frames do not contribute the 3D reconstruction process. Key framing provides the selection of the frames which are identical and fulfill the view angle. The algorithm [6, 7] used in the key framing process is explained below.

- Select the first frame as a key frame.
- For each of the frames after the key frame, compute the similarity between the key frame and the frame.
- If the similarity is above a similarity threshold, eliminate the frame.
- If the similarity is under a threshold, store it and select as the last key frame.

In the next step, the camera positions are extracted and point cloud of the scene is created. This step is handled using a technique known as structure from motion. The study uses VisualSfM [8] as the structure from motion application. The application takes key frames as input then produces the camera positions and the point cloud of the scene. The most important reason to select this application is that this application uses SIFT feature descriptor. SIFT [9] feature descriptor gives the best precision results [10], which are very important for the study.

The final step of the pipeline is dense reconstruction. The study uses an MVS technique known as Clustering Views for Multi-view Stereo (CMVS) [11]. CMVS tool can be integrated to the VisualSfM application and they can be used in the same interface. The output of the VisualSfM becomes the input of the CMVS. The output of the CMVS, in other words the output of the pipeline because CMVS is the last step of the pipeline, is 3D dense of the scene. **Figure 2** shows an overview of the pipeline.

4. Architecture

Architecture refers to how the agents of the system are constructed and how they differ from each other. There are two main architectures [12]. These are homogeneous and heterogeneous architectures. Architecture selection should be problem dependent. Both of them have some advantages and disadvantages against each other. According to problem and facilities, one of them can be selected.

4.1 Homogeneous architecture

In homogeneous architecture, all the agents have same capabilities and all of them are identical. A system which has agents from same brand can be an example of homogeneous architecture. The example can be understood well from **Figure 3**. The advantage of this architecture is simplicity. Implementing a homogeneous architecture is simpler than heterogeneous architecture.

4.2 Heterogeneous architecture

In heterogeneous architecture, the agents can have different capabilities and they can be different from each other. There can also be different agent groups to form a heterogeneous architecture. A system which is implemented with a heterogeneous architecture should not constrain the number of agents in these groups. All the agent groups should have desired number of agents and their agent number can also be different from each other. A system which has agents from some different brands can be an example of heterogeneous architecture. **Figure 4** illustrates a heterogeneous architecture.

Heterogeneous architectures can be more flexible and cheaper than homogeneous architectures using some optimizations. Tasks can be allocated according to features of an agent. For example, while the agent which has a better camera is capturing photos, the other one which has a better processing power can handle task sharing issues. Although a multiagent system is not constructed heterogeneous agents, it can be better to design an architecture suitable for heterogeneous agents.

4.3 Architecture of the study

The study is implemented with a fixed brand agent but the agents from different brands or having different capabilities can be used. This feature is provided by the connection mechanism. The system uses a local area network (LAN) in order to communicate. The communication is handled via messages. There are some types of communication messages in our system. These messages are addressed in

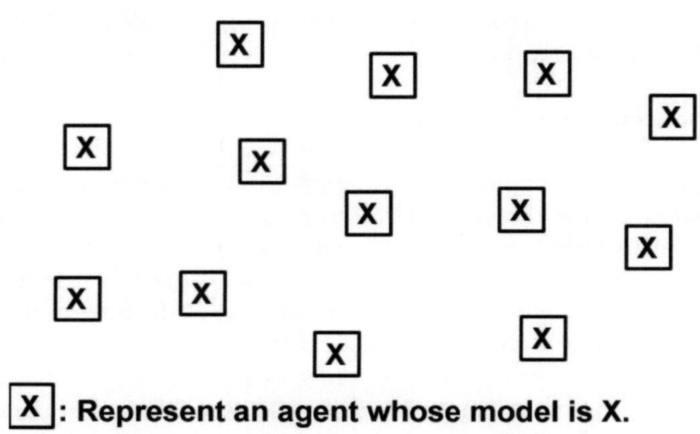

Figure 3.
A homogeneous multiagent system.

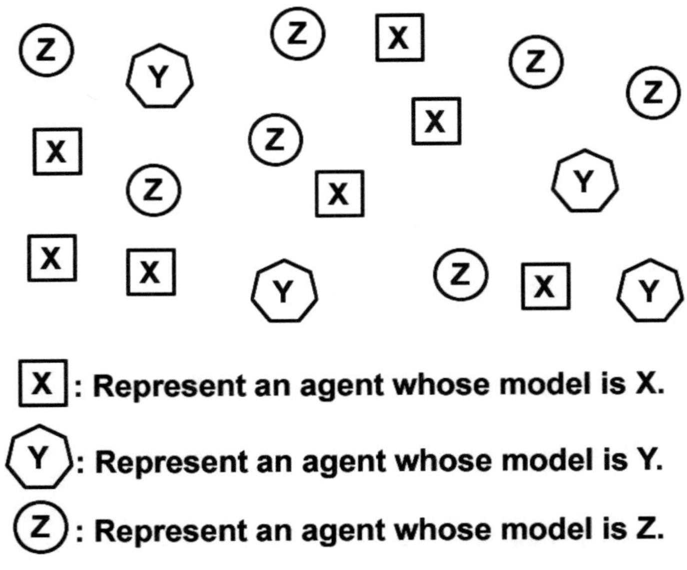

Figure 4.
A heterogeneous multiagent system.

Section 6. One of the reasons to select this type of communication structure is providing a heterogeneous architecture. When an agent implements these messages, it can easily join our system. For example, there is a message type whose purpose is transferring command messages. This message carries information about the coverage area and the task. An agent which has features suitable for our problem and which has implementation to parse the information can take command messages and be a part of our system.

The architecture does not restrict the number of different heterogeneous agents or number of agent. There can be any number of agents as much as an agent can store the address of other agents. This property is provided by implementation of the architecture. In our implementation, all the agents have a list to store the address of other agents. This list does not keep agent dependent information but it only store the address of other agents. In this way, the agents need just the address of the other agents. This improves scalability of the system and gives the power of working with desired number of different agents. This implementation also does not restrict the number of agents from different groups. There can be any number of groups and any number of agents in these groups. These properties make our system more robust, flexible and scalable.

4.4 Implementation of another architecture

When the study uses a homogeneous architecture, a different model agent could not be added and this would constrain the abilities of the system. For example, assume that we want to add an agent and we have an agent from different brand. If the system does not provide heterogeneous agents, we cannot use the agent. Instead, we have to buy a new agent whose brand same as the ones in the system. This increases our costs and this is not a desired situation. On the other hand, some products can be sold in a specific time intervals. Even if we do not buy a constructed agent, its internal components are sold in same way too. This situation results a system which only can be used as long as the agents can be constructed or bought.

When our agent list would have been designed to some fixed different agents, it results a system which is heterogeneous but whenever a different agent must be added, the implementation of the system must be updated according to the agent, which is wanted to add. This situation would be laborious and could not be applied in some situations. For example, if the implementation is not proper to add a new type of agent or an agent is not proper for the system, it cannot be added. This situation has some drawbacks which are same as in the previous case.

5. Control mechanisms

Control mechanism is one of the challenging and vital components. They affect the whole system from agents to communication styles. A control mechanism determines how the agents are controlled; in other word, it determines how the agents decide for coordination.

Choosing a right control mechanism depends on some parameters. These are performance of agents, communication style of the system, environment, cost and mission type. There can be some parameters depending on the problem. This situation leads to finding different types of control mechanism or variating the existing ones in order to build effective systems. In this chapter, the main three control mechanisms [13] are addressed. These are centralized, distributed and hierarchical control.

5.1 Centralized control

In centralized control, there is a fixed agent to control the coordination of the system. This agent can be called master or mediator. The other agents are called slaves. There is a centralized control illustration in **Figure 5**. All slaves take orders from master. This approach creates a system in which the master agent is constructed a bit different or completely different than slaves. Depending on the problem or the facilities, differences can be set. But, these differences determine the ability of the master and the system. For example, if the master is used only in order to control of the system, it does not need to have a payload. On the other hand, if there are limited numbers of agents and the master must contribute to completion of the task, then it must have a payload.

Centralized control has some advantages and disadvantages. It requires a simple consensus mechanism in which the agents just obey the master. But on the other hand, implementation of centralized control is somehow difficult because it requires design of agents and implementation of the system in two different perspectives. These are how the master and slaves are constructed and how the system is implemented. These can result a master whose cost is higher than slaves and a system which is implemented in a master perspective and in slaves perspective. For example, there must two different programs, one of them is for master and

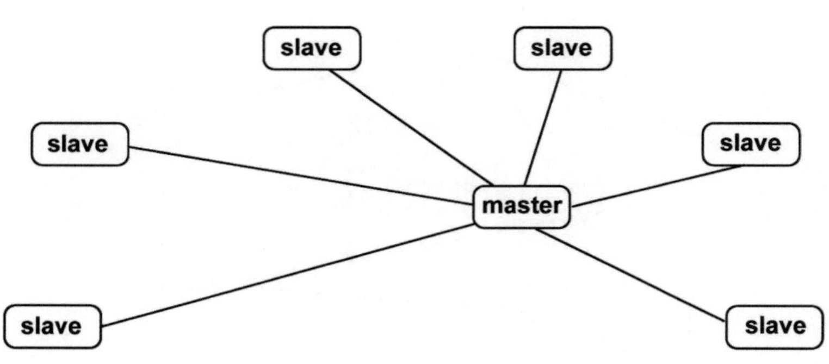

Figure 5.
A centralized control.

the other one is for slaves. The other important disadvantage is that, operational capability of the system depends on the master. If the master is damaged, the system cannot be used or the task cannot be completed.

5.2 Distributed control

In distributed control, all agents are equal for the control. There is not any master agent to control the slaves. Instead, all the agents contribute control equally. This is done by consensus. In multiagent systems, consensus means that the agents decide on an agreement which determines the behavior of the system. There are various consensus algorithms in literature [14, 15]. All of them have some differences and come with advantages and disadvantages against each other. But all of them have the same objective and all of them have the characteristics of distributed control.

Using distributed control mechanism can be advantageous. It results a system in which design and implementation are easy because all the agents are in same level, there is not any need to think about in master and slave perspectives. The other important advantage is that if any of the agents is damaged, the task can still be completed. On the other hand, implementation of a consensus algorithm is a challenging task. They are problem dependent and they affect the communication styles of the system (**Figure 6**).

5.3 Hierarchical control

Hierarchical control acts like a tree and it has a tree characteristics. All agents can have children and can have parent. All agents are responsible for control of their children. There is a root agent at the top of the control. Actually, the root is responsible for the control of the system. It shares the task to its children and its children can share the task among their children. **Figure 7** can give an idea about the mechanism. Depending on the situation, this mechanism can lead a system in which there are one type, two types or three types of different agents. In the case of three different agents, there can be a root, controllers, and leaves. The root can be responsible for sharing task among controllers. The controller can be responsible for the control of the leaves and only the leaves can contribute to completion of the task. In the case of two different types of agents, there can be a root, controllers and leaves but instead of only controlling the leaves, the controllers contribute to completion of the task. In the case of a one type of agent, there can be a root, controllers and leaves but all the agents can contribute to completion of task.

Hierarchical control mechanism generally used in problems which requires multiple tasks and which spreads on a wide area. There are some advantages and disadvantages

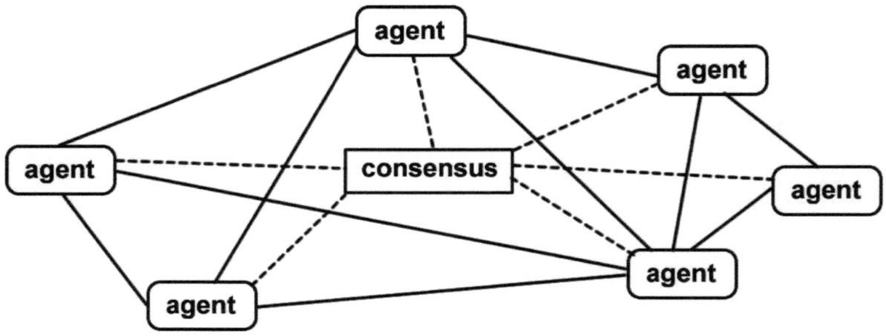

Figure 6.
A distributed control.

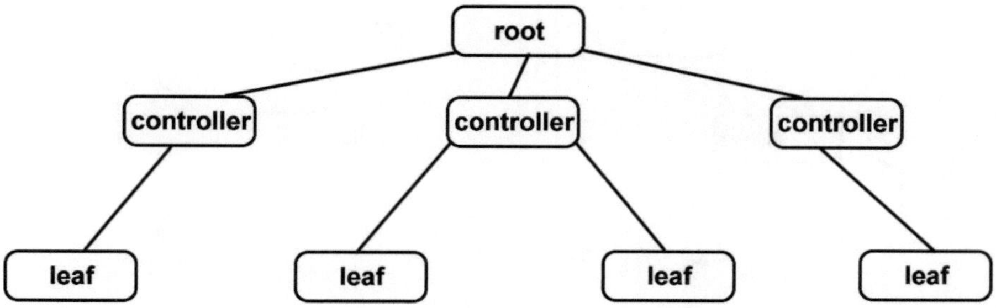

Figure 7.
A hierarchical control.

using hierarchical control. One of the advantages is that it has a simple consensus mechanism in which children obey the order of parents. The other important advantage is that the system is well suitable for multiple tasks which must be done simultaneously. On the other hand, implementation of the system can be difficult in both agent perspective and the system perspective. It is difficult in agent perspective because the system can have different types of agent. This allows constructing different types of agent whose requirements and capabilities are different from each other. It is difficult in system perspective because different types of agents require different implementation.

5.4 Designed control mechanism for the study

A different control mechanism is designed for the study which is mixture of centralized and distributed control. In the mechanism, there is not any fixed master. Instead, all agents can be a master as long as they have mission. When any of the agents have a mission, it shares the mission among others including itself and it became a master until the mission is completed. It is similar to distributed control because there is not any fixed master in the system. It is similar to centralized control because the tasks are shared among agents by a master. This hybrid control mechanism results a system which is very suitable for our problem. **Figure 8** shows the control mechanism of the system.

There are some reasons to design such a control mechanism for the study. The most important reason is that this mechanism offers some advantages against the other control mechanisms. One of the advantages is that it provides a simple consensus algorithm because whenever an agent has a mission, it just gives the mission to others and they just accept the order and then try to complete it. This algorithm is as simple as the consensus algorithm of a centralized control. The other advantage is that it provides easy design and implementations. It provides an easy design because all agents can be constructed same, there is not any need to design different types of agents. It provides an easy implementation because all agents act the same, and there is not need to implement different types of agents. The other important advantage is operational capability. When an agent is damaged, the others can still complete the mission or they can still take a mission because the master is not fixed. Thus, the system does not depend on a single agent.

5.5 A different view

If centralized control is selected for the study, there must be a fixed agent in order to control the slaves. This situation enforces the study designing two different implementations for each of the agent type. On the other hand, the study became depended to the master. If the master gets some damages, the study cannot be used.

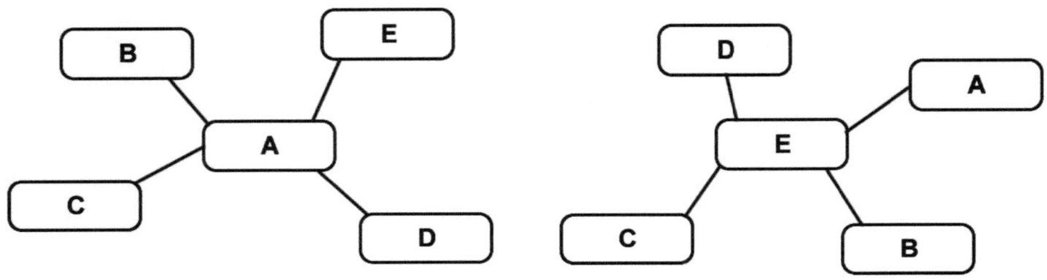

Figure 8.
Control mechanism of the system.

If distributed control is selected, a consensus algorithm is needed for coordination. But, our problem is more suitable for a consensus algorithm like the one in centralized control because our area, which is reconstructed in 3D, is selected in advance. This makes our problem static and can easily be solved with the consensus mechanism of centralized control.

If hierarchical control is selected, there must be a hierarchy among agents but our problem is not suitable well for a hierarchy. A hierarchy may be needed in situations in which the mission has several tasks or it has a large task. But, our problem requires only one task and the areas are not very large.

6. Communication mechanisms

Communication is another challenging and vital component in multiagent systems. Unlike other vital components, it does not affect the coordination directly. Instead, it provides a basis and coordination is provided using it. A communication mechanism determines how the agents communicate.

Communication is effected from components of multiagent systems and some other factors. These factors and components are environment, agents, control mechanism, architecture and weather. These have a critical role in order to select a mechanism. There are three [13, 16] main communication mechanisms. These are direct communication, communication using sense and communication using environment. Each of them has advantages and disadvantages. These are discussed in this section. Depending on the problem and facilities, one of them can be selected.

6.1 Communication using environment

In this mechanism, the agents do not interact with each other. Instead, they use environment as a medium. Thus, they adapt to the changes in the environment. In other word, they make their next movement according to environment. This provides communication among them. This mechanism generally is known as stigmergy [17, 18]. It can be found in nature. Some insects and termites complete their tasks using this type of communication. It is inspired from nature and applied to multiagent systems.

In multiagent systems, this mechanism is provided by implementation of agents and input devices like sensors, cameras or others. Implementation of the agents determines what the agent does when it encounters with an object. Input devices provides observing and identification of the objects which are used as communication medium. All agents have the input devices. While they are observing the environment, they collect information and this information is parsed.

When the information is parsed, the agents act how they are implemented according to information. For example, there can be an obstacle type whose purpose is turning the agents to left. When the agents are implemented suitable for the purpose of the obstacle type and when the agent encounters with the obstacle, they turn to left.

There are some advantages and disadvantages of the mechanism. One of the advantages is that ones the mechanism is set, it can provide a communication mechanism for a lot of agents and number of agents does not affect the system. The other important advantage is that it can be used in complex and large tasks without considering connection range. On the other hand, there are some important disadvantages of the mechanism. One of them is that the cost of using the mechanism can be very high because it can require multiple sensors and multiple sensors require more performance. This approach comes with high cost. Another important disadvantage is that designing such an environment is generally difficult. There are a lot of things to consider. These are objects in the environment, different objects which do not affect the communication, input types of the agents. When these things are determined, the system can be set.

6.2 Communication using sense

In this communication mechanism, the agents communicate with local interactions. One of the agents senses another. In this way, they make inferences about their next movement or their next states and they contribute completing the task according to these inferences.

The mechanism is realized by sensors and implementation of the agents. The sensors sense the other agents, in other words, they gather information about the states of others. Implementation of the agents determines what the agent does when it senses an agent which is desired type or which carries desired features. According to problem, the agents can be implemented in order to sense any agents or any desired features. While they are sensing the other agents, they determine them according to their implementations and when they sense the appropriate ones, they behave according to their implementations. For example, the agents can be implemented for sensing the ones whose distances are 50 cm away from them and when they sense them, they can try to keep the distance constant.

The most important advantage of the mechanism is that it can used to solve some kind of problems. These problems are pattern formation and flocking. In order to solve these, the agents sense their neighbors and they adjust themselves according to them. In contrast, the mechanism is more suitable for distributed control and using a centralized control is much harder.

6.3 Direct communication

In this communication mechanism, the agents communicate with direct messages. Every agent can get and send messages to others. The messages are determined when the system is designed and all the agents use these pre-determined messages.

This mechanism is generally set on a network. Thus, all the messages are sent and get through it. The mechanism is realized using implementation of agents and a component which let agents join the network. The implementation handles what the agents do when a message is received or what kind of message will be send to other agents. The component handles the communication issues. It provides getting messages which are released to the network and sending messages to other agents, in other word, it provides an interface in order to release messages. According to implementation and the need of the system, the agents can send or get messages from any agents. While agents wait messages from others, they can do whatever they want but when they get a message from other agents, they must behave according to their implementation. For example, an agent can be programmed to sleep when any mission is not assigned to the agent but when it gets a message which carries a mission, it must start completing it.

Direct communication mechanism can be used to implement any type of control mechanism. It can be even used for a control mechanism which is derived from other control mechanisms or whose design is unique and it can be used for any type of problem. In addition, there can be any number of agents in the system but in case of sending or getting too many messages simultaneously, the system can be slower. Or it cannot be used in case of a mission which spreads on a large area. Because, a network which provides connection for long distance is required and this requires a high cost which cannot be afforded.

6.4 Communication used in the study

Direct communication mechanism used in the study. The UAVs used in the study has a feature to connect a network and the system is suitable for any kind of networks. Thus, any network can be used for communication.

The system has tree type of communication messages. These are command messages, communication messages and mission completed messages. All of them have different purpose and all of them contribute to system in different perspectives. In order to send and get these messages, the agents uses their IP address as a communication address. Thus, the agents must know IP address of other agents to send and get messages from them. All the agents have an agent list which stores other agents IP addresses. Agents can get and send these messages according to the agent list and they must behave according to messages. The following subsection explains how these message types are used in the study.

6.4.1 Connection messages

Connection messages set up a connection between two agents. In other words, it allows two different agents to recognize each other. The agent lists are filled using connection messages. These messages carry the IP address of the agent. There are two connection messages in the system. These messages are add agent and confirm agent. They are in following form and each agent can send and get these.

- ADDAGENT#ip_address
- CONFIRMAGENT#ip_addres

An add agent message is sent when an agent wants to add another agent to its list. Its purpose is sending an add request to other agents. In order to add an agent, the agent list of the sender must first be checked to ensure that the agent has not been added yet. If it is so, sender agent send an add agent message to the receiver agent.

Confirm agent message is sent whenever an add message is received. Its purpose is confirming the sender about the connection. A receiver agent does not need to check if the sender is on the list or not. If it takes an add message, the sender is not on the list because when a connection message is completed, both the sender and the receiver add the other agent to its list. This approach yields a system in which the agent is on same level. When an agent gets confirm agent message, it adds the sender of the message to the list. The algorithm is explained step by step below. **Figure 9** shows the sender and receiver side briefly.

1. The sender checks if the receiver has not been added yet.

2. If the receiver has not been added, sends an add message.

3. If the receiver gets an add message, adds the sender of the message to the agent list

4. The receiver sends a confirm message to the sender.

5. When the sender gets the confirm message, it adds the receiver to its agent list.

6.4.2 Command messages

When any of the agents takes a mission, it shares the mission with its agent list. Before the agent shares the mission, the mission information must be defined. The agent which shares the mission is responsible for defining mission information. The mission is shared in a command message.

In the implementation of the study, a mission information message is defined by a class. The class carries the location of the area, the location of the mission which is assigned to the agent, the number of agents in the system, the ID of the agent. The location area is the location which the master agent takes, in other word, it is the whole scene. The location of the mission is the task which is given an agent to cover. This information is required to defining the area. The number of agents in the system is required because the agent must know how many agents are there in the system. Whenever a mission is shared, all the agents are given an ID by the master agent. The ID of the master agent becomes 1 and the ID of the other agents

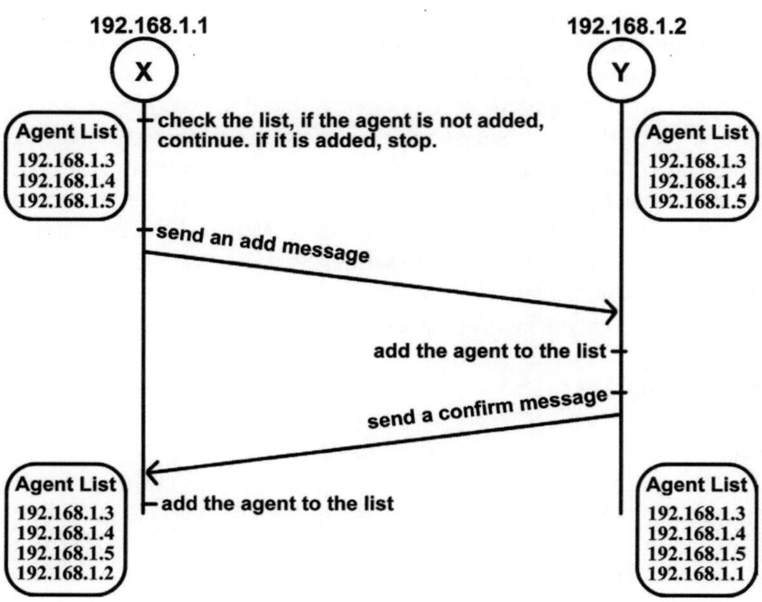

Figure 9.
Connection message.

determined relatively with the master agent. This information is required because it is used in coverage of the area and for checking if the agents complete the mission successfully.

6.4.3 Mission completed messages

The system must be sure that the mission is completed successfully. In order to be sure of the completion of the mission, mission completed messages are sent. There are four types of mission completed message in the system, these are error, state, success and not completed messages. They carry an IP address and they are in the following form.

- ERROR#ip_address
- STATE#ip_address
- SUCCESS#ip_address
- NOTCOMPLETED#ip_address

Actually, there are three types of scenarios to realize mission completed messages. These scenarios arise because there are differences among mission completion of master as first, mission completion of slaves as first and in the case of not taking a response from a slave.

When any of the slaves completes its mission before the master, they send a success message to the master. The purpose of the success message is informing the master about the completion. When the master agent completes the mission before the slaves, it sends a state message to the slaves which have not sent a success message yet. The purpose of state message is determining if the slave completes its mission or not and if it does not complete, determining the reason. The reason can be an error. When the slaves get the state message, they send not completed message if they have not completed their mission but they think they can complete it successfully, in other word, if they have power and facilities to complete the mission. The purpose of not completed message is informing the master about the state of the slave. When the master agent gets a not completed message from a slave, it sends states messages until the agent sends a success message or an error message. The error message is sent in the case of there is an error in the agent or the agent cannot complete the mission because of facilities or power. The purpose of error message is informing the master about the state of the slave. When the master gets an error message, it completes the mission of the sender of the message. When the master sent a state message and a slave does not response in a given time interval, it is counted as error too. The following algorithms explain scenarios and **Figure 10** and **Figure 11** shows the scenarios briefly.

When a slave finishes first:

1. The slave sends a success message to master.
2. Master gets the message and will not send it a state message.

When a master finishes first:

1. The master sends a state message to slaves.

2. The slaves get the message.

3. The slaves send a not completed message if it can complete the mission.

4. The slaves send an error message if it cannot complete the mission.

5. If the master gets a not completed message, it sends states messages until it gets a success or error message.

6. If the master gets an error message, it completes the mission of the sender agent.

When a slave does not response:

1. The master sends a state message and waits for a while.

2. If the slave does not response, the master completes its mission.

6.5 Implementing other communication mechanisms

If communication using environment is selected, there must be some objects whose purpose is defining the coverage area for each of the agents in the scene.

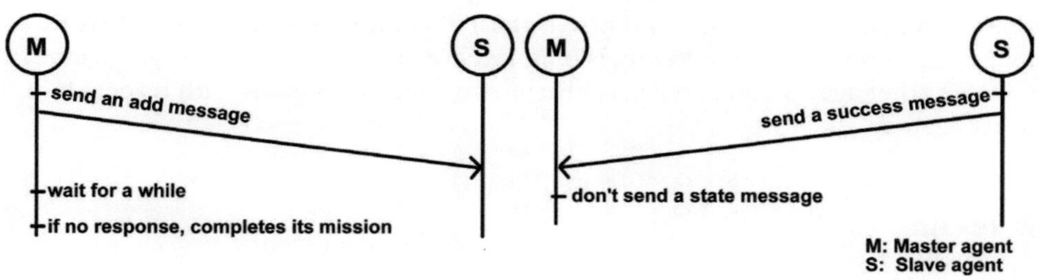

Figure 10.
A slave finishes first and a slave does not response.

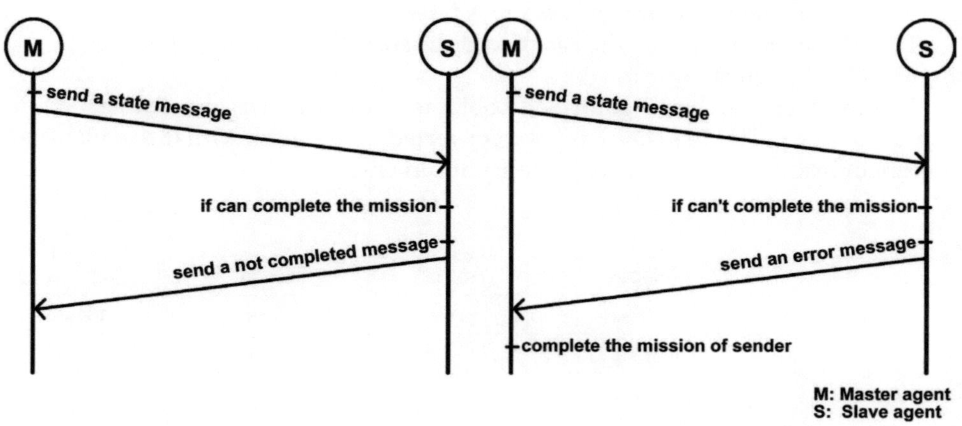

Figure 11.
Master finishes first.

There must also be additional sensors or a camera implementation whose purpose is determining the objects in order to communicate. In the case of having sensors on the agent, the agents collect the information which comes from the sensors and tries to determine the coverage area from the collected information. The sensors add additional cost to the agent and the system. They add additional cost to the agent because buying and integrated a sensor to an agent requires additional time and money. In addition, the performance of the agents must be upgraded because the sensors also need process power. They add additional cost to the system because the system requires objects and buying objects requires money. In addition, positioning the objects to the scene requires a human interaction or designing a different study whose purpose is just positioning the object to the scene. In the case of using a camera implementation, while the cameras record the scene, they try to determine the coverage area. This case adds additional complexity to the system because a camera implementing requires detecting objects in the scene and integrating this implementation to the main implementation results a more complex system.

If communication using sense is selected, there must be additional sensors on the agent and there must be different implementation of the system. The additional sensors are required because the agent uses information which comes from the sensors in order to communicate. The types of the sensors can vary according to desired communication range. For example, one sensor type can sense 100 m distances but another can sense 1000 m. This situation restricts coverage area with respect to sensors and results a system whose capabilities is strictly depended on the sensors. In addition, the sensors add the system additional cost to the agent. The reason of the cost is same as with the cost of communication using environment. A different implementation is required because in this case the agents must observe other agents and determines their own coverage regions with respect to other agents.

7. Results

The study is executed with one, two and four agents in four areas. The sizes of the fields are 1600, 2500, 3600, and 4900 m^2, respectively. When they start their mission, a chronometer is starter and it lasts until they finish their missions and the results are recorded. The results are shown in **Table 1**. The results show that when the number of agents is more, the system is faster.

The relationship between the agents and the size of the agents can be seen in **Figure 12** and **Figure 13**.

Figure 14 depicts the 3D point cloud obtained by the multiagent reconstruction approach. The point cloud can easily be converted in to a mesh with the available texture information acquired from the agent cameras.

	1600 m^2	**2500 m^2**	**3600 m^2**	**4900 m^2**
1 Agent	69 sec	83 sec	96 sec	104 sec
2 Agents	39 sec	46 sec	51 sec	55 sec
4 Agents	24 sec	28 sec	31 sec	34 sec

Table 1.
Results for 1, 2 and 4 agents for various scenarios.

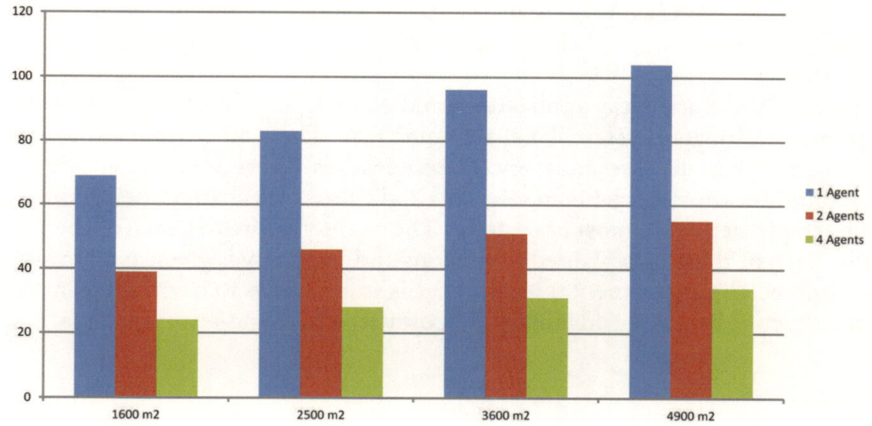

Figure 12.
Relationship between the number of agents and the size of the fields.

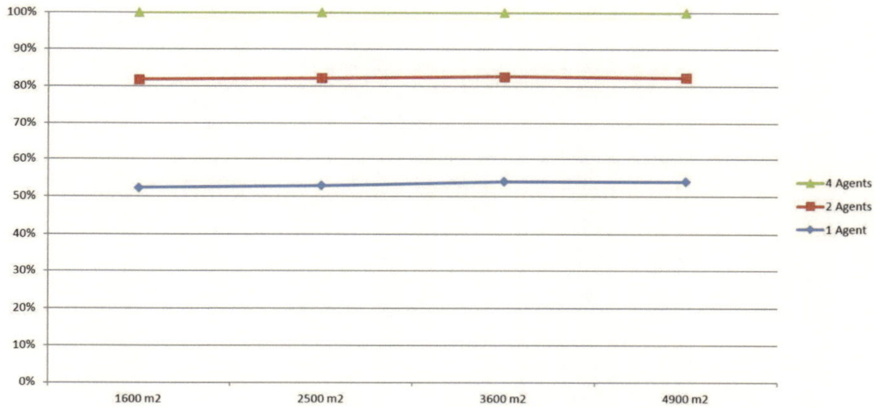

Figure 13.
Percentage relationship between the number of agents and the size of the fields.

Figure 14.
An output from the study.

8. Conclusion

Multiagent systems deal with coordination of more than one agent in order to complete a task. There are several features of these systems. These features are robustness, scalability and flexibility. These features give some advantages to multi agent system. These advantages make multiagent systems cheaper, faster and more reliable. There are many applications of multiagent systems ranges from networking to robotics.

Although there are many applications and advantages of multiagent systems, designing a multiagent system is a challenging task. There are several issues to consider. The chapter addresses most encountered issues. These are architecture selection, communication mechanism selection and control mechanism selection. They must be implemented in most of systems. The chapter addresses each of them with a study. Each of them is explained in sections and the study is given as an example in each sections. The experimental results of this study shows that a multiagent system is more effective and more advantageous compared to single-agent systems.

Author details

Metehan Aydın[1], Erkan Bostancı[1*], Mehmet Serdar Güzel[1] and Nadia Kanwal[2]

1 Department of Computer Engineering, Ankara University, Ankara, Turkey

2 Lahore College for Women University, Lahore, Pakistan

*Address all correspondence to: ebostanci@ankara.edu.tr

References

[1] Şahin E. Swarm robotics: From sources of inspiration to domains of application. In: Şahin E, Spears W, editors. Swarm Robotics Workshop: State-of-the-Art Survey. Lecture Notes in Computer Science, No. 3342. Berlin, Germany; 2005. pp. 10-20

[2] Navarro I, Matía F. An introduction to swarm robotics. ISRN Robotics. 2013;**2013**:10. Article ID 608164

[3] Balaji PG, Srinivasan D. An introduction to multi-agent systems. In Innovations in multi-agent systems and applications-1. Berlin, Heidelberg: Springer; 2010. pp. 1-27

[4] Ali D, Salil K, Raja J. Multi-agent systems: A survey. IEEE Access. 2018;**6**:1. DOI: 10.1109/ACCESS.2018.2831228

[5] Mutlu B, Hacıömeroğlu M, Serdar GM, Dikmen M, Sever H. Silhouette extraction from street view images. International Journal of Advanced Robotic Systems. 2014;**11**(7):114

[6] Bostanci E. 3D reconstruction of crime scenes and design considerations for an interactive investigation tool. International Journal of Information Security Science. 2015;**4**(2):50-58

[7] Bostanci E. Crime scene investigation in 3D using video frames. In: International Symposium on Digital Forensic Science; Ankara, Turkey. 2015. pp. 8-13

[8] Wu C. VisualSFM: A Visual Structure from Motion System. 2011. Available from: http://ccwu.me/vsfm/

[9] Lowe DG. Distinctive image features from scale-invariant keypoints. International Journal of Computer Vision. 2004;**60**(2):91-110

[10] Güzel MS. Performance evaluation for feature extractors on street view images. The Imaging Science Journal. 2016;**64**(1):26-33

[11] Furukawa Y et al. Towards internet-scale multi-view stereo. In: 2010 IEEE Conference on Computer Vision and Pattern Recognition (CVPR); IEEE. 2010

[12] Stone P, Veloso M. Multiagent systems: A survey from a machine learning perspective. Autonomous Robots. 2000;**8**(3):345-383

[13] Cao YU, Fukunaga AS, Kahng A. Cooperative mobile robotics: Antecedents and directions. Autonomous Robots. 1997;**4**(1):7-27

[14] Yu W, Chen G, Cao M, Kurths J. Second-order consensus for multiagent systems with directed topologies and nonlinear dynamics. IEEE Transactions on Systems, Man, and Cybernetics, Part B. 2010;**40**(3):881-891

[15] Gao L, Liao X, Li H, Chen G. Event-triggered control for multiagent systems with general directed topology and time delays. Asian Journal of Control. 2016;**18**(3):945-953

[16] Gregory D et al. A taxonomy for multi-agent robotics. Autonomous Robots. 1996;**3**(4):375-397

[17] Heylighen F. Stigmergy as a universal coordination mechanism I: Definition and components. Cognitive Systems Research. 2016;**38**:4-13

[18] Dorigo M, Bonabeau E, Theraulaz G. Ant algorithms and stigmergy. Future Generation Computer Systems. 2000;**16**(8):851-871

Chapter 3

A Q-Learning-Based Approach for Simple and Multi-Agent Systems

Ümit Ulusoy, Mehmet Serdar Güzel and Erkan Bostanci

Abstract

This study proposes different machine learning-based solutions to both single and multi-agent systems, took place on a 2-D simulation platform, namely, Robocode. This dynamic and programmable platform allows agents to interact with the environment and each other by employing a variety of battling strategies. Q-Learning is one of the leading and popular machine learning-based solutions to be applied to such a problem. However, especially for continued spaces, the control problem gets deeper. Essentially, one of the main drawbacks of reinforcement learning (RL) is to design an appropriate reward function that the function can be described by only employing few parameters for simple tasks, whereas estimating the goal of the reward function may be a challenging problem. Recent studies prove that neural network-based approaches can handle these challenges and achieve to learn control strategies from 2-D or 1-D data. Besides those problems of RL algorithms for single robots, once the number of robots increases and the systems need to behave as multi-agent systems, the overall design requirements become more complex. Accordingly, the proposed system is validated by considering different battle scenarios. The performance of the Q-Learning-based system and the supervised learning techniques are compared by employing different scenarios for this problem. Results reveal the superiority of the ANN-based approach over other methods.

Keywords: multi-agent systems, Q-Learning, Robocode, auto-encoder, neural network, battling strategy

1. Introduction

Swarm intelligence is a scientific field that integrates the fields of swarm intelligence and cooperative robotics to establish and coordinate robots to achieve challenging tasks within a reasonable time [1, 2]. Multi-agent systems, on the other hand, are considered to be coordination of autonomous agents so as to complete tasks by exchanging or sharing information over a network. This resembles the swarm intelligence discipline in similar ways [3, 4], as it has been previously noted that multi-agent systems mainly deal with the coordination of multiple interacting agents so as to complete different tasks. The key objective of those systems is to coordinate rather simple agents instead of using a complex agent [5]. The coordination ability of agents gains different skills to these systems that individual agents may not be allowed to achieve, which are, namely, robustness, scalability, and flexibility [5, 6]. The Robocode platform on the other hand is a game developing platform and allows developers to design robot battle tanks to battle against other tanks [7]. The battles are running in real time, and the game is played on a two-dimensional simulation environment by employing single or multiple robots, as shown in **Figure 1**. These robots can be defined as single robot, or some of them can be marked as team robots. Each of them is possessed with battling behaviors which allows them to decide movement, fire, and targeting in order to keep their energies high and destroy their opponents. The time is measured with ticks, and each robot is allowed only one movement for each tick. At the end of each round (game), the total score for each attendee is calculated by their "fire damage," "ram damage," and "survival status." This lets a team to obtain the highest score even if their robots did not survive.

The flexibility, scalability, and robustness of the Robocode platform encourage authors to employ machine learning-based approaches for multi-agent system problems. Despite their advantages, the platform also offers some challenges that should be handled in an appropriate manner. The critical issues are detailed as follows:

- Opponent rounds are not visible and the environment is not fully observable.
- Sensors used by robots are limited.
- The number of action is quite high which makes learning harder.
- The speed of robots slows down during firing and turning behaviors.
- Once the gun of robot's temperature is high, firing behavior does not work, which forces users to consider all parameters.

Robocode gathers great deal and attention from a big community including researcher, students, and engineers, in which design concepts and source codes are

Figure 1.
An example screenshot from the Robocode environment [7].

shared. Tournaments and leagues are arranged via websites. Hence, the rankings of customized robots are continuously updated [7]. Therefore, game strategies are very critical and continuously evolve by utilizing different approaches. Robocode game strategies are characterized as trees of atomic elements agreeing to actions and observations in a battle.

Machine learning has been widely used in single [8, 9] and multi-agent systems [2, 3]. This also encourages researchers to apply machine learning or meta-heuristic-based methods to train and prepare robotic teams for this battling process of Robocode environment. For instance, there exist studies employing genetic algorithm in order to generate various and evolving behaviors using genetic algorithm [8, 10]. Besides, decision tree and neural network-based solutions have been employed to estimate a strategy to obtain a higher rank in the league [11, 12]. Those studies prove that machine learning is an efficient way of designing and implementing strategies for such an environment. Accordingly, this study is inspired from those previous studies and introduces three different machine learning-based approaches to train and prepare robots for the battle. The first approach mainly employs reinforcement learning to train a single and team robot separately so as to allow them to survive in a tank battle. It is proven that despite its discrete structure, Q-Learning can be adapted for such a complex game. In addition, a neural network-based design is also implemented in order to compare the results, which has been previously employed in a similar study [13]. Finally, an auto-encoder-based model is designed to train a number of robots, allowing them to battle to the death in an arena. Similar studies can be seen in [14–16]. Next section mainly introduces the proposed methods separately. The experiments are defined, and results are evaluated in a detailed manner at the experimental section. Lastly, the study is concluded at the conclusion section.

2. Methodology

This study proposes three different machine learning-based solutions to the multi-agent battling game. The first of them employs reinforcement learning approach, aiming extracting the maximum award from the network used in learning procedure. The second approach, on the other hand, relies on a supervised learning algorithm based on an artificial neural network architecture. Finally, an auto-encoder-based model has been designed and implemented to train the robots for the challenge. Each of those solutions will be detailed, respectively.

2.1 Q-Learning robot for Robocode

Reinforcement learning (RL) aims to take suitable action to maximize reward in a specific situation. It is employed by various software and machines to find the best possible behavior in particular situation. Reinforcement learning differs from the supervised learning that the agent agrees what to do to achieve with the given task. Instead of employing a training dataset, the agent learns from its experiences. Q-Learning is the most popular RL algorithm and preferred for this study due to its efficiency and popularity [17]. The agent mainly observes the environment and performs the action by employing the previously defined action. The agent then obtains the action consequence or award from the environment. This state and action pair is kept for future usage since it gives clues about the reward. The algorithm mainly aims to generate a Q-Table which illustrates maximum expected future rewards for action at each state. Q-Learning update rule is designed based on the Bellman equation so as to estimate the optimal Q-Value, and the Q-Learning update rule is given as Eq. (1):

$$Q(s_t, a_t)^{new} = (1 - \alpha)\boldsymbol{x}Q(s_t, a_t)^{old} + \alpha x(r_t + \gamma \boldsymbol{x}\ \text{maxQ}(s_{t+1}, a_t)) \tag{1}$$

where, at each time "t," the agent selects an action "a_t," observes a reward "r_t," and enters a newer state "s_{t+1}." Besides, α refers to learning rate, whereas γ illustrates discount factor. Within the given algorithm and approach, a Q-Learning robot is designed according to the rule and environment of Robocode. Accordingly, any robot knows enemy position, bearing angle, and distance to enemy by employing its radar; then at each step, a robot selects an action that maximizes the upcoming reward for the current state. These state and action pairs are stored in table that is updated during the game, and robot collects rewards at each "thick" to update the table (Q-Table) as a result of applied actions. The lookup table contains following states and actions for the proposed Q-Learning robot for the Robocode problem (see **Table 1**). The flow chart of the Q-Learning robot is given in **Figure 2**.

The pseudocode of the Q-Learning algorithm is given as follows:

Q-Learning algorithm:

Requires *States s:1 to n;*
Actions a:1 to m;
Reward Function;
α (learning rate), γ : (discount factor)
Ensures *Updated Q-Table for action state coordination*
Procedure *Q-Learning*
Initialize state-actions table *Q(s,a)*
Current state "s" should be selected
While(A final state or threshold value is obtained)
Basing on the action selection policies select and action **a**
Obtain reward **r** for selected action alongside with the next state.
Update Q value for current state **s** and for following state according to (1) and parameters
EndWhile
EndProcedure

2.2 Artificial neural network robot for Robocode to approximate Q-Values

Artificial neural network is considered as universal approximators that can be adapted in many different and challenging problems. Several studies have already been applied to Robocode environment; some of those references can be seen in Section 1. Accordingly, a multilayer perceptron inspired from those studies has been adapted and designed for this study. It mainly aims to search the best output for

States	Actions
Robot location	Run away from the enemy
Enemy location	Move toward the enemy
Bearing angle with the enemy	Hold the current position
Energy level	Spin clockwise or anticlockwise

Table 1.
List of states and actions for Q-Learning robot of Robocode.

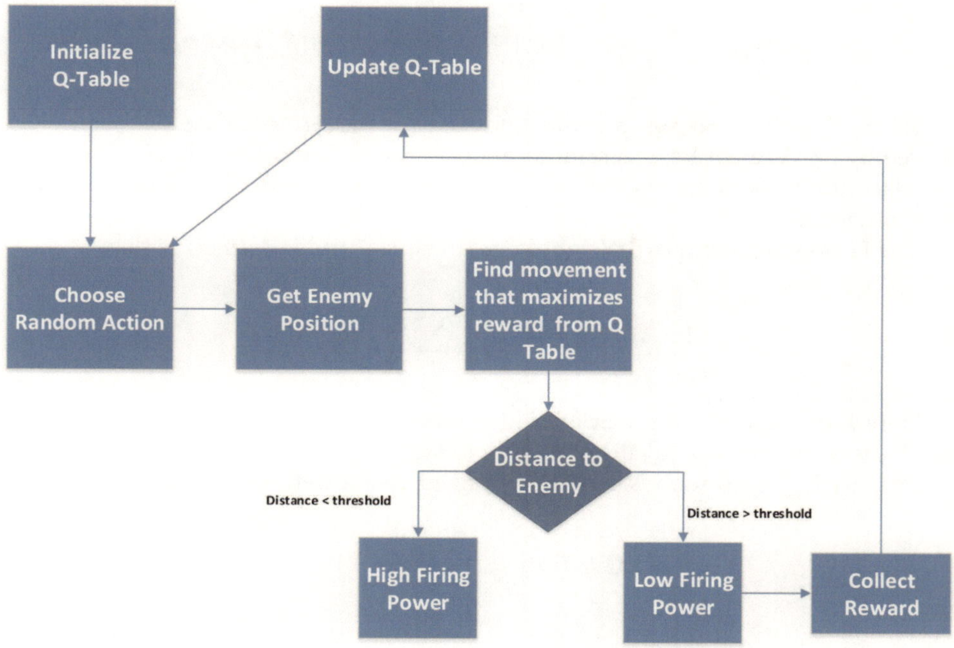

Figure 2.
Q-Learning robot training flow chart.

each Robocode thick based on actions and states that mainly allows us to approximate maximum Q-Values.

The proposed neural network has a very simple structure which consists of two layers. The first layer represents inputs, namely, X position, Y position, the distance between the robot and the opponent, the bearing angle, action, and bias values. The second layer on the other hand is a fully connected layer. The final layer represents the Q-Values, as seen in **Figure 3**. Sigmoid function is employed as the activation function, and also, node numbers at the hidden layer are estimated by trial and error method that results in higher learning accuracy.

2.3 Deep auto-encoders applied Robocode to approximate Q-Values

Stacked sparse auto-encoder is a type of deep neural network involving stacking sparse auto-encoders, and a classifier is regularly used as the final layer for mainly classification or regression problems [18]. This model has not been applied in such a problem which encourages authors to employ the technique into the current problem. Consequently, an example model is designed and given for this problem shown in **Figure 4**.

Accordingly, the first auto-encoders are trained by utilizing an unsupervised training method [18]. Fundamentally, the output of the first sparse auto-encoder is considered as an input to the second one, and the output of second auto-encoders becomes an input to the classifier as shown in the corresponding figure. The auto-encoders and the classifier "SoftMax" are stacked and qualified in a supervised manner by employing the backpropagation algorithm for estimating the optimum Q-Value. Each auto-encoder is trained by employing using the cost function illustrated in Eq. (1). E_r value is regulated by employing mean square error (MSE) approach:

$$E_r = \frac{1}{M}\sum_{m=1}^{M}\sum_{t=1}^{T}(x_{tm} - \hat{x}_{tm})^2 + \lambda * \Omega\, weights + \beta * \Omega\, sparsity \tag{2}$$

where *Er* is the error rate, x is the input and $\hat{x}$ is the restored data, $''\lambda''$ coefficient is used by L2 "Weight Regularization" and $''\beta''$ coefficient is used for the "Sparsity Regularization," m is the number of observations, and t illustrates the training data label number.

The $\Omega\, weights$ illustrates "Weight Regularization" and is defined as flows:

$$\Omega\, weights = \frac{1}{2}\sum_{x}^{X}\sum_{j}^{J}\sum_{k}^{K} w_{jk}^{(x)^2} \tag{3}$$

Here X indicates the number of hidden layers, n signifies observation numbers, and k shows hidden layers [18].

Sparsity Regularization is on the other hand can be defined as follows:

$$\Omega\, sparsity = \sum_{i=1}^{D} KL(\rho \| \hat{\rho}_i) \tag{4}$$

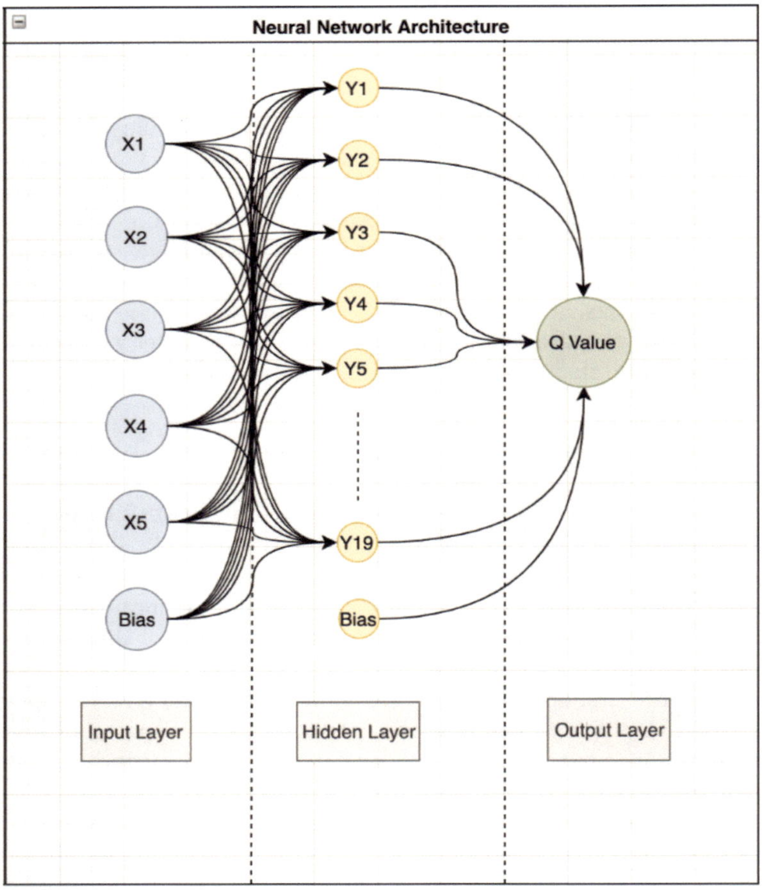

Figure 3.
ANN architecture to approximate Q-Values.

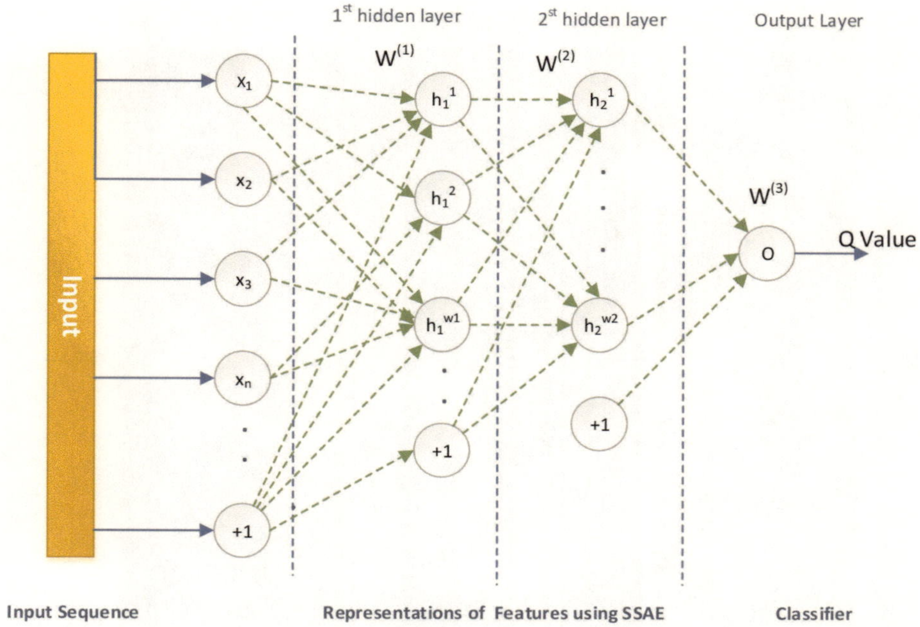

Figure 4.
A stacked sparse auto-encoder (SSAE) having two hidden layers and softmax classifier.

where anticipated value is represented by ρ, $\hat{\rho}_i$ denotes the average output activation of each neuron *"i, "* and "KL" is the function that evaluates the variance between two probabilities distribution over the same data. The details of those equations can be seen in [18].

3. Experimental results

Aforementioned Robocode is a tank-combat emulator developed by IBM alphaWorks [7]. Basically the tank or teams must navigate the environment to avoid being shot by its rivals. Three different machine learning-based approaches are employed to train the single and multi-agent systems to win the battle against their opponents in an autonomous manner. A desktop computer having Intel Core i7-6700 CPU @ 2.60-GHz and 16-GB RAM is employed to conduct experiments. Each method and results are illustrated separately by defining scenarios.

3.1 Scenario 1

This scenario illustrates a single robot battle, in which a Q-Learned customized robot (AUQRobot) fights against the Spin Robot. An example screenshot is illustrated in **Figure 5**. Within the scenario up to 12,000 round took place to train the robot. **Figure 6** illustrates the change of the winning percentage along the rounds. Regarding to the graph, it is very clear that winning percentage is up to 87% with the power of reinforcement learning that provided greedy method. Collaterally, collected cumulative reward change along the rounds gives a same curve. This result is obtained under Robocode maximum data storing constraints. Results are experienced with a Q-Table includes 9216 elements, and it is also noted that increasing the table size will probably increase the overall winning performance.

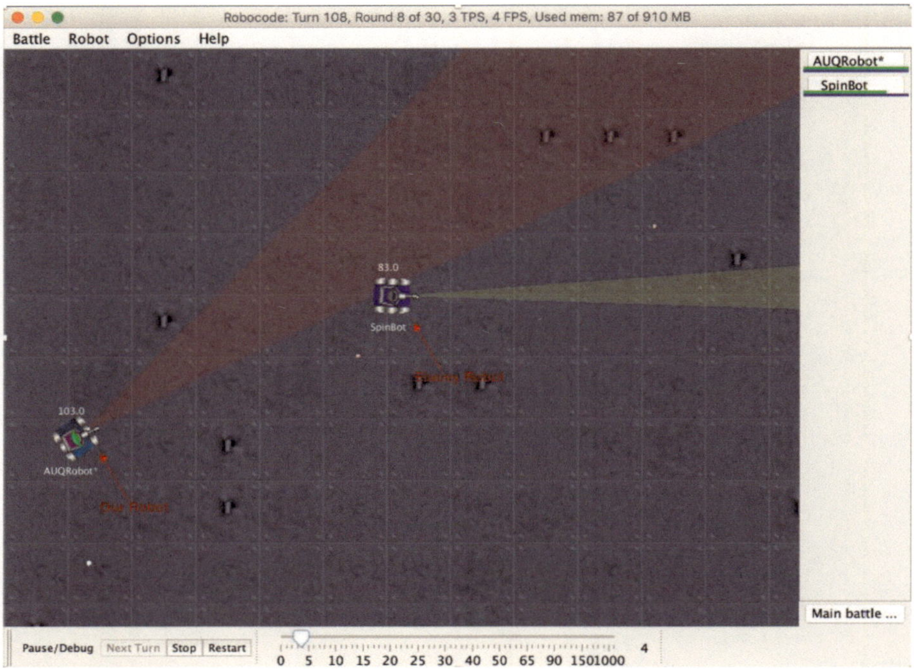

Figure 5.
A screenshot obtained from Scenario 1 (SpinBot Robot).

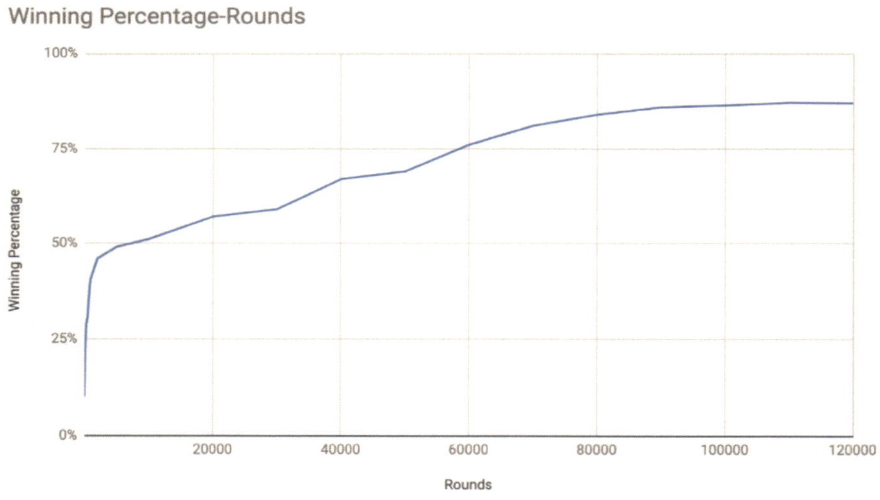

Figure 6.
Winning percentage of AUQRobot within rounds.

Within this scenario, Q-Learned customized robot (AUQRobot) fights against the TrackerBot Robot (see **Figure 7**), which is also a popular robot used in Robocode. For this scenario, the same training configuration is also applied, and 92% winning rate is also obtained. An example screenshot obtained from the Robocode platform is shown in **Figure 8**. Regarding to the results, Tracker Robot never survived during a 20-round battle. AUQRobot has lost 8% against to the opponent.

3.2 Scenario 2

This scenario illustrates a single robot battle, in which a customized robot (AUNNRobot) fights against the Spin Robot. The robot, which was implemented according to the artificial neural network architecture described above, was trained against SpinBot within 200 and 50,000 iterations. **Table 2** illustrates the configuration of ANN-based system.

The neural network performing linear regression and Q-Value, obtained from Q-Learning algorithm, was employed to train the system. **Figure 9** illustrates the

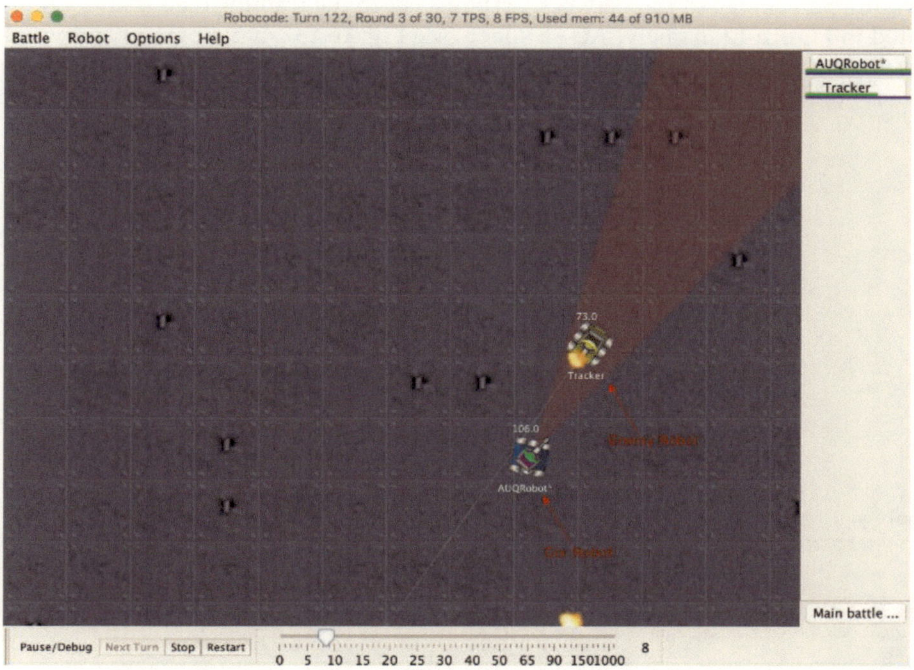

Figure 7.
A screenshot obtained from Scenario 1 (Tracker Robot).

Results for 20 rounds

Rank	Robot Name	Total Score	Survival	Surv Bonus	Bullet Dmg	Bullet Bonus	Ram Dmg * 2	Ram Bonus	1sts	2nds	3rds
1st	uu.AUQRobot*	3407 (92%)	1000	200	1835	367	5	0	20	0	0
2nd	sample.Trac...	293 (8%)	0	0	292	0	1	0	0	20	0

Save OK

Figure 8.
A screenshot illustrating Total score for Scenario 1 (Tracker Robot).

Input name	Parameter range	NN input range
Position X	0–800px	{0.0, 0.1 ... 7.9, 8.0}
Position Y	0–600px	{0.0, 0.1 ... 7.9, 8.0}
Distance to enemy	0–1000px	{0.0, 0.1 ... 5.9, 6.0}
Bearing angle between robot and enemy	0°–360°	{0.0, 0.1 ... 5.9, 6.0}

Table 2.
Configuration of ANN-based system.

winning percentage of the ANN-based robot within training procedure. Results reveal that the ANN-based method starts learning rapidly but converge lately when compared with reinforcement-based approach.

Accordingly, it has been considered that a battle between AUQRobot and AUNNRobot, both have already been trained for same robot class, may compare both systems performance appropriately (see **Figure 10**). In general, none of the participants are able to outperform the opponent clearly, but AUNNRobot has an advance as 54–46% over the AUQRobot based on 50 rounds as can be seen in **Figure 11**.

The results of deep auto-encoder-based method have also been trained that the winning percentage of the network with respect to the training data is also illustrated in **Figure 12**, namely, AUAERobot (see **Figure 13**) that, however, provides less wining rate compared with AUNNRobot. It should be noted that if raw image data is employed as input instead of giving position values to the network, the deep

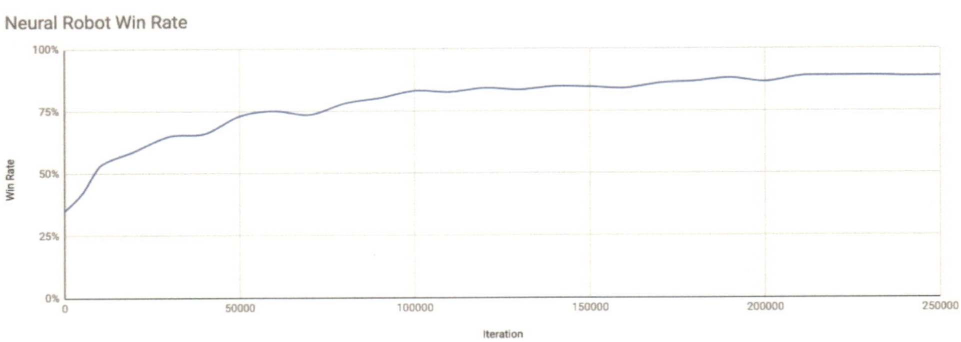

Figure 9.
Winning percentage of AUNNRobot within rounds.

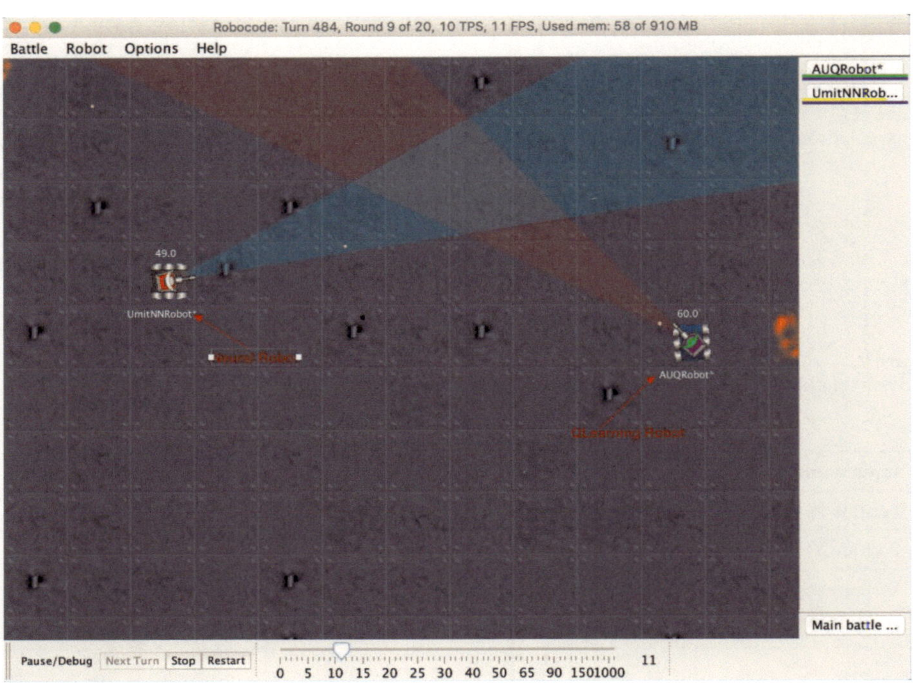

Figure 10.
A screenshot obtained from Scenario 2 for AUQRobot vs. AUNNRobot.

Results for 50 rounds

Rank	Robot Name	Total Score	Survival	Surv Bonus	Bullet Dmg	Bullet Bonus	Ram Dmg * 2	Ram Bonus	1sts	2nds	3rds
1st	uu.UmitNNRobot*	3771 (54%)	900	180	2474	215	1	0	20	30	0
2nd	uu.AUQRobot*	3149 (46%)	1500	300	1186	158	6	0	32	18	0

Save OK

Figure 11.
Results for 50 rounds for Scenario 2.

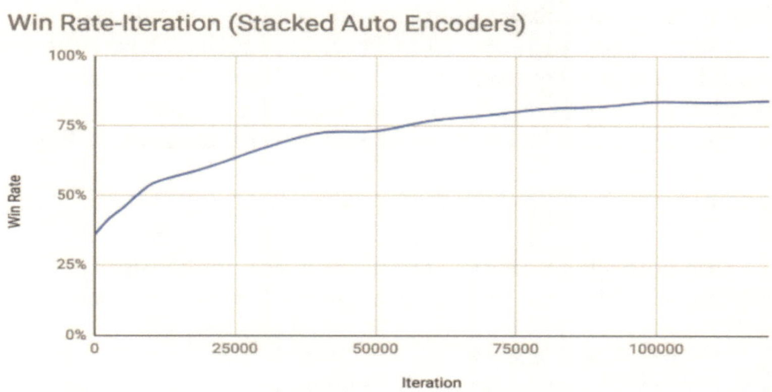

Figure 12.
Winning percentage of AUAERobot within iterations.

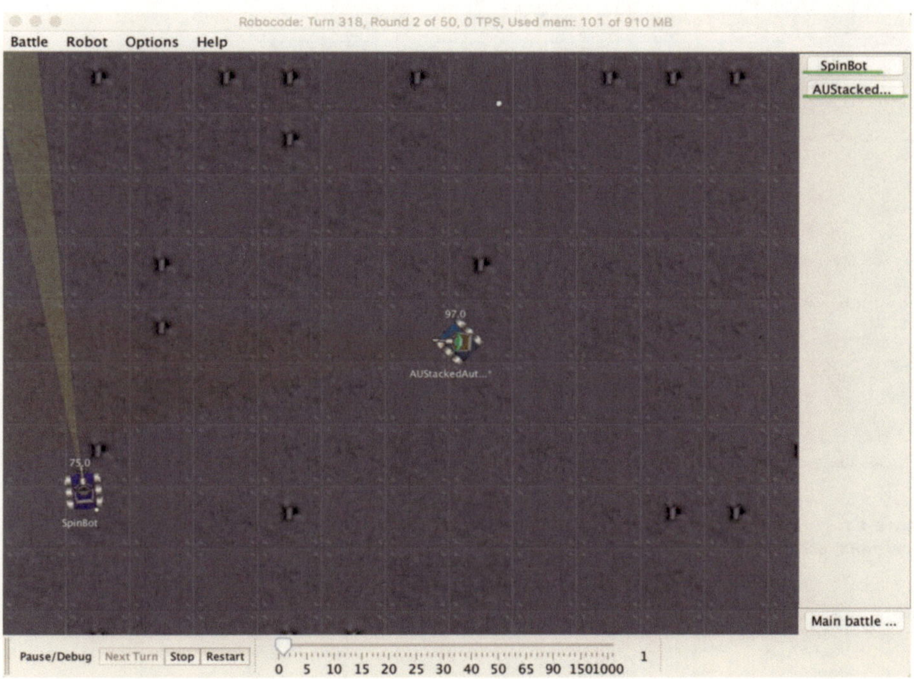

Figure 13.
A screenshot obtained from Robocode for Scenario 2 (AUAERobot).

auto-encoder and also CNN-based architectures may outperform the AUNNRobot architecture, which is, on the other hand, costly in terms of obtaining training data as well as performing training process compared with aforementioned approaches. Despite given challenges, it is planned to apply those architectures to the given problem as future works. Consequently, instead of AUAERobot, AUNNRobot is preferred to compete with AUQRobot.

3.3 Scenario 3

This scenario illustrates a multi-agent robot battle, in which a customized robot (AUQRobot) fights against with SpinBot Team. Since one of the starting points of this study aims to perform multi-agent team battles, first the trained robot forms a team against a single robot class. Afterward, the members of this team are programmed not to strike each other. Finally, the robot class, where the training is achieved, is defined as a robot team of AUQRobot. **Figure 14** illustrates a screenshot from the battlefield. Results reveal that customized decentralized AUQRobot teams outperform "SpinBot Team" with an average of 65–35% as shown in **Figure 15**.

3.4 Scenario 4

This scenario illustrates a battle of multi-agent systems consisting of five robot tanks. According to which, the first team is inherited from AUQRobot, whereas the

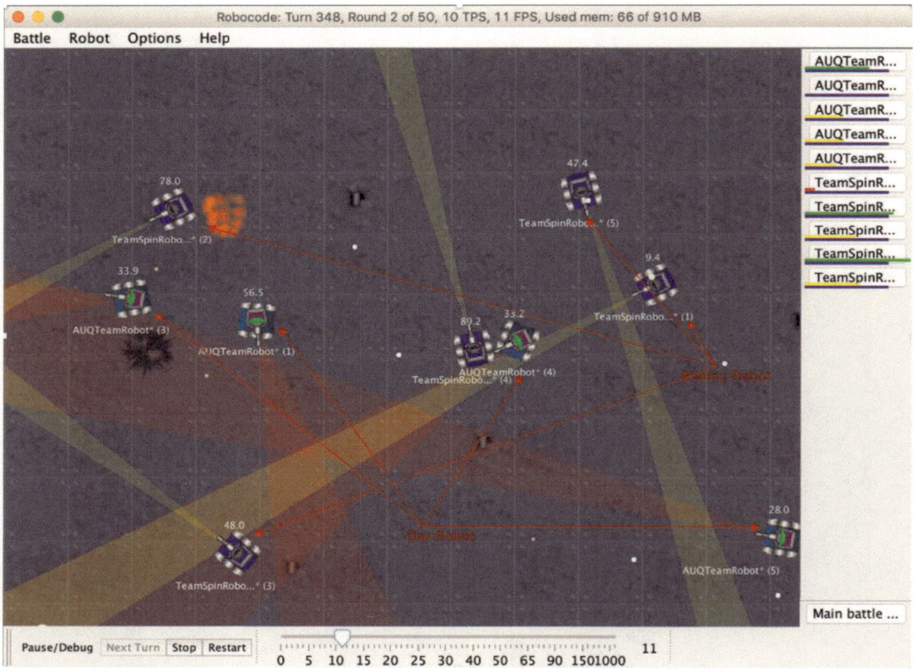

Figure 14.
A screenshot obtained from Scenario 3 (multi-agent battle).

Rank	Robot Name	Total Score	Survival	Surv Bonus	Bullet Dmg	Bullet Bonus	Ram Dmg * 2	Ram Bonus	1sts	2nds	3rds
1st	uu.AUQTeamRobot* ...	5897 (17%)	3450	450	1833	96	67	0	5	0	1
2nd	uu.AUQTeamRobot* ...	5251 (15%)	3250	0	1806	104	90	0	1	3	3
3rd	uu.AUQTeamRobot* ...	4836 (14%)	2750	180	1748	80	67	11	3	0	0
4th	uu.AUQTeamRobot* ...	4401 (13%)	2550	0	1687	77	88	0	0	2	2
5th	uu.TeamSpinRobot* (1)	3171 (9%)	2500	90	383	9	178	12	1	1	2
6th	uu.TeamSpinRobot* (4)	2978 (9%)	2250	90	415	10	210	3	1	0	0
7th	uu.TeamSpinRobot* (2)	2487 (7%)	2000	0	350	3	128	5	0	2	0
8th	uu.AUQTeamRobot* ...	2052 (6%)	950	0	1014	33	55	0	0	0	0
9th	uu.TeamSpinRobot* (5)	1939 (6%)	1450	0	348	1	140	0	0	1	2
10th	uu.TeamSpinRobot* (3)	1655 (5%)	1300	0	249	3	103	0	0	0	0

Save OK

Figure 15.
A screenshot obtained from Robocode to illustrate results for Scenario 3.

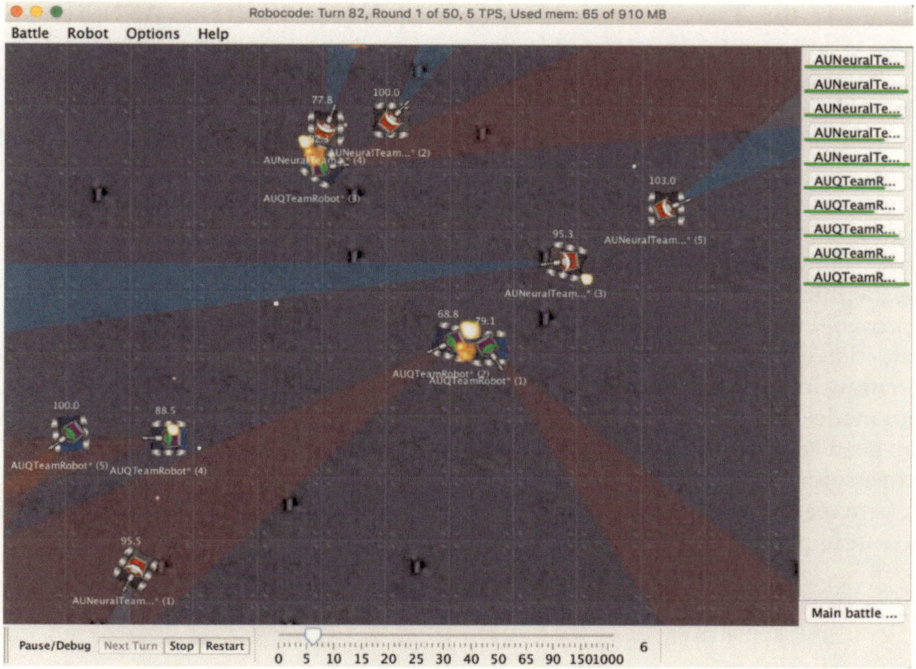

Figure 16.
A screenshot obtained from Robocode for Scenario 4.

Results for 50 rounds

Rank	Robot Name	Total Score	Survival	Surv Bonus	Bullet Dmg	Bullet Bonus	Ram Dmg * 2	Ram Bonus	1sts	2nds	3rds
1st	uu.AUNeuralNetworkTeamRobot* ...	25653 (16%)	16500	990	6945	401	784	33	11	13	8
2nd	uu.AUNeuralNetworkTeamRobot* ...	24132 (15%)	15100	810	7045	390	779	8	9	7	7
3rd	uu.AUNeuralNetworkTeamRobot* ...	23626 (15%)	14850	990	6773	336	672	5	11	7	7
4th	uu.AUNeuralNetworkTeamRobot* ...	23419 (15%)	14950	810	6657	296	688	18	9	9	8
5th	uu.AUNeuralNetworkTeamRobot* ...	23025 (14%)	14700	630	6687	304	680	24	7	8	11
6th	uu.AUQLearningTeamRobot* (1)	9019 (6%)	8000	180	763	13	64	0	2	3	2
7th	uu.AUQLearningTeamRobot* (4)	8275 (5%)	7350	0	831	3	90	0	0	0	3
8th	uu.AUQLearningTeamRobot* (5)	8174 (5%)	7250	0	876	4	44	0	0	1	4
9th	uu.AUQLearningTeamRobot* (2)	8075 (5%)	7100	90	831	1	53	0	1	3	0
10th	uu.AUQLearningTeamRobot* (3)	7274 (5%)	6450	0	756	3	65	0	0	0	2

Save OK

Figure 17.
A screenshot obtained from Robocode to illustrate results for Scenario 4.

second one is inherited from the AUNNRobot model. An example screenshot obtained from this scenario is shown in **Figure 16**. Several different competitions (experiments) were conducted between those robot teams, and results reveal that the AUNNRobot team outperforms its opponent from 67% (minimum) to 74% (maximum) winning rate. **Figure 17**, generated from the Robocode platform during the experimental procedure, includes 50-round battle and illustrates the team performance of AUNNRobot against its opponent.

4. Conclusion

This paper introduces and compares some of the popular machine learning-based approaches for the single and multi-agent systems by employing a popular 2-D game simulator, namely, Robocode. This platform essentially allows researchers to design customized robot teams so as to join the competition and perform tank battle players and designers all around the world. Despite the challenges of continued space problem with respect to the characteristics of the games, a

Q-Learning-based model is introduced for the problem. Besides, an ANN-based model is designed to approximate Q-Values instead of constructing a huge Q-Table, which in essence is not a realistic approach. In addition, previous experiences prove that stacked auto-encoders (SAEs) may offer an alternative supervised learning approach once the labeled data is obtained. However, as position data is employed instead of a raw image, SAEs do not provide any advances such as denoising on images or reducing the input size. Within these results, it should be noted that raw images, illustrating game states, should better be employed by the deep architectures, as input to design a stronger architecture than an ANN architecture. However, within the given input, the ANN model outperforms both machine learning approaches on both single and multi-agent systems. The experimental results and evaluation of those results encourage authors to design a SAE- or CNN-based model using raw images as future works. Those models will only need raw image data to train models, which will probably outperform both RL- and ANN-based models but may need larger amount of training data, and also require excessive training time to form a suitable model. Despite the given explanation, it is not clear to estimate the performance of those algorithms on different multi-agent systems except Robocode without implementing and evaluating their overall performance.

Author details

Ümit Ulusoy, Mehmet Serdar Güzel* and Erkan Bostanci
Department of Computer Engineering, Ankara University, Ankara, Turkey

*Address all correspondence to: mguzel@ankara.edu.tr

References

[1] Şahin E. Swarm robotics: From sources of inspiration to domains of application. In: Swarm Robotics Workshop: State-of-the-Art Survey; Şahin E, Spears W, editors, Lecture Notes in Computer Science; no. 3342; Berlin, Germany; 2005. pp. 10-20

[2] Brambilla M, Ferrante E, Birattari M, Dorigo M. Swarm robotics: A review from the swarm engineering. Swarm Intelligence. 2013;**7**(1):1-41

[3] Guzel MS et al. A novel framework for multi-agent systems using a decentralized strategy. Robotica. 2019; **37**(4):691-707

[4] Rodriguez-Angeles A, Vazquez CL. Bio-inspired decentralized autonomous robot mobile navigation control for multi agent systems. Kybernetika. 2018; **54**(1):135-154

[5] Jiménez AC, García-Díaz V, Bolaños S. A decentralized framework for multi-agent robotic systems. Sensors. 2018;**18**(2):417

[6] Dorri A, Kanhere S, Jurdak R. Multi-agent systems: A survey. IEEE Access. 2018;**6**:28573-28593. DOI: 10.1109/ACCESS.2018.2831228

[7] Jin-Hyuk H, Sung-Bae C. Evolution of emergent behaviors for shooting game characters in Robocode. In: Proceedings of the 2004 Congress on Evolutionary Computation (IEEE Cat. No. 04TH8753). Vol. 1; Portland, OR, USA. 2004. pp. 634-638

[8] Sanjay MS, Chirag ST, Dharm S. Multimedia based fitness function optimization through evolutionary game learning. In: 2011 International Conference on Emerging Trends in Networks and Computer Communications (ETNCC). 2011. pp. 164-168

[9] Nattharith P, Güzel MS. Machine vision and fuzzy logic-based navigation control of a goal-oriented mobile robot. Adaptive Behavior. 2016;**24**(3):168-180

[10] Harper R. Evolving Robocode tanks for Evo Robocode. Genetic Programming and Evolvable Machines. 2014;**16**(4):403-431. DOI: 10.1007/s10710-014-9224-2

[11] Deep Q-Learning for Robocode, Baptiste DEGRYSE [thesis]. Ecole polytechnique de Louvain; 2017

[12] Gade M, Knudsen M, et al. Applying machine learning to Robocode. Technical Report. 2003

[13] Shichel Y, Ziserman E, Sipper M. GP-Robocode: Using genetic programming to evolve robocode players. In: Proceedings of 8th European Conference on Genetic Programming; Lecture Notes in Computer Science. Vol. 3447. Germany: Heidelberg: Springer-Verlag; 2005. pp. 143-154

[14] Abdellatif AJ, McCollum B, McMullan P. Serious games quality characteristics evaluation: The case study of optimizing Robocode. In: 2018 International Symposium on Computers in Education (SIIE); Jerez; 2018. pp. 1-4

[15] Alaiba V, Rotaru A. Agent architecture for building Robocode players with SWI-Prolog. In: 2008 International Multiconference on Computer Science and Information Technology; Wisia; 2008. pp. 3-7

[16] Safak AB, Bostanci E, Soylucicek AE. Automated maze generation for Ms. Pac-Man using genetic algorithms. International Journal of Machine Learning and Computing. 2016;**6**(4):226-240

[17] Sharma A, Gupta K, Kumar A, Sharma A, Kumar R. Model based path

planning using Q-Learning. In: 2017 IEEE International Conference on Industrial Technology (ICIT); Toronto, ON. 2017. pp. 837-842. DOI: 10.1109/ICIT.2017.7915468

[18] Karim AM, Güzel MS, Tolun MR, Kaya H, Çelebi FV. A new generalized deep learning framework combining sparse autoencoder and Taguchi method for novel data classification and processing. Mathematical Problems in Engineering. 2018:1-13

Chapter 4

Multi-Agent Systems, Simulation and Nanotechnology

Alexandre de Oliveira Zamberlan, Rafael Heitor Bordini, Guilherme Chagas Kurtz and Solange Binotto Fagan

Abstract

Multi-agent systems (MAS) are used in investigations with different purposes, mainly in computational simulations. These systems are composed of autonomous software entities, named agents, that act and interact in a shared environment, changing the state of the environment. Simulation environments for nanostructures can be considered essentially reactive, that is, suitable for reactive agent architectures. A significant feature in agent-oriented theory is autonomy, which also exists in small-scale structures such as atoms and molecules, despite the strong interaction. Regarding the organisation of a reactive or cognitive multi-agent system, there are events, constraints and interactions that occur in a nanoscale environment. So, MAS paradigm has methodologies and tools that could guarantee simulations of Brownian motion, at the nanoscale, generating and monitoring collision systems. Experiments for the nanocapsule production and characterisation should be supported by computational simulations, mainly to reduce experiment time, equipment wear and material waste. Therefore, this paper presents how MAS can increase the investigations in nanoscience through simulations of moving bodies.

Keywords: event-driven simulation, nanoparticles, reactive systems, distributed artificial intelligence

1. Introduction

Artificial intelligence is widespread in many areas of knowledge. It increases the quality of processing solutions of different problems. One of the areas in which artificial intelligence can also collaborate is in nanoscience [1], through multi-agent systems.

Nanoscience is the study of phenomena and manipulations of materials at atomic and molecular scales, where properties differ significantly from those at a larger scale. Nanotechnology is concerned with the design, characterisation, production and application of nanoscale structures [2]. Production and characterisation of polymer nanoparticles (PNPs), colloidal dispersion, are processes that require time and technical skills to produce accurate results. Computational simulations in nanoscience have aided in these processes, providing support and agility to achieve better results [3].

In order to help and reduce this gap, a simulation environment for nanocapsules —colloidal dispersion—was designed and built: multi-agent system for polymeric nanoparticles (MASPN) [3, 4]. This tool can be considered innovative and unprecedented, as it combines event-driven simulation resources and the multi-agent system paradigm. This environment allows the researcher to enter input parameters, visualise particle interactions and monitor whether the dispersion is stabilising or not. The manipulation parameters are amount of particles, maximum and minimum particle sizes, mean particle distribution, zeta potential, pH, polymer, drug and drug content.

There are different types of polymeric nanoparticles (PNP), in which nanocapsules and nanospheres differ according to composition and structural organisation. Nanocapsules are defined by vesicular structures consisting of a thin polymeric shell and a normally oily central cavity where the active substance may be dissolved [5, 6]. Due to this, it is considered a reservoir system, which has a submicron diameter of less than 1 mcm, typically between 200 and 400 nm. The active component may be dissolved in the oily central cavity or may adsorb to the polymer wall [7–9]. Nanocapsules are composed of the drug, polymer, oil, surfactant and water and are produced by different methods with size distributions smaller than 1 μm. The nanometric size generates greater surface area, thus correlating their biological responses [10]. For this reason, the nanoparticles are suitable for applications in composite materials, transport and delivery of drugs and storage of chemical energy, for example, [7, 11]. PNPs attract researchers' attention because their bioavailability, biodegradability and photostability characteristics of drugs, to modulate interaction with cells and tissues, reduce drug adverse effects, increase encapsulation efficiency, increase solubility and reduce therapeutic doses and biological fluids during storage [7–10].

The nanocapsules can be produced with natural or synthetic polymers and can be used to encapsulate bioactive drugs and compounds. In addition, the polymers protect the lipophilic nucleus and control the release of lipophilic drugs. Therefore, the proper choice of the polymer is important to achieve specific purposes and modulate the release and degradation characteristics of the particles [7, 10].

Thus, computational modelling and simulation are resources that can produce accuracy in results, decrease production time and characterisation and preserve the life of laboratory equipment. Modelling and simulations through the multi-agent approach has been used in numerous investigations in biology, chemistry, physics, etc. [12].

We organise the text into sections. Sections 2 and 3 deal with computation applied to nanotechnology, and MAS paradigm focused on computational simulations. Section 4 presents the related works that investigated MAS as a tool to support nanotechnology. In the sequence, we present Section 5 that discusses the MASPN tool, its characteristics and functionalities. Finally, the conclusions and bibliographical references are presented.

2. Computational nanotechnology

Nanotechnology can be categorised in relation to applications, structures and tools. The tools are mechanisms to assist in the measurement, manipulation and development of nanostructures, and the area of computing provides innumerable resources to contribute to both measurement and manipulation of nanomaterials. Thus, we assume that computational nanotechnology contributes to molecular modelling, nanodevice simulation, high-performance computing, etc. [1].

We believe that computation applied to nanotechnology focuses on the design and construction of tools to aid the understanding of physical and chemical phenomena occurring on a nanometric scale, for example, in electronics, logic and computing, sensors, drugs, cosmetics and new materials with specific characteristics.

Systems and computational simulation are carried out in time and space using analytical models and physical, chemical and material science fundamentals [1, 12, 13].

Molecular modelling involves computational methods and techniques to mimic the behaviour of atomic and molecular systems. We assume that modelling is the process of extracting really relevant information from a given system, such as structural aspects (set of attributes or characteristics and their possible values) and functional aspects (operations or methods and their constraints).

3. MAS and simulation

The MAS form an area of research in distributed artificial intelligence, manipulating aspects related to distributed computing in artificial intelligence systems [14]. These systems consist of several entities (agents) that interact in a shared environment in order to achieve some individual or collective goal.

The simulation studies the modelling of the functionalities (behaviours) of a physical or conceptual system over time [12]. These same authors state that for more than 20 years, the MAS field and the simulation field were combined into lines of research.

On the one hand, agents have been used as a tool for modelling and simulation of problems; on the other hand, simulation has often been used for MAS design in a variety of application domains. Thus, Uhrmacher and Weyns [12] believe that joint research efforts promise benefits between the two research areas and their work aims to integrate and consolidate the knowledge and experience gained in both areas.

The definition of the internal architecture of the agent is related to the task type that the agent will perform and its role in the multi-agent society.

In this way, what characterises an agent and the society that it is inserted in are the interactions with the environment and the internal processes that make possible the accomplishment of these interactions [14]. The specification of what and how these internal processes are is called architecture. Different architectures have been proposed with the objective of characterising the agents with a level of intelligence and autonomy. Therefore, the architectures can be classified according to the mechanism used by the agent to select actions [15].

Once considered this, agent can be classified as [14]:

- Reactive, in which the choice of action (response) is directly situated in the occurrence of a set of events (stimuli) that it perceives in the environment, captured by its sensors or by messages sent by other agents.

- Cognitive or deliberative, because it has an explicit process to choose the action to be performed. This action can be chosen, also, through a utility function and carried out by plan and a symbolic representation of the environment. A cognitive agent is a rational agent who has some explicit representation of his knowledge and goals. An agent may be more cognitive than another, depending on the degree of explicit rationality of his behaviour [14, 16].

Cognitive agent architectures [14] can be classified into functional architectures, in which the agent is composed of modules that represent each of the functionalities necessary for its operation. The agent has knowledge, set of objectives, perception skill, communication, decision and reasoning. There are also architectures based on mental states, which adopt a psychologically inspired perspective to define the structure of agents, which are entities in which the state consists of mental components such as beliefs, desires, capacities, choices and commitments. It may be that a mental state-based architecture also has functional aspects and vice versa [15].

Definitions and properties that characterise an agent are not meant to divide the world between entities that are and are not agents but serve as tools for analysing systems as well as specifying, designing and implementing systems whose basic elements are agents [17].

Thus, we assume all approaches to modelling and development of multi-agent systems can be classified as top-down and bottom-up. Top-down approach specifies the organisation towards the structure and behaviour of agents, while the bottom-up approach starts from the individual aspects of an agent in a way that the collective aspects emerge. This classification is very similar to nanostructure development methodologies, with the same principle, top-down and bottom-up.

3.1 MAS modelling and implementation tools

In recent years, many agent-based system development tools or environments have been deployed (or released). Each environment has a variety of features and functionalities. There are some studies comparing these tools, for example, [18]. The research evaluated whether tools have some features and functionalities, such as (i) an integrated development environment, (ii) what the programming language is, (iii) the operating system, (iv) manuals and examples, (v) integration with other libraries and (vi) 2D or 3D visualisation.

The modelling and verification of multi-agent systems present many challenges, especially when it comes to reliability, robustness and visualisation of the simulated system (spatial properties) [18]. Thus, visualisation property of simulation scenarios is also an important property in the construction of simulation systems.

Multi-agent simulation environments suitable for the context of nanoparticulate systems are:

- FLAME[1] is a general agent-based model building system that generates highly efficient simulation software that can run on any computing platform, such as high-performance parallel supercomputers and GPUs. You can set up large-scale models with millions of agents.

- JASON[2] is a multi-agent system development environment with many user-customisable features. It is the interpreter for the AgentSpeak language.

- MASON[3] is a discrete event library for multi-agent simulation in Java language.

- Netlogo[4] is a simulation environment, that is, it is both a programming language and a programmable modelling environment for the simulation of multi-agent systems. It has a graphical interface for visualisation of the simulations.

---

[1] http://www.flame.ac.uk

[2] http://jason.sourceforge.net/wp

[3] http://cs.gmu.edu/eclab/projects/mason

[4] https://ccl.northwestern.edu/netlogo

- Repast[5] is a set of free and open-source platforms for multi-agent modelling and simulation. It has Java versions for workstations and small clusters of computers and C++ for supercomputers and high-performance computing clusters.

- SeSAm[6] is a generic environment for the modelling and experimentation of agent-based simulation. It is a tool for building complex models, which include dynamic interdependencies or emerging behaviour.

- SWARM[7] is a general-purpose simulator, mainly of social complexity based on the programming languages Objective-C and Java.

Of the tools analysed, only JASON and SWARM do not have an integrated development environment, but JASON can be incorporated (as a plugin) in other development environments. All tools run on major operating systems and have excellent developer support. FLAME and Repast are the only ones that do not have an open source, that is, they do not allow you to change the source code of the tool. The NetLogo tool stands out because it also has the integrated simulation execution environment. FLAME and Repast can be executed in computational clusters or in graphic cards, allowing the large-scale simulation of many agents.

We did not investigate issues of performance and robustness of the analysed tools.

4. Related works

In this section, we will present some works in the context of nanotechnology that used MAS as an evaluation or simulation tool.

4.1 Multi-agent system simulation of nanorobotic drug delivery in tumours of body tissues

The paper discusses the simulation of specific drug delivery in tumour tissue through MAS simulation [19]. The simulation was designed, implemented and evaluated with reference to some initial requirements, such as energy consumption, drug loading capacity and the perception of some agents. The work has simulated the behaviour of nanorobots, the agents responsible for drug delivery. The use of nanorobots was proposed as a hypothetical situation, and the main characteristics were biocompatibility, minimum energy for operation, communication and navigation skills (e.g., target search) and decentralised and cooperative coordination. The proposal of the nanoparticle simulation experiment was recognition and binding to the target, with the release of the drug and with biodegradation protective surface. For this, three types of nanorobots were designed: searcher, digger and killer (drug delivery).

Due to the complexity of the biological system, it was necessary to apply layers of abstractions and to focus on some parameters and functionalities. For example, the way nanorobots are injected has been disregarded. However, blood flow (velocity) and obstacles in blood (macromolecules) were taken into account.

---

[5] http://repast.sourceforge.net

[6] http://130.243.124.21/sesam

[7] http://xenia.media.mit.edu/nelson/research/swarm

The limitations of the simulation tools for time, size, density, viscosity, size of nanorobots in relation to body cell size and energy resources by the nanorobots were all considered in the simulation.

The NetLogo simulation platform was used for the construction and execution of the simulation. The results obtained were the visualisation interface generated and the analysis of some situations, as if the tumour was eliminated, if there was failure to eliminate the tumour or failure to complete the experiment. For this, 500 simulations were executed for each experiment, with the following parameters: number of searcher type agents, number of load capacity and radius of diggers, number of load capacity and energy of killers and agents and agent collaboration.

The purpose was to estimate the ideal parameter values for the possible experiments (qualitative analysis). The conclusions were as follows: it is possible to have a combination of values in the parameters that eliminate the tumour; large numbers of diggers do not eliminate the tumour; the amount of drug loading influences tumour clearance rather than the radius of perception; mean values in the parameters cause tumour elimination; and the greater the energy allocated to the agents, the greater chance of elimination of the tumour.

Finally, the authors conclude that drug delivery through nanostructures is a promising area, as nanotechnology is more widely used, be it in the development of structures to coat pharmaceutical substances and proteins or in the design of chemical sensors and structures with "stealth" property (are not detected by the immune system).

4.2 Agent-based modelling of stem cells

Here, MAS was used for biological simulation of complex system (modelling and simulation) known as haematopoietic stem cell (HSC) system in adults [20].

Biological systems have reactive and complex behaviour, such as self-regulation and self-organisation, and it is a challenge to understand the mechanisms and processes of interaction. Therefore, in the use of MAS, as they are recognised for modelling and simulation of these complex systems [20], since they explicitly represent the environment, the cells are modelled as agents containing the physical, chemical and biological properties, and there is facility in changing experiment parameters.

The haematopoietic stem cell system in adults has limitations, such as difficulty in tracking stem cells in adult human bodies, making it impossible to observe the behaviour of the system. The alternative presented is to use modelling and simulation to understand both individual and collective behaviours (prediction). In the research, a framework was proposed containing the base structure of the simulation environment, agents representing the cells, stochastic processes of the simulation system, etc.

For the experiment, the MASON library was used. The main components of the structure were modelled and implemented separately. Cellular agents were used to model the individual cells of the system. The environment represents the physical, biological and chemical environment where the cells meet. The simulation mechanism promotes the "movement" of the simulation of a cell system. This is done by updating the environment in response to agent requests and signals.

An important point to note in the work is environment initialisation that includes chemical and topological information that reduces the need to resort to stochastic processes. In addition, it is possible to model the physical movement of cells to ensure self-organisation in stem cell systems.

4.3 Coordinating microscopic robots in viscous fluids

In [21], the multi-agent control (by simulation) is discussed that provides strategies to agglomerate microscopic robots (named in the text as nanorobots) in environments of fluids relevant for medical applications. Unlike larger robots, viscous forces and Brownian motion tend to dominate behaviour. Examples range from modified microorganisms (programmable bacteria) to robots used in the development of molecular computing, sensors and motors. Controls were evaluated for the location of a cell of specific size by emitting a type of chemical signal in a moving fluid. Parameters corresponding to chemicals released in response to injury or infection in small blood vessels were also considered.

These authors state that robots, with sizes comparable to bacteria, could provide new skills through their ability to feel and act in small-scale environments. Robots could be useful in a variety of biological and medical research contexts. For example, robots and nanoscale materials inside the body can improve the diagnosis and treatment of diseases [21]. However, making these robots is beyond the capacity of current technology, but progress in nanoscale engineering devices could eventually allow the production of such robots.

In that paper, they affirm that it is possible to evaluate control methods, before constructing the robots, by means of simulation, thus guaranteeing an environment with chemical signals, movement of cells and robots according to the characteristics of the fluid. Robots could act independently, for example, by detecting specific patterns of chemicals. Such coordinated action would produce an agglomeration effect, necessary for a rapid and adequate response to infection [21]. The agglomeration of small-scale robots differs significantly from larger robots in several respects. First, the physical environment is dominated by the flow of viscous fluid and requires movement in three dimensions. Second, thermal noise is significant for sensors, and Brownian motion limits the ability to follow precisely specified paths. Third, targets are recognisable through chemical signatures rather than visual markings or specific forms. Fourth, tasks involve a large number of robots, each with limited capabilities in sensing, communication and computing.

Thus, these characteristics suggest that control by multi-agent simulation with reactive architecture is particularly well suited for robots on a very reduced scale.

4.4 Related work considerations

In nanoscience investigations, nanostructured drug delivery research is conducted in a number of research centres and can be considered one of the most promising.

In [19], the drug delivery and MAS areas were combined. The relation with this work happens through the use of the simulation tools, statistical model for the evaluation process and the layers of abstractions. In relation to the work presented in dinverno:2009, this research also specifies, performs and evaluates the behaviour of interacting particles obeying a dynamics of self-organisation. Another relation is there is the possibility of changing the values of the input parameters.

A contribution in [21] is how groups of robots were collectively controlled (individual vs. collective behaviour in response to the environment and other agents).

Generally, computational studies of controlling groups of robots complement the studies to control individually. And this can be extended to a system with particles that exhibit coordinated behaviour in response to different stimuli, for example, the agglomeration effect generated by physical-chemical properties of the environment, as ionic strength of the environment.

5. MASPN: multi-agent system for polymeric nanoparticles

Finally, we present MASPN simulation environment [3, 4, 17], an environment built with the Java language that integrates JASON and the *algs4* simulation package. The *algs4* package contains the entire implementation of equations of the Brownian model that guarantee elastic and inelastic collisions. MASPN has been developed according to the feature-driven development methodology of software design and the methodology of multi-agent systems.

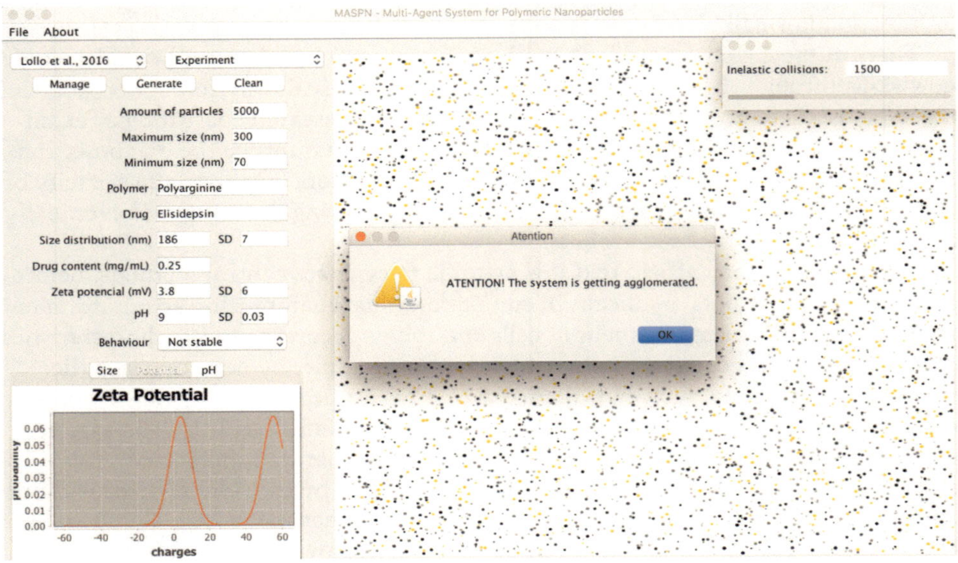

Figure 1.
MASPN tool interface.

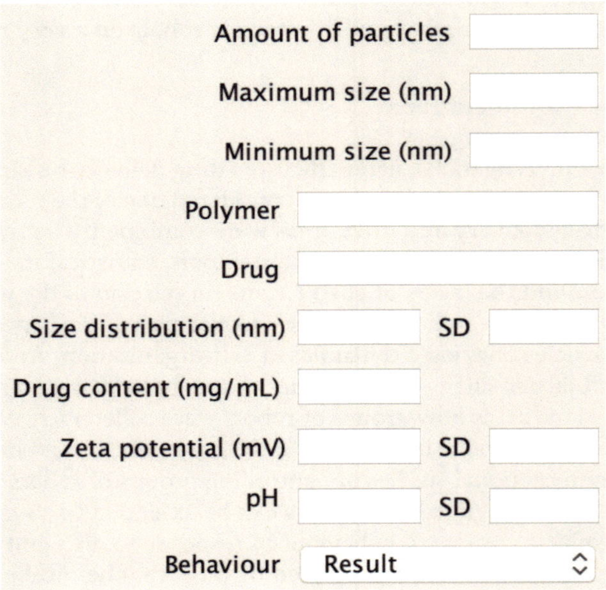

Figure 2.
Simulation parameters in MASPN.

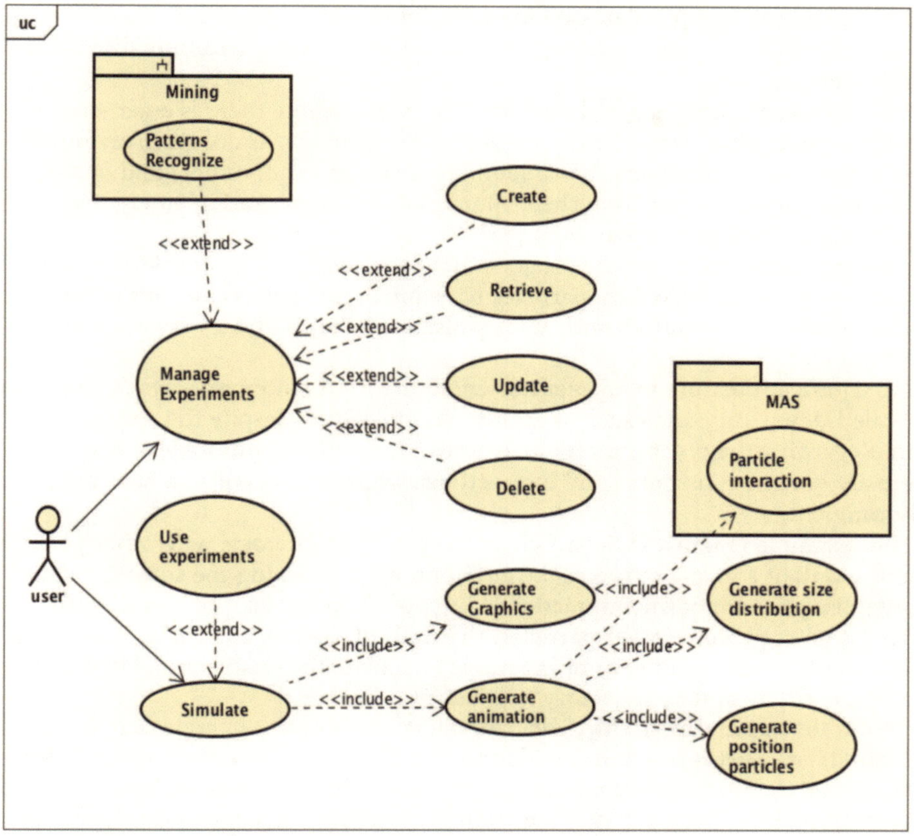

Figure 3.
Use-case diagram: MASPN main features.

The MASPN environment emerges as the main result of this research, since it is an alternative simulation tool, containing graphical interface with integrated physicochemical parameters, distribution graphs (particle size, particle zeta potential and environment pH) and particle animation under the Brownian mathematical model (**Figure 1**).

The parameters of the simulations, for evaluation of the agglomeration effect, are size, size distribution, surface electric charge, mass, drug content and pH (**Figure 2**). The simulation environment designed and built, integrating areas, methodologies and technologies can be considered a resource in the production and characterisation of polymer nanoparticles, since the simulations performed had significantly accurate results.

Figure 3 shows use-case diagram that represents all the possible functionalities of the system, for example, managing experiments and performing simulations. The results of the simulations are the interactions between the particles (agents) and the environment. The interactions obey Brownian motion of collisions, and the collisions that generate agglomeration are counted and announced in the system.

6. Conclusions

Nanostructured simulation environments can be considered reactive, ideal for reactive agent architectures. Some computing researchers would tend to indicate the use of distributed problem-solving techniques rather than MAS. However, MAS makes it possible to design complex simulation systems in a naturally distributed and bottom-up way.

The MAS paradigm is based on natural systems, where there is emergence of intelligent behaviour from the interaction of its elements, as occurs in an anthill (the colony has an intelligent behaviour, whereas the ant does not) and in the neurons (simple cells but from their interaction and organisation emerges a complex and intelligent behaviour) [16].

The group has characteristics that cannot be reduced to its base elements. At this point, we do not say that nanoparticles have intelligent behaviour, but rather complex, once they interact with an organisation scheme and a very reactive environment.

A significant feature in an agent-oriented theory is autonomy, which also exists in scaled-down structures such as atoms and molecules, despite the strong interaction. Regarding the organisation of a reactive or cognitive multi-agent system, there are events, constraints and interactions, which also occur in a nanoscale environment.

For example (**Figure 1**), a particle is an agent that interacts with other particles and the wall of a box. The box is the environment containing the solvent (which would dissipate or not the interaction energy of the particles). In this way, the particles must perceive other particles, the walls of the box and the solvent of the environment. Next, plan your next actions (calculate the elastic or inelastic collision forces), and act (update trajectory and velocity data).

From the approaches to MAS development, the bottom-up approach is well indicated, first, because agents are designed independently of some specific problem; second, because inter-agent interaction is not built in advance but in generic situations by specifying a communication protocol for agents; and third, because there is no centralised control. Thus, there are advantages such as the feasibility of adaptive and evolutionary systems, in which MAS has the ability to adapt to new situations (inclusion or exclusion of agents or changes in the organisation).

As already mentioned, it is naturally suitable for the modelling of complex and concurrent (or distributed) systems, that is, suitable for simulations in nanostructured environments.

The MAS area is consolidated, with methodologies and tools for the design and implementation of multi-agent systems, both reactive and cognitive.

Acknowledgements

We want to thank the Postgraduate Program in Nanosciences of the Franciscan University. We also need to thank researcher Ana Julia Dalcin for her support in the production and characterisation of colloidal systems.

Conflict of interest

The authors declare no conflict of interest.

Multi-Agent Systems, Simulation and Nanotechnology
DOI: http://dx.doi.org/10.5772/intechopen.88529

Author details

Alexandre de Oliveira Zamberlan[1*†], Rafael Heitor Bordini[2†],
Guilherme Chagas Kurtz[1] and Solange Binotto Fagan[1]

1 Franciscan University, Santa Maria, Brazil

2 PUCRS, Porto Alegre, Brazil

*Address all correspondence to: alexz@ufn.edu.br

† These authors contributed equally.

References

[1] Neto OPV. Intelligent computational nanotechnology: The role of computational intelligence in the development of nanoscience and nanotechnology. Journal of Computational and Theoretical Nanoscience. 2014;**11**:1-17

[2] Dowling A, Clif R, Grobert N. Nanoscience and Nanotechnologies: Opportunities and Uncertainties. London, UK: The Royal Academic of Engineering; 2004

[3] Zamberlan A, Kurtz GC, Gomes TL, Bordini RH, Fagan SB. A simulation environment for polymeric nanoparticles based on multi-agent systems. Journal of Molecular Modeling. 2018;**25**:5

[4] Zamberlan A, Dalcin AJ, Kurtz G, Bordini R, Raffin R, Fagan S. Simulation environment for polymeric nanoparticle: Experiment database. Disciplinarum Scientia. 2016;**17**(3): 429-446

[5] Jo DH, Kim JH, Lee TG, Kim JH. Size, surface charge, and shape determine therapeutic effects of nanoparticles on brain and retinal diseases. Nanomedicine: Nanotechnology, Biology and Medicine. 2015;**11**(7): 1603-1611

[6] Patra CN, Priya R, Swain S, Jena GK, Panigrahi KC, Ghose D. Pharmaceutical significance of eudragit: A review. Future Journal of Pharmaceutical Sciences. 2017;**3**(1):33-45

[7] Mali AD, Bathe RS. Updated review on nanoparticles as drug delivery systems. International Journal of Analytical, Pharmaceutical and Biomedical Sciences. 2015;**4**(9):18-34

[8] Mora-Huertas C, Fessi H, Elaissari A. Polymer-based nanocapsules for drug delivery. International Journal of Pharmaceutics. 2010;**385**(1–2):113-142

[9] Santos SS, Lorenzoni A, Pegoraro NS, Denardi LB, Alves SH, Schaffazick SR, et al. Formulation and in vitro evaluation of coconut oil-core cationic nanocapsules intended for vaginal delivery of clotrimazole. Colloids and Surfaces B: Biointerfaces. 2014;**116**: 270-276

[10] Frank LA, Contri RV, Beck RCR, Pohlmann AR, Guterres SS. Improving drug biological effects by encapsulation into polymeric nanocapsules. Wiley Interdisciplinary Reviews: Nanomedicine and Nanobiotechnology. 2015;7(5):623-639

[11] Barua S, Mitragotri S. Challenges associated with penetration of nanoparticles across cell and tissue barriers: A review of current status and future prospects. Nano Today. 2014; **9**(2):223-243

[12] Uhrmacher AM, Weyns D. Multi-Agent Systems: Simulation and Application. Computational Analysis, Synthesis, and Design of Dynamic Models Series. Boca Raton, FL, USA: CRC Press; 2009

[13] de Barbosa RC, Krott LB, Barbosa MC. Structural behavior of an anomalous fluid under hydrophobic, hydrophilic and heterogeneous confinement. Journal of Physics. 2016; **686**. VIII Brazilian Meeting on Simulational Physics

[14] Wooldridge M. Introduction to Multiagent Systems. New York, NY, USA: John Wiley & Sons, Inc.; 2001

[15] Bordini RH, Hübner JF, Wooldridge M. Programming Multi-Agent Systems in AgentSpeak Using Jason. Liverpol, UK: Wiley; 2007

[16] Hübner JF, Bordini RH, Vieira R. In: Itakura FT et al., editors. Introdução ao

Desenvolvimento de Sistemas Multiagentes com Jason. Paraná: XII Escola de InformÃ¡tica da SBC; 2004. pp. 51-89

[17] Zamberlan AO. Sistema Multiagente para avaliação do efeito de aglomeração em nanopartículas poliméricas [thesis]. UFN—Universidade Franciscana; 2018

[18] Petreska I, Stamatopoulou I. A comparative study of tools for visualisation of state-based spatial multi-agent models. In: Proceedings of the 6th Balkan Conference in Informatics, BCI '13. New York, NY, USA: ACM; 2013. pp. 53-60

[19] Ntika M, Kefalas P, Stamatopoulou I. Multi-agent system simulation of nano-robotic drug delivery in tumours of body tissues. In: 2013 17th International Conference System Theory, Control and Computing (ICSTCC). Sinaia: IEEE; 2013. pp. 777-782

[20] d'Inverno M, Howells P, Montagna S, Roeder I, Saunders R. Chapter 13: Agent-based modeling of stem cells. In: Uhrmacher AM, Weyns D, editors. Multi-Agent Systems: Simulation and Application, Computational Analysis, Synthesis, and Design of Dynamic Models Series. Boca Raton, FL, USA: CRC Press; 2009. pp. 389-418

[21] Hogg T. Coordinating microscopic robots in viscous fluids. Autonomous Agents and Multi-Agent Systems. 2007; **14**(3):271-305

Section 2

Multi-Agent Systems Applied to Energy Distribution

Chapter 5

Applications of Multi-Agent System in Power System Engineering

G.S. Satheesh Kumar and S. Tamil Selvi

Abstract

Power system needs a continuous upgrade to overcome the challenges like distributed control, self-healing, power quality, demand side management and integration of renewable system. At present, power system needs an advance and intelligent technology to perform various system level tasks. Centralized control of the system has efficient operation during integration of the renewable resources and lag of communication between the stations. Smart grid provides the intelligent and efficient power management system. Upgrade of present power system with multi-agent system (MAS) provides the solution for most of the power system issues. More number of MAS are used in the power system network based on acquires of the system. MAS are communicating with each other for the more acquired result. Better implantation of MAS can achieved by providing the high speed and secured communication protocol. In this chapter, we discussed about the MAS fundamental architecture and intelligent controller design tools and case study of real time tariff management using MAS.

Keywords: multi-agent system, power system, self-healing, MAS platform centralized control, decentralized control

1. Introduction

Nature has various forms of energy that exist in the world, among these electrical energy is very important. The modern world is mainly depending on electrical energy. Electricity is an important part of the day-to-day life of every human. Energy is the basic need for the development of any country. Availability of the energy in various forms depends on the geographical location of the country. Demand for energy is increasing rapidly due to industrialization and modernization. The energy availability in the world is decreasing gradually. Energy that is developed and supplied all comes under power system engineering. This will consist of power generation, transmission, distribution and analysis. The main drawback in the present power system is inefficiency due to lack of infrastructure [1, 2].

One of the highly risk system is known as power system. The analysis of the system in different conditions at the real time is more important for the smooth operation of the system. Error information costs the shutdown of the whole system. Implementing the sophisticated controls in all the levels improves the economy and reliability in the system. For this, detailed study about the operation, control, analysis and interconnection of the system is essential [3–5].

Power system is responsible for maintaining the adequate level of power in the network by adding or removing the power generation units in the network. It also supplies the power uniformly to the loads with high quality at any time. In past decade, the power system uses the low-level AC transmission lines which have low efficiency. Now the power system networks are developed to support the high-voltage AC transmission. This improves the efficiency of the system and derives many number of loads, also high-voltage direct current (HVDC) system is developed to reduce the transmission loss and conductor cost. Implementing power system network with closed loop system will improve the efficiency of the system and also reduce the power outage. Fast growing power system structure needs and high responsible intelligent and self-healing system to upgrades the system for future world.

The scientific community is not only searching for next generation computing but also searching for next breed of processing machines. This should be smaller, faster and more potent to process more data in a short span of time. To develop such kind of machines, one needs to consider the following points: (1) theories that explain what intelligence is, how it processes imprecise information and stores, recalls, associates, correlates, infers and extract precious values, (2) technology with a small amount of circuitry to process vast amount of imprecise information in a very short time and provide precisions, and (3) architecture that encompasses the new theories and technologies [6, 7].

2. What is multi-agent system?

It is related to the computer with intelligence programming. Various definitions for agent are available based on their environment and how it is used. An advantage of using agent is its flexibility in all types of environment and autonomy. Complex system control and monitoring can be done using intelligent controllers. Agent is a fully referred as software and it mainly depend on the environment. Agent is used in the power system, it known as power system environment are agent may be a part of an environment like sensors, relay, etc.

The agent is mainly interconnected between the hardware and software components. The agents will take the decision based on the signals received from the work environment. More numbers of agents are used in the network for the efficient operation and hence it is named as multi-agent system (MAS). Basic property of the MA is not varied but depends on the location. For example, in a power system use MA in substation and control center is same, only the program that feed in the MA depends on the location. The function of the MA related with the other MA system connected in the network. Autonomy places a major role in the MA for the real time decision making it performed based the present and future data analysis. MA data are stored and is shared through the network for the references of MAS [8–12].

3. MAS design

3.1 Introduction

Present power systems are espoused with the centralized control it leads to delay of the operation, reliability, power management and control. Utilization of renewable energy and energy management needs advanced technology with autonomous control and operation.

A smart grid is a hope to efficiently control and operate the future power system. The centralized grid required communication between hardware and software protocol. Nowadays, grid is automated through the exchange of control signals and status of the grid. Monitoring and controlling purpose automated technology agents used this so-called multi-agent system (MAS). It is one of the sound technologies to implement into the present grid. In this approach, a number of agents are interlinked together to obtain the objective of the complex system. The main function of the MAS in function autonomously and take the decision locally while a grid suffers from the unexpected operating condition. Implementation of MAS technology into the power system is due to lake of awareness. A major application of the MAS is to integrate renewable resources into the power grid in an efficient and controllable way. In this chapter organizing as follows, deals with MAS structure, intelligent technology and the implementation related to this work.

Single agent system denotes, it communicates particularly to one device for control and monitoring purpose. It will not help to achieve the entire goal of the systems. MAS has more numbers of agents working together to achieve the common goal by means of effective communication, coordination and cooperation between the agents.

3.2 Multi-agent system

In a present power system, effective communication and control were done using supervisory control and Data Acquisition System (SCADA) as a centralized system. SCADA did not allow any autonomous function of the device. Command and control signals are sending by the SCADA, it leads to absences of real-time performance. Multi-agent system is overcoming the drawback of the existing system. It provides distributed control over the system. Intelligent electronics devices or software is used as a control agent. This will have the rights to take the decision based on the environment condition [13–17].

Each agent has set goals to perform at a specified time period. Agents are classified into many types based on the operation namely control agent, distributed agents, monitoring agent, centralized control agent, date base agent, etc.

3.3 Structure of multi-agent system (MAS)

Integration of hardware and software was done by the multi-agent system. An agent may be hardware or software based on the operating condition. Every agent has its own set of goals. In a complex power system, a number of agents used at different levels with its own set of goal. Collectively, the objective of the agents is to implement the smart grid technology into the power system. The agent may be hardware or software interlaced with an operating condition and able to perform autonomously. Characteristics of agents are reactivity, pro-activity and social ability. **Figure 1** shows the basic structure of MAS [18].

The complex power system problems are cracked into small problems. These small problems are handled by individual MAS. This will reduce the complexity of the system easy to identify and isolate the system. MAS have the right to take the decision individually, no need to wait to get the signal from the control center. An agent can communicate with the nearby agent about its task completion status and provide information about some nearby agents and its status. Coordination and cooperation between the MAS are very essential for the intelligent operation of the system to achieve the overall goal. Coordination is need between the MAS for effective exchange of the information at a real-time to obtain the overall objective

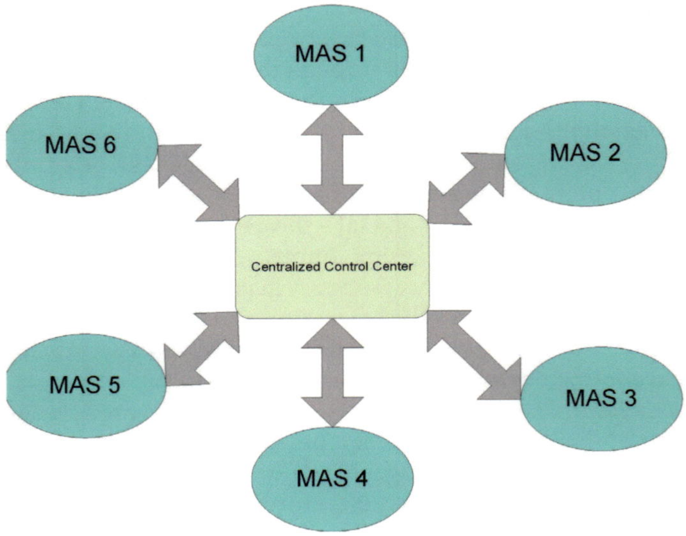

Figure 1.
Structure of MAS.

of the system. Cooperation in this agent has the right to reject, accept and defend the signal from the other agents. In this regard, cooperation is a very critical thing in MAS function.

The agents can communicate about status and goal achievement. This supports other agents to obtain the goal in the fastest way. Throughout the operation, common commanding language is used for communication.

3.4 Features of a multi- agent

- An agent can perform partly with the environment like it has information about the current bus systems voltage level and a voltage level of the generation bus. Decisions are taken in the consideration of other bus parameters also (autonomous and decision making).

- An agent has a facility for communicating nearby agent through high-speed communication network to interchange their real-time data. For example, the current power generation cost are collected from the center control agent, based on this information, the consumer can change their load pattern (coordination and cooperation).

- An agent has the decision making capability for certain level. Based on the resources date available with the agent, it will perform independently to obtain the objective. If anyone of the generation is failed, agent will take the decision to give reliable supply based on the real-time data available to end user (self-healing).

3.5 Multi-agent system in power system

Power system needs to reward with upcoming technology to operate the grid professionally. The power system has a huge network with a high sense of risk in the control and operation. The areas include generation control, monitoring, fault location, overload and surplus power generation, etc. It needs a more sensible operation. These high-risk factors are addressed by the MAS without disturbing the reliability of the system.

The present structure of the system falls under the inefficient operation due to the aging of the power system devices like circuit breakers, switching devices and transformer. Replacement of the entire system leads to huge investment. The smart grid with intelligent devices provides the solution to avoid the huge investment by adaptability with present system devices with slide modifications. **Figure 2** shows the smart grid structure [19, 20].

Computational intelligence is required in the smart grid in all levels for better operations. The fuzzy logic, neural networks and other intelligent technology are necessary for the implementation. The sensor devices are more sensible and it will decide the entire system efficiency during real-time operation. Intelligent operation of the system is based on the received from the sensor to control center. Malfunctioning of the sensor causes the entire system failure. The devices receive a number of dates from the sensor devices at a periodic interval of time from generation to end users. The devices also know the normal and up normal operations of the sensor data based on the reference value to avoid the uncertainty of the system.

The wireless communication between the devices also places the main role for the smart grid. Advanced communication technology with high-security date transfer is essential to avoid the cyberattack. Wrong information from the remote center leads the system under the block out condition.

3.6 Use of fuzzy in power system

Fuzzy mathematics is adopted in all traditional mathematical area. Implementation of Fuzzy in to power system provides better results. Fuzzy logic plays a vital role in the engineering area and also commercial market. This provides

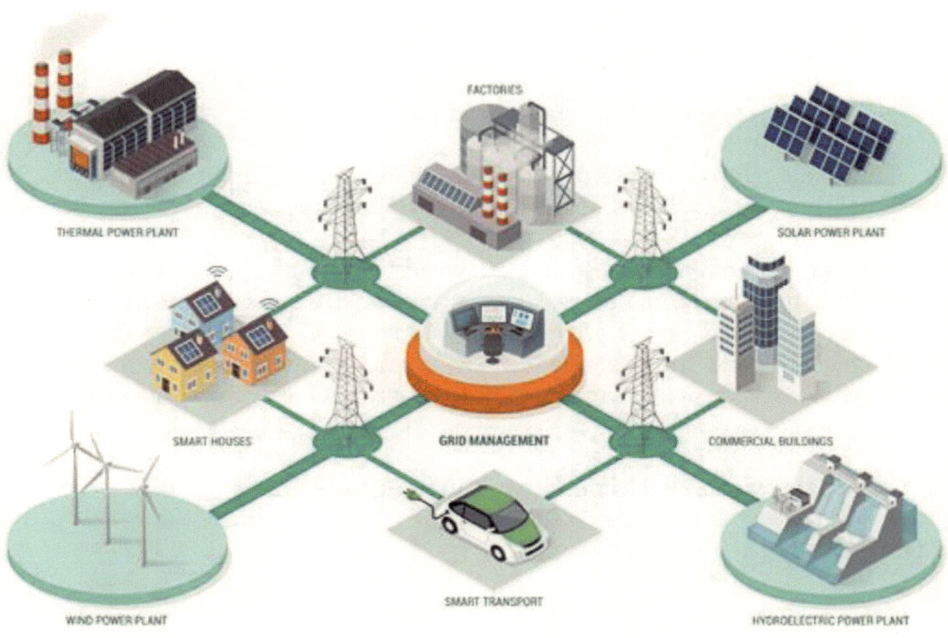

Figure 2.
Smart grid structures.

a user friendly approach for the consumer with sophisticated decision and control problems. Some of the features and capability of fuzzy set approaches are

- Integration between logical and numerical methods.
- Models for soft constraints.
- Models for resolving multiple conflicting objectives.
- Strong mathematical foundation for manipulation of the above representations.

Improbability is developed in many ways in power systems problems. This can be modeled using the fuzzy. Independent problem arise in the knowledge of the system. This problems need to be addressed to achieve the goal of the system. The ways of uncertainty in the system is caused due to models of the system and constraints and objectives arise from the decision-making process.

Fuzzy sets have to be applied for many power system application like Contingency analysis, diagnosis/monitoring, distribution planning, load frequency control, generator maintenance scheduling, generation dispatch load forecasting, load management, Reactive power/voltage control and security assessment.

Rule-based fuzzy sets are used in power system and improbability is associated with the each rule in the rule-base. Example, the circuit breaker trips in the distribution due to the over current in the circuit. The two uncertainties to be modeled are "often" and "high," which are most easily represented as a fuzzy measure and fuzzy set, respectively. The mathematical modeling is developed to address the numerical values associated with the improbability.

Fuzzy controller is a traditional control design for the development of fuzzy set. The controller follows a set of laws to take the decision that are

IF Temp is high and positive

AND Temp change is large and negative

THEN control output is small and negative

This membership functions depend on the valid range of input and output values. Within power systems, fuzzy logic controllers have been proposed primarily for stabilization control.

Fuzzy decision-making and optimization consider optimal power flow. Objectives could be cost minimization, minimal control adjustments and minimal emission of pollutants or maximization of adequate security margins. Physical constraints must include generator and load bus voltage levels, line flow limits and reserve margins. Fuzzy mathematics provides a mathematical framework for these considerations.

4. Applications of MAS in power system engineering

4.1 Case Study

4.1.1 Introduction

In this section, case study is carried out using multi-agent system for tariff management in power system. This method uses various types of multi-agent systems for control center, data collection and intelligent operation. Solar with battery storage and wind power plants are simulated using MATLAB Simulink, solar and wind simulation are done in systems 1 and 2 this is connected in the grid. The fuzzy logic controller was developed in system 3, communication between the systems is done using TCP/IP protocol [21].

The simulation of the smart grid demand side management using MATLAB/Simulink was done. In this, work was carried out in three different simulation environments. Simulation of solar power generation using photovoltaic is done in system 1 with battery storage as shown in **Figure 3**. In these, batteries are connected to the solar power module through the intelligent circuit breaker and it is controlled by the fuzzy controller. In this work, solar radiation is taken as a constant value. For load analysis, critical and non-critical loads are connected in the grid. This solar output is connected to the power grid through circuit barker 1. Measuring of grid parameters like line voltage, line current, load voltage, load current and frequency are measured in every stage using the measuring devices. The measured values are converted and sent to the fuzzy logic controller.

4.2 Controller design and functioning

Fuzzy logic intelligent controllers (FLC) are used in this work because of the compactness of the controller design. There is a possibility to add more number of inputs and outputs variables in FLC. The output of the FLC gives better result based on the else-if statement. More number of statements formed using else-if condition for enhanced result. Fuzzy inference learning system model that converters input to the resultant output are used in this case study. Fuzzy system has two types namely Mamdani and Sugeno or Takagi-Sugeno. This two methods are common for their fuzzing operation and the only different is output that it generates in Sugeno model generates linear or constant output, whereas the Mamdami generates variable output [22–25].

Solar power plant was designed using PV solar modules with 36 number of solar cells connected in series and power output of 230 W. Series and parallel combination are made for the maximum power output of 20 kW. This system is also enhanced with the batteries to store the excess power from the solar plant. Connection of solar power plant is done using internet protocol (IP)-enabled circuit breaker. **Figure 3** shows the solar power plant for the simulation model.

In MATLAB Simulink, self-excited wind power plant for 5 MW with capacitor bank was designed in order to provide steady power quality. Output of the wind power plant is connected to the main grid using the IP-enhanced circuit breakers as shown in **Figure 4**. Wind voltage, current, power and power factor are monitored using various sensors. The outputs from the sensors are converted into predefined values and send to the FLC. FLC receives the values from solar power plant and main grid for the intelligent tariff management system functionality. The output from the FLC are defuzzing, it is in the range of 1–10. Input to the IP-enabled circuits breakers are taken from the defuzzing output. The circuit breaker states will change accordingly with respect to the type of fuzzy rules employed.

The design of 20 kW solar power plant and 5 MW wind power plant using MATLAB simulation are shown in **Figures 3** and **4**. For better understanding, simulation models are developed in three different environments. Solar power plant was designed in system 1 and wind power plant was designed in system 2. Fuzzy logic system was created in the system 3. Measured parameters from sensors are converted and stored in the excel file for future references. The breakers get activated through step pulse from FLC which is controlled by energy control center command (ECC). The control parameters are converted into excel values through fuzzy commands

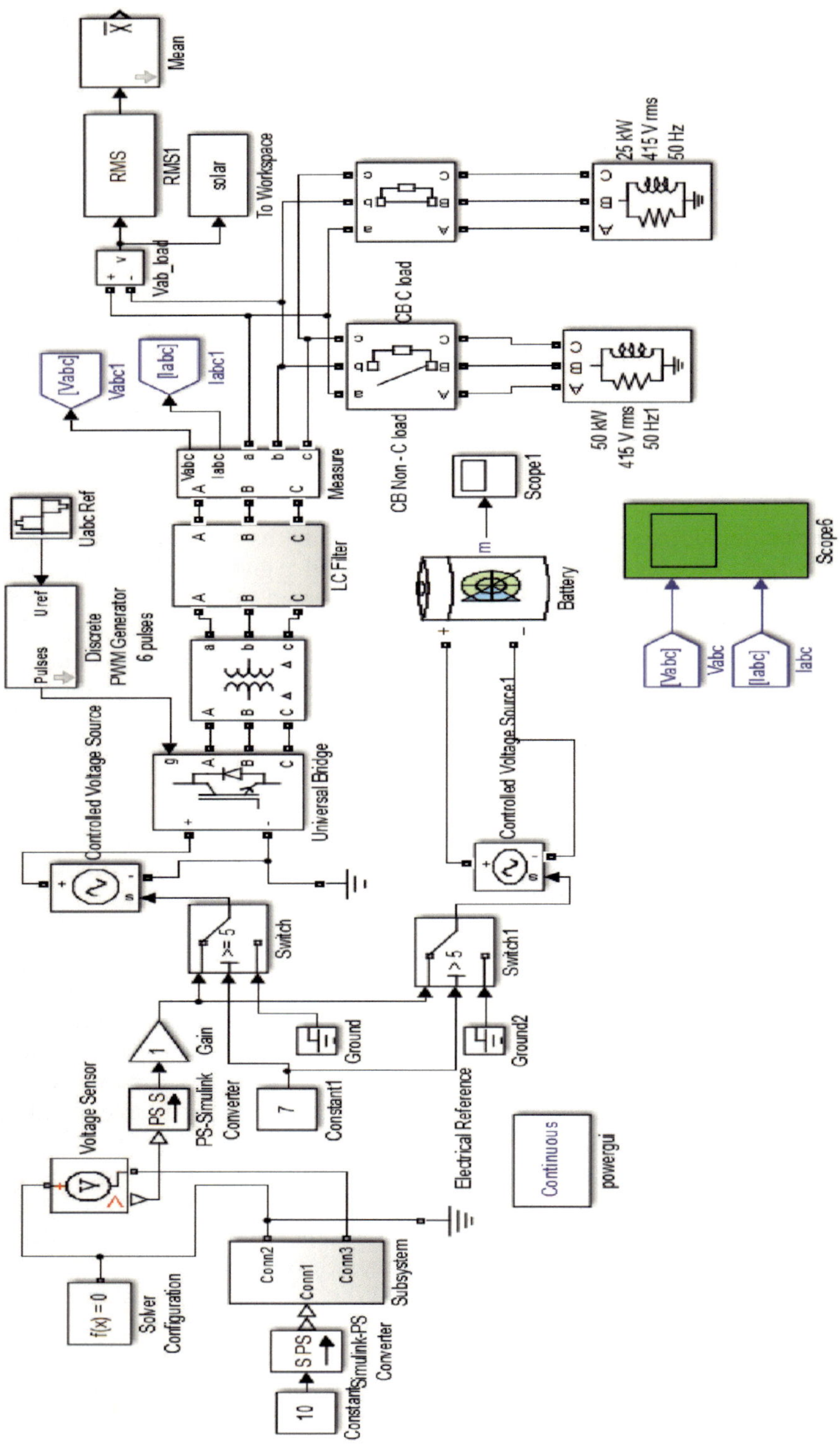

Figure 3.
Simulation of the solar power plant.

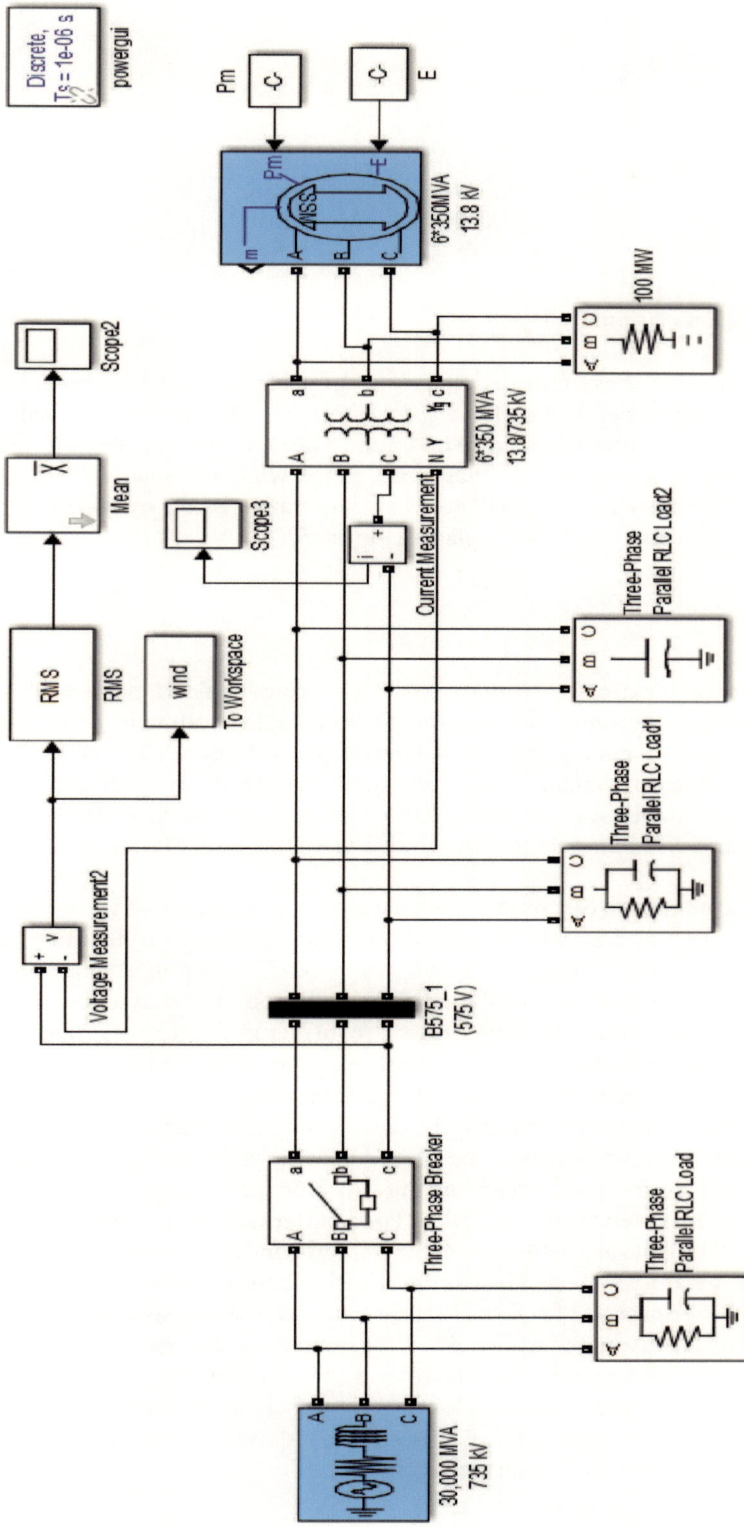

Figure 4.
Simulation of the wind power generator.

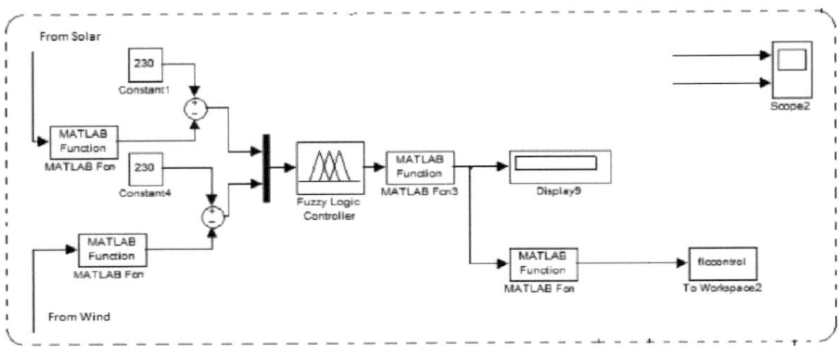

Figure 5.
Fuzzy logic controllers in operation in system 3.

and these excel files are transferred into a database agent using MATLAB command and loaded to the workspace before it simulates. Based on the voltage value received from the input, FLC decides upon the course of action. The ECC takes the responsibility of monitoring and controlling the magnitude of the wind and solar voltage production in a regular time frame. TCP/IP network data transmission are used to transfer the data for solar and wind power plants (**Figure 5**).

5. Conclusion

The standard communication techniques and TCP/IP communication are used to develop the multi-agent system. The purpose of a multi-agent system is to implement effective demand-side management in the smart grid/microgrid. The system implements the algorithm for demand responses based on time of day tariff and real-time tariff management using the MATLAB command and Simulink model. Simulation of solar and wind models are developed in two different Simulink environments.

Design and implementation of a multi-agent using fuzzy logic tool kit were described; it includes import and exports the data from the grid, solar and wind modules using MATLAB command. The multi-agent system development requires parameter specification, design process, data flow and environment that will generates the multi-agent codes. This constrains are consider to develop the code in the fuzzy logic controller. In the data agent, control agent, database agent and renewable agents are developed for the efficient function of the system. In solar power generation, the excess power in the systems is stored using batteries. These agents are collecting the present status of the system to achieve the over goal of the system. MATLAB command is used to convert the data from various agents into an excel sheet and it is again given to the controller. For a better understanding of the two simulation environments are developed for solar and wind, the control agents are developed in the separate system. The communication between the systems established using TCP/IP protocol for reliable and secure were discussed. At last, the system was tested; a consumer gets benefited for implement the real-time tariff method compared with a time of day tariff and show in table and graphical representation. In this study is more useful for the researchers to analysis functions of the multi-agent system in a smart grid. Furthermore, it develops the new system architecture for smart grid demand-side management.

Acknowledgements

We sincerely thank Management, Principal and Faculty of Erode Sengunthar Engineering College, Perundurai, Tamil Nadu, India for their support and continue motivation for this work.

Author details

G.S. Satheesh Kumar* and S. Tamil Selvi
Erode Sengunthar Engineering College, Erode, Tamil Nadu, India

*Address all correspondence to: satheeshgs22@gmail.com

References

[1] Zamora R, Srivastava AK. Controls for microgrids with storage: Review, challenges, and research needs. Renewable and Sustainable Energy Reviews. 2010;**14**(7):2009-2018

[2] Di Somma M, Graditi G, Heydarian-Forushani E, Shafie-khah M, Siano P. Stochastic optimal scheduling of distributed energy resources with renewables considering economic and environmental aspects. Renewable Energy. 2018;**116**:272-287

[3] Akpojedje FO, Ogujor EA, Folorunso O. A comprehensive review of optimal demand side management and its influence on enhancing distribution network congestion management. International Journal of Research in Engineering and Technology. 2018:107-113

[4] Rajeswari N, Janet J. Load scheduling using fuzzy logic in a home energy management system. International Journal of Engineering and Technology. 2018;**10**(5):1263-1272

[5] Hussain HM, Javaid N, Iqbal S, Hasan QU, Aurangzeb K, Alhussein M. An efficient demand side management system with a new optimized home energy management controller in smart grid. Journal of Energies. 2018:2-28

[6] Alsaif AK. Challenges and benefits of integrating the renewable energy technologies into the AC power system grid. American Journal of Engineering Research. 2017;**6**(4):95-100

[7] Arcos-Aviles D, Pascual J, Marroyo L, Sanchis P, Guinjoan F. Fuzzy logic-based energy management system design for residential grid-connected microgrids. IEEE Transactions on Smart Grid. 2017:1-14

[8] Javor D, Janjic A. Application of demand side management techniques in successive optimization. Communications in Dependability and Quality Management An International Journal. 2016;**19**(4):40-51

[9] Jagatheeswari K, MannarMannan J. An effective demand side management in smart grid using cloud computing. International Research Journal of Advanced Engineering and Science. 2016;**1**(2):96-99

[10] Rasheed MB, Javaid N, Awais M, Khan ZA, Qasim U, Alrajeh N, et al. Real time information based energy management using customer preferences and dynamic pricing in smart homes. Energies. 2016

[11] Fossati JP, Galarza A, Martín-Villate A, Echeverría JM, Fontán L. Optimal scheduling of a microgrid with a fuzzy logic controlled storage system. International Journal of Electrical Power & Energy Systems. 2015;**68**:61-70

[12] Pascual J, Barricarte J, Sanchis P, Marroyo L. Energy management strategy for a renewable-based residential microgrid with generation and demand forecasting. Applied Energy. 2015;**158**:12-25

[13] Rahbar K, Xu J, Zhang R. Real-time energy storage management for renewable integration in microgrid: An off-line optimization approach. IEEE Transactions on Smart Grid. 2015;**6**(1):124-134

[14] Khan MA, Javaid N, Mahmood A, Khan ZA, Alrajeh N. A generic demand-side management model for smart grid. International Journal of Energy Research. 2015;**39**:954-964

[15] Bacha S, Picault D, Burger B, Etxeberria-Otadui I, Martins J. Photovoltaics in microgrids: An overview of grid integration and energy

management aspects. IEEE Industrial Electronics Magazine. 2015;**9**(1):33-46

[16] Barbato A, Capone A, Chen L, Martignon F, Paris S. A distributed demand-side management framework for the smart grid. 2014 preprint. http://arxiv.org/abs/1405.1964

[17] Qudaih YS, Ali R, Mitani Y. Microgrid design including fuzzy logic controlled storage system. Journal of Power and Energy Engineering. 2014;**2**:374-380

[18] Palma-Behnke R, Benavides C, Lanas F, Severino B, Reyes L, Llanos J, et al. A microgrid energy management system based on the rolling horizon strategy. IEEE Transactions on Smart Grid. 2013;**4**(2):996-1006

[19] Jiang Q, Xue M, Geng G. Energy management of microgrid ingrid-connected and stand-alone modes. IEEE Transactions on Power Apparatus and Systems. 2013;**28**(3):3380-3389

[20] Fan S, Hyndman RJ. Short-term load forecasting based on a semi-parametric additive model. IEEE Transactions on Power Apparatus and Systems. 2012;**27**(1):134-141

[21] Logenthiran T, Srinivasan D, Khambadkone AM, Aung HN. Multi-agent system for real-time operation of a microgrid in real-time digital simulator. IEEE Transactions on Smart Grid, Special Issue on Applications of Smart Grid Technologies on Power Distribution Systems. 2012;**3**(2):925-933

[22] Celebi E, Fuller JD. Time-of-use pricing in electricity markets under different market structures. Power Systems, IEEE Transactions on. 2012;**27**:1170-1181

[23] Satheesh Kumar GS, Nagarajan C. Design and implementation of intelligent energy control for tariff management using multi agent system in smart/micro grid. In: Concurrency and Computation: Practices and Excises. Wiley; 2019

[24] Palensky P, Dietrich D. Demand side management: Demand response, intelligent energy systems, and smart loads. IEEE Transactions on Industrial Informatics. 2011;**7**(3):381-388

[25] ChengQi O, Charlene X, Jingxia X, Feihong L. Time-of use price decision model of natural gas based on simulation and grey relationships. In: Information Management, Innovation Management and Industrial Engineering (ICIII), 2010 International Conference on. 2010. pp. 176-179

Chapter 6

Architecture of a Microgrid and Optimal Energy Management System

Muhammad Waseem Khan, Jie Wang, Linyun Xiong and Sunhua Huang

Abstract

With the growing population trends, the demand for electricity is accelerating rapidly. The policy planners and developers have great focus to utilize renewable energy resources (RERs) to encounter the scarcity of energy since they offer benefits to the environment and power systems. At present, the energy generation is evolving into a smart distribution system that assimilates several energy resources assuring to generate clean energy, to have reliable operational procedures, and to enhance the energy supervision and management arrangements. Therefore, the model of a distributed microgrid (DMG) with optimal energy management strategies based on multi-agent systems (MASs) technique has been focused in this chapter. Distributed energy resources (DER) have been considered for the generation of electrical power to fulfill the consumer's load demands. Thus, a fully controlled architecture of a grid along with concept of MAS and its development platforms, implementation, and operational procedures have been discussed in detail. In addition, agent's operations and their coordination within the MG arrangements have been focused by considering the supervision of the entire system autonomously. Moreover, optimal procedures of a microgrid (MG) energy supervision and power distribution system have also been presented considering the cost control and optimal operations of the entire MG at the distributed level.

Keywords: distributed microgrid, multi-agent system, distributed generation, energy management, optimization, agent-based solutions, renewable energy resources

1. Introduction

The microgrids (MGs) which have a low energy arrangement involves a fragment of power-driven delivery system specifically situated at the consumer's premises of the distribution network and comprises a variety of distributed energy resources (DER) such as solar photovoltaic (PV), wind energy turbines, fuel cells (FC), and other microlevel turbines, along with storage system including chargeable battery arrangements, capacitor banks, and flywheels with diverse features and dimensions at the culmination manipulators of electrical energy to accomplish their load requisition competently [1]. Certain controllable rudiments are usually installed in order to offer smooth and clean electrical energy in the optimal way.

In current period, the petition of electrical energy is rising rapidly; to satisfy such requests on regular basis, renewable energy resources (RERs) are pledged very productive. Operational accomplishment and governor of disseminated generating units with their incorporation with power storing approaches, manageable load arrangements like heaters for water boiling, and air-conditioning schemes are the vital acuity of the distributed microgrid (DMG). A variety of electricity clients serves at MG level in a form of domestic/residential customers, commercial/industrial manipulators, and also including some recreational parks. Thus, the architecture of the distributed hybrid MG is presented in **Figure 1.**

Nevertheless, the complication carried about by consuming two or more different RERs together develops the hybrid structure more problematic to inspect. These forms of energies are environmentally friendly and do not harm the atmosphere by excreting any harmful gases during the generation process. Thus, solar PV and wind energy system have developed and are broadly popular due to being segmental and environmentally friendly in nature [2–5]. Normally, solar PV and wind systems for power generation works isolated or grid-connected mode, but due to stochastic behavior of such resources, the efficiency of the generation reduces. Therefore, a model to quickly enhance turbine blade geometry, to boost power generation for the applications of the wind tunnel, is accessible in [6]. The momentous characteristics of the hybrid system are to associate two or more RERs to establish the suitable practice of their operational features and to acquire effectiveness higher than that might be gained from a single renewable source technology. Several linking facilities such as optical fibers, microwaves, 4G, and GPRS/GSM are now attractive incorporated parts of the power networks [7–10].

To integrate multi-agent system (MAS) into the power network applications, it significantly leads to make the system smoother, quicker, easier, feasible, and relatively more consistent. Likewise, in [11] architecture of distributed control is created using MAS for monitoring complex energy management of disseminated power production network. A noncooperative game theory accomplishes significant job in interlinking MAS to the organization. Arrangement was assessed by simulation, generation capabilities, cyclical load demands, variations in RERs, and certain grid instabilities; it was confirmed to deliver relatively high-performance

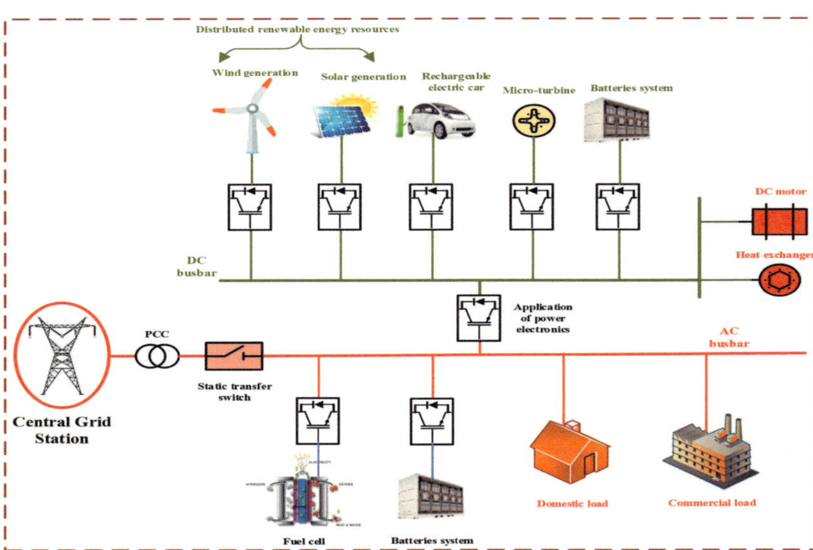

Figure 1.
Architecture of the hybrid MG at the distributed level.

supervision and additional robustness to that of conventional centralized energy managing arrangements. Similarly, based on MAS smart restoration edifice is practiced to a distribution network, simulated by an open spreading classification simulator. The uniqueness of the agent structure comprises fading the network losses while restoring the provision to the loads according to their priority deprived of disturbing the system impairments [12]. Construction built on original resident data, to complete the arrangement procedures steadily and effectively, and DG fundamentals inside the MG are delimited and constructed on energy management scheme using MASs [13, 14]. Consistently, virtual bidding is created for arrangement of scheduling progression and competency reserve, recognized on alteration impairment, drop, or upsurge on the energy request received from single or multiple manageable feeding rudiments operating in the scheme.

Numerous optimization practices, such as graphical construction technique, probabilistic method, and iterative practice, have been suggested by scientists and researchers, promising investment at the lowest price with the complete usage of solar arrangement, wind scheme, and storage system. A graphical construction practice for supposing the finest amalgamation of battery-operated and PV collection in a hybrid solar-wind arrangement has been presented in [15]. Such type of graphical approaches usually has only two constraints (wind turbine and PV, wind turbine and storage system, or PV and storage system) which were involved in the optimization procedure. In an article [16], authors offered a probabilistic method constructed on the convolution performance to integrate the unstable performance of the resources and load, therefore removing the essential for time-series statistics, to measure the long-term operation of a hybrid arrangement. In [17, 18], an iterative optimization method was used ensuring the loss of power supply probability prototype for a hybrid wind-solar organization. From this iterative technique, numerous conceivable combinations of wind-solar power generation measurements were attained. The assessment of wind resource with power generation competency along with solar stills with varied temperature storing materials was carried out to investigate the efficiency and performance improvements in [19, 20]. The entire annual cost for individual arrangement is then considered, and the mixture with the minimum price is designated to signify the optimum combination [21].

2. Concept of multi-agent systems

Agents are usually referring to an entity that have enough intelligence ability to operate in an environment autonomously and continuously to perform tasks efficiently and have the competency to interact with the neighbor agents where they share the desired information to take place in the system together to attain both their specific goals and the cooperative objective within the system. To be more specific, agents must have the following abilities to provide enough intelligence to the entire system in order to make the network more consistent [22]:

- To observe
- To supervise the system
- To communicate and cooperate
- To quick operate in case of any uncertainties
- To accomplish the tasks autonomously

2.1 Agent development platforms

To implement MAS, several open-source agent development platforms are available online that basically provide the software environment or setting where agents activate and run by the use of programming. These platforms help the agent developers to design a complex task agent system in a simplified way. Four stages are very important to be considered in the early development stage of the MASs [23]. First, the investigation stage deals with demonstrating the agent's performances and characteristics, which can be easily achieved to recognize the proper zone and issues arising in the network. Second, the designing phase is quite complicated and significant for categorizing composite difficulties and handling by using improved technique achieved in the first part. Third, the expansion period usually deals to achieve the targets of the intelligent agents in an efficient way to enhance the process of the organization. In the final phase, initiation of the created MAS, agent's interaction capabilities with different RERs, their progressive management aptitudes, and production and circulation of the data are involved.

2.2 Implementation and operation of agents

The agent's implementation stage typically requires a precise prototypical system design, which completely improves prior design models to acquire a specification that is competent enough to be operated by code generators or complier tools automatically. Several agents are needed to be considered in the modeling phase of the system having sufficient ability to activate in a particular position to serve exact information. Making such comprehensive model normally needs matching the theoretical/conceptual entities, assembled from investigation and architectural design deliverables to the real industrial items that are profitable to be used to form the system. By employing the MAS technology, a complete intelligent design can be achieved to follow a prescribed method of providing the information and carrying it to the individual assigned agent optimally. Thus, the NetLogo/Skeleton, Java Agent Development Framework (JADE), JANUS, ZEUS, and VOLTTRON are several foremost tools which are used for the implementation of MASs. Such tools allow the designers to interface their design with the system by applying the MAS technology [1].

The operation of agents is also very significant in the system environment that allows the entire system to operate accurately and efficiently. Thus, the operation of agents comprises the following three phases:

1. Perception and awareness: the operation of assembling information in the location either by monitoring existing working state of the arrangement or by foreseeing responsibilities to be complete in upcoming.

2. Decision-making and alternation: by intellectual reasoning they act and vary the setting freely. It might be possible that making the decision and the system alteration movements fixed either offline or online.

3. Action and execution: the agent's action changes the setting either physical or nonphysical, and the execution of the agents can be done either by hardware or software actions.

2.3 Role of MASs in MG dependability

The MASs play an important role in the MG dependability especially in the applications of agents at the energy management of the MG at the distributed side. In order to make the power system faster and more secure, the employment of agents has the ability to achieve the goal of protection by a competent way compared to other traditional technologies. In addition, MASs have the aptitude of self-learning, flexibility, cooperation, and autonomy, which demonstrate the efficiency of their practice in MGs reconfigurations and diagnosis. Similarly, by focusing on the self-healing MG systems using MAS, the efficiency and safety of the entire system boost up, because its development is directly associated with the system to increase the system reliability. Many researchers have focused on the submission of the self-healing of MG using MASs. For instance, the self-healing of a MG in an emergency situation using the MAS architecture has been proposed in [24]. Moreover, the employment of MASs in multiple MGs that associate altogether and working in cooperation to control the flow of reactive power, to keep the stability works (voltage and frequency), to perform the synchronization jobs, and to consider the economic aspects of the system.

2.4 Key features and shortcomings of MASs

MAS technology has a variety of advantages upon employing agents in a power system, especially at the distributed level of the MG. Agents have been considered one of the most intelligent approach practices with RERs at the distributed level when compared to other traditional systems; the benefits can be seen in the form of smooth operations of the system, improving the stability jobs and also enhancing the entire system reliability.

2.4.1 Key features of MASs

MAS has offered numerous benefits to the organizations with different aspects; some of the key advantages are considered and have been listed below:

- *Robust and flexible*: MASs provide the platform to the formation of flexible, robust, and extensible network. To transform the system, the agents should be modeled considering the demands of the users, and thus it leads to offer a flexible system to accomplish the tasks according to the user's demands.

- *Distributed in nature*: the MASs best fits into the distributed generation system where the agents can perform tasks independently by the use of their local installed programs and best fits into the arrangement that rely on local data and selection creation.

- *Supervision*: the agents have strong supervision ability; they observe the discrepancies in their network or in their neighbor agent network and supervise the entire system according to the nature of their goals.

- *Stability and efficiency*: MASs have the ability to quickly respond to the faults and adjust them in a possibly minimum time to prevent the arrangements from the blackout or even to maintain the efficiency of the entire system.

- *Data reduction and cost control*: the agents are usually responsible to operate distinctly in their location. Therefore, the data processing of the agents limits to their local network which leads to minimize the processing of the data along with their costs. In addition, by processing the limited data, the communication burdens among the two agents also decreases, and thus the system leads to reliable operations.

2.4.2 Shortcomings of MASs

MASs have some shortcomings which have also been discussed below in order to improve the agent's performances in the future [25]:

- *Agent's emergent behavior*: the goal of the intelligent agents is usually pre-programmed to operate according to the instruction inserted by the developer, which might lead to unpredictable results because the effect of run-time operations cannot be predetermined. The result might be beneficial for the market operations but may be problematic for the system service restoration.

- *Practical consideration and implementation*: usually, most of the MASs designs are conceptual based and practiced on software or simulation based that it might be challenging to install such designs in real-time MG. Therefore, such designs should be widely tested on real-time actual MG hardware to validate and implement for the transparent use of the agents.

- *System scalability*: recently, more computational power is accessible that allow scholars to design larger MG with various agents coordinating activities on a single podium. However, the capability of MAS to measure such system with rise in problems for an agent across multiple platforms or for an agent of multiple types is not well understood.

- *Security and safety*: MAS technology is smarter enough to control the space of the MG. Therefore, the change of large physical setup of the system toward smarter technology increases the risks of safety and security from malicious external or disruptive elements.

3. Agent-based architecture of the MG

3.1 The MG architecture

To boost the outcomes of the integrated distributed generating units (DGUs) and to overcome the difficulties associated to the supervision and management of a grid components, DGUs, storage system, load demands, control arrangements and other equipment-from MG utility viewpoint because of their multi-dimensional behavior, the concept of MG has invented. MGs are considered the low-voltage scheme situated at the distribution side that includes DGUs to generate electrical power from the RERs (solar PV, biomass, FC, wind energy, thermal energy turbines, diesel engines, etc.), storage system to store electrical energy during excess generation of power (ultra-capacitor banks, battery system, and flywheels), and including certain supervisory arrangements to protect the entire system during failure in the MG arrangements to deliver smooth energy to the power consumers optimally. All such elements in the MG environment ensure the stable frequency and voltage profiles and reliable flow of power within a particular distribution region. Therefore, the hybrid MG architecture at the distribution side is depicted in **Figure 1**, and the relative features of the MG compared with centralized and decentralized system are given in **Table 1.**

3.2 Unit sizing and proper technology

The unit sizing in MG organization is very important because the use of proper technology and unit sizing leads to make the system more reliable and efficient. It is understood that the unit sizing issues are complex tasks since they require high costs and steadiness but later always lead to control the load demands efficiently. In the MGs which are grid-connected, the sizing of the components is less difficult as they require the area where the unit has installed and the time period to transfer the power to the load, while the self-sustainable MGs unit sizing is complex as they involve many components and guarantee to transfer quality power to the consumers within the allocated boundaries.

S. no.	Characteristic	Details	Comparison	
			Centralized system	**Decentralized system**
1.	Multiple distributed generating units	• Photovoltaic • Wind • Fuel cell • Biomass • Thermal, etc.	√	√
2.	Multiple storage arrangements	• Batteries • Capacitor banks • Flywheels, etc.	√	√
3.	Construction	Can be constructed at the centralized and distribution or remote area	Complex	Easy
4.	Supervision or monitoring	• Voltage • Power • Frequency	√	√
5.	Protection and control of power flow	• Controls the power supply during both grid-connected and islanded operations • Use information to control the power flow of DG units	Use the central controller instructions	Use the local controller instructions
6.	Processing the data	Processing of data and tasks execution in the arrangements	Time-consuming	Quick processing
7.	Connecting MG with distribution network	Separation switch known as point of common coupling (PCC)	√	√
8.	Subset of multiple voltage levels	• Medium voltage • Low voltage	No	Yes
9.	Two operating modes	• Grid-connected mode • Islanded mode	√	√
10.	Costs	MGs can be easily constructed with low/high capital costs	High	Low
11.	Supply multiple voltages	Supply both types of voltages • AC • DC	√	√
12.	Fault detection and recovery	The capabilities of controlling arrangements to detect and recover the faults	Difficult	Easy

Table 1.
Characteristics of MG and their comparison.

Assortment of technology and system sizing can sometimes be as concise and precise as accomplishing certain local necessities such as utilizing the accessible technology for power production within power rating of the device, or it can be as multifaceted as sustaining numerous constrictions and attaining several goals at the same time to govern the system effectively. Generally, based on accessible statistical data about power extraction from RERs, consumer load demand, consistency of the anticipated scheme, fiscal limits (amount of interest), cost factors, geographical facets, and supplementary case-specific information, power production technologies and their sizes can be enhanced to satisfy exact purposes, for example, minimizing functioning and developmental charges, ecological impact, and remuneration stages on asset and/or increasing the overall consistency of the system. Therefore, various optimization techniques are available that solve the unit sizing issues employed at the MG level and realize the progress in the development of the MG system, for instance, computational approaches, such as artificial intelligence and classical techniques. The classical approach uses dynamic programming, linear and nonlinear programming, and optimal power flow, while artificial intelligence, which are stimulated by natural behavior that includes harmony search, ant colony, simulated annealing, interior point method, evolutionary algorithm, and heuristic methods such as genetic algorithms and particle swarm optimization, can be used for the sizing of the units to enhance their capabilities to make the arrangements more consistent, to control the costs, and to improve the operational schedules.

3.3 Distributed power generating systems

In present time, as petition of energy is growing quickly to accomplish the requirements on regular basis, RERs are considered enormously effective. Actual accomplishment and governor of circulated power production sources and its incorporation with energy storage arrangements such as capacitor banks, flywheel, electrical batteries system, and certain governable loads like water boilers/heaters and air-conditioner system are the main perception of MG at distributed level [26]. The main DGUs at commercial and domestic regions are given in **Table 2.**

S. no.	DGS	Operational region		Comment
		Domestic	Commercial	
1.	Solar	Yes	Yes	—
2.	WTs	Yes	No	Variable speed
		No	Yes	Fixed speed
3.	FC	Yes	Yes	—
4.	CHPS	No	Yes	—
5.	Hydropower	No	Yes	Microlevel turbines only
6.	Biomass	No	Yes	—
7.	AGSG*	Yes	Yes	Normally diesel/gas/gasoline fueled
8.	WMCG**	No	Yes	Need extra environment protection

**Alternative grid-supporting generators are expensive but in practice to fulfill the load demands.*
***Waste material combustion generators are expensive because they need extra environmental protection system.*

Table 2.
Most commonly used distributed generating systems at domestic and commercial zones.

3.3.1 RERs and their impact on the environment

Different technologies are usually installed at the MG level that operate proficiently to generate power where the consumers need environmentally friendly generating system with reasonable prices. Hence, RERs have been considered the best way to generate power since they deliver electrical power to the energy consumers locally without producing any harmful gases. The RERs are usually installed at the distributed level to overcome the load demands locally by less comparable costs and transmission losses including the environmental impact on producing the electrical energy. Therefore, different RERs that include solar PV, wind turbines, biomass, FC, etc. are usually installed in the MG system to generate and distribute electricity locally. These generation resources assure the reliable operational procedures and produce clean energy without causing any harm to the environment in the form of generating harmful gases. In addition, due to unpredictable nature of the wind and solar, it is necessary to consider the fluctuation in the system due to different levels of energy generation at different intervals. Thus, employing the RERs having storage arrangement at the distributed level will lead to produce clean energy, to control the instabilities, and to deliver clean energy with less operational, generation, and distribution costs.

3.3.2 Storage system

The storage of energy in the MG arrangement is very important and offers a wide range of benefits to the power generation companies. The electrical power during off-peak period can be stored in batteries, flywheels, and in super capacitor banks that can be used during peak hours or even blackout of the grid. Therefore, the grid operations, costs, and dependability of the entire system can be guaranteed upon installing the storage system. In addition, by incorporating storage system in RERs power generation system at the distributed level, it helps to minimize the instabilities and enhances the stability jobs during load deviations. Thus, a series of batteries are usually installed with biomass, solar PV, wind turbines, and microturbine power production system to store electrical energy. Similarly, FCs and hydropower plants contain supercapacitor bank and flywheel technologies to store electrical power during off-peak hours, respectively.

Storage of electrical energy has been extensively evaluated for MG arrangements; a wide collection of submissions persevere for energy storing arrangements. In [27], the authors discussed improvement of power quality, dynamic distribution organizations, supporting operations of MG in islanded process, and plug-in electric vehicles technologies. Storing of electrical energy has significant benefits, including refining dynamic constancy, transient steadiness, provision of voltage, and deviations in frequency [28, 29]. Moreover, such arrangements can also be functional for diminishing the entire charges and impact on the environment. An extensive range of applications exists for storage system, and the existing RERs power production at MG are now intelligent enough to operate efficiently by receiving benefits from MAS technology. In [30], batteryless schemes are being experienced and have been identified as what has been termed as green substitutes. In Ref. [31], the power delivery difficulties along with storage arrangements deal with interaction with numerous diverse MG components, including energy storage schemes, RERs power generation capabilities, and predicting agents.

3.4 Implementation of MAS in the DMG

MAS technology offers the smart intelligence approach that make the MG system more competent to operate efficiently with less instabilities at the distributed level than centralized approach. The initial designing and implementation of the agent has already been discussed in detail in Section 2, including different tools that the agents can be implemented. The agent works independently and locally, that is why they perform their tasks autonomously with less communicational data processing which makes the system more reliable and competent. In the MG arrangements, different agents are usually inserted in each power generating unit, protection arrangement, and even at the consumer's load side to evaluate the current process of the system and create the feasible protection and operational arrangements upon causing any instability in the assigned location autonomously. Hence, the main steps of the implementation and task accomplishment of the agents at the MG level are discussed below and are also deliberated in the flowchart in **Figure 2**:

1. The system operation starts with no initial fault.

2. The activation of the agents takes place in order to supervise the grid efficiently.

3. Upon fault condition, the system checks the current status of the agents.

4. The neighbor agents check for the cooperation, and the agents start cooperation among themselves.

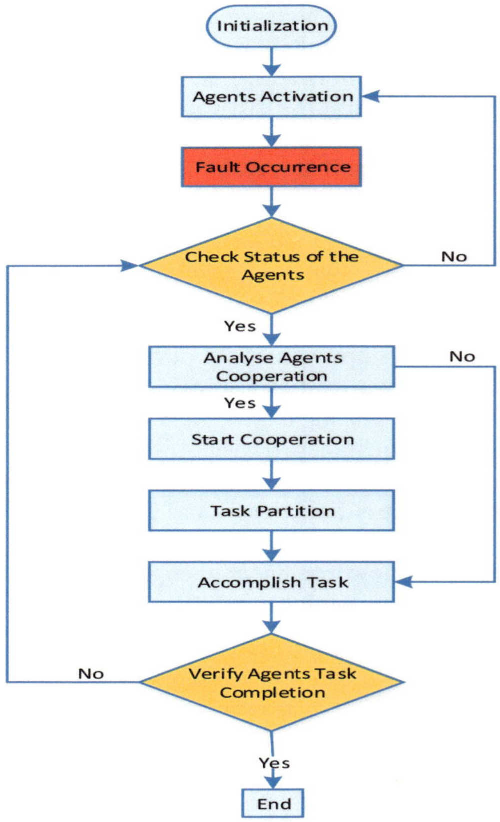

Figure 2.
Implementation and task accomplishment of the agents at the DMG.

5. The agents divide the task and perform their operation to overcome the specific fault within the system.

6. The assigned agent accomplishes the task in the specific fault location with the cooperation of the neighbor agents.

7. The control agent verifies the specific task completion and activates the agent or terminates the current situation according to the agent's performance.

3.5 Control strategies and operations

The matching of active and reactive power plays a significant role in the enhancement of the power system reliability. As an evidence, the authors in [32, 33] proved that imbalanced active and reactive powers lead to voltage deviation and frequency instability from their rated values, respectively. Therefore, management of active power, and controlling the frequency are observed the identical governor petition, and thus voltage controlling, and coordination of reactive power can be led to a reliable system operation. In islanded mode, MG missing support from the central grid, and it is quite difficult for MG arrangements to stay in a steady state. Thus, recent research resolves such difficulties by applying MAS technique in MG at distributed level. The agents offer an effective and appropriate governor functionality in current advances of the MGs. The technology comprises several supervisions and controlling operative procedures, which make the MG arrangements more intelligent and reliable; such roles cover the matching difficulties of active/reactive powers, enhance the system stability, and uphold the voltage and frequency balancing roles in grid operation mode.

3.5.1 Centralized MG control system

In the centralized MG control arrangement, the main central controller takes the responsibility to process all the instructions and perform the jobs within the grid. Several local controllers are also in operation in such approach, but due to being centralized in nature, all local controllers send instructions to the main central controller, and thus the decision-making and supervision of the entire system are only carried out by the central controller. This system has the advantage of accomplishing complete optimization calculated on all current information in the multi-objective energy management system. However, due to increasing energy demands, the structure of the system becomes more complex and expensive to build. In addition, the processing of data is also complicated, and in case of any short circuit or mishappening, the entire system leads to blackout. Thus, the reliability of the grid is also challenging.

3.5.2 Decentralized MG control system

The decentralized control arrangement is also known as distributed control system. Several local controllers are usually installed in every DER and with protection arrangement to supervise the system independently. The local controllers measure the signals and perform tasks locally within their assigned location that make the system more intelligent and reliable. Such controllers process less data and also have the competency to communicate with their neighbor controllers to perform tasks according to the nature of the system autonomously. Similarly, as every sub-level controller is responsible for their assigned location to handle, thus the processing of data reduces that leads to make the system structure simpler and control the costs as well. However, the complexity of communication in the MG arrangement is still an issue; therefore the intelligent algorithms discussed earlier in Section 3.2 should be considered along with their hybrid groupings to handle such issues efficiently.

3.6 Protection arrangements

The hybrid system that delivers both direct current (DC) and alternating current (AC) powers to the load needs certain controllable arrangements to supervise the whole system. Thus, application of power electronics has widely been in practice to achieve the anticipated outcomes. Lopes et al. [34] explored dual control method for triggering an inverter in the system. Although inverter model is ensuing consulting to subsequent governor method, the PQ inverter controller is in practice in which inverter establish specified active/reactive power set points. Voltage source inverter (VSI) control technique is applied in which inverter is monitoring "provender" consignment based on pre-defined values for system frequency and voltage. Depending on active/reactive powers of the arrangements, load demand outputs of VSI are illustrated. MG-allied VSI is anticipated in [35]; power delivery supervisor is considered for creating system frequency and magnitude of significant output voltage allowing by droop features and by identical action of traditional synchronous generator; voltage controller is implemented to generate position filter-inductance current path; also, current controller is applied to generate vector command voltage to be created by pulse width modulation technique. Linking inductor outlines with inverter output impedance, consequently active/reactive power connection is minimized precisely.

In [36], Gandomi et al. proposed a multilevel system voltage utilizing a single DC source which minimizes the number of power switches, not signifying the minor voltage matching problem. Such type of inverter has also a competency to improve voltage at the input without any additional boost electronic circuitry. In [37], authors offered segmental cascaded multilevel H-bridge PV inverter considering maximum power point tracking at distributed grid-connected applications. Such topology advantages to increase flexibility and efficiency of the PV schemes. In addition, to uphold the system constancy, linear and nonlinear switching loops can easily control the operational capabilities and has the competency to manage capacitance/inductance current of the filter at the output to accomplish dynamic and fast responses within the scheme [38].

3.7 Cost control and safe operations of the MG

The MG at the distributed level needs proper equipment, protection arrangements, and storage system to generate and store electrical energy optimally [39]. Thus, such arrangements usually cover a huge initial investment cost. The implementation costs of such scheme are high but have positive impact on the environment and consumers. The main points that show that the costs of the MG could be minimized with optimal operational procedures are given below:

- The RERs are usually in practice to generate electrical energy and distribute it locally that leads to produce clean energy without the creation of any harmful gases that pose a hazard to all living organisms.

- Generate and distribute the power locally to eliminate the high transmission losses.

- In case of emergency, the whole scheme is prevented from the blackout, and only the specific grid is affected.

- Due to limited components installed at that MG level, the maintenance becomes easy.
- Easy to connect with the central grid to share electrical power upon surplus generation.

Considering the above points, it is noteworthy that installing the MGs integrated with RERs at the distributed level is very productive, and the outcomes become more economical. Moreover, employing the MAS technique in the MG organization makes the grid more intelligent and provides enough supervision competency that lead to optimal operations.

4. Advanced energy management system for the DMG

A very promising and reliable approach to handle problems and operate the system efficiently at the distributed level is MAS approach. A MAS operation consists of three stages, perception, decision-making, and action. Perception can be performed by collecting information in the location either by monitoring the existing operational data or by forecasting duties to be performed in upcoming. In decision making, by cognitive intelligence conducts and altering the environment freely (might be either online/offline), while in actions, arrangements of the agents affect the system either by software or hardware actions, which work together and will lead to achieving a comprehensive global objective. MAS has been widely used for integration of power systems, power system reconfiguration, restoration, and management of electrical power in MGs [40, 41].

4.1 Structure of the proposed supervision system

The proper supervision arrangements in the MG organization are very important. Due to unpredictable nature of the RERs, it is very difficult to supervise and predict the actual amount of power that will be generated in a specific interval of time; therefore, the use of MASs in the MG energy management plays a vital role that leads to supervise and optimally operate the entire system. In order to get the appropriate amount of energy from the RERs and to fulfill the consumer's energy demands, the MASs technique has been presented and inserted in the MG organization that spreads throughout the system and supervises the system properly as shown in **Figure 3.** Different agents have been installed in power generating units, storage, protection system, and load demand side. Each of these agents supervises their assigned location tasks in the MG system and manages the electrical energy efficiently. Moreover, the supervision of the MG system is also important in order to smoothly operate the system, to control the costs, and to prevent the system from any mismatches or failure to enhance the system reliability.

4.2 Agent's communication arrangements

The agent's communication technique and exchanging of data are significant to identify and perform the task according to the current status of the MG. Khan et al. in [42] presented the three levels of agent's communication technique in the MG organization which are shown in **Figure 4.** The agent's communication has been carried out in order to make the system more intelligent and to supervise and operate the MG at the distributed level optimally. The proposed three levels of agent's communication system are discussed below:

1. The RERs have been considered for the generation of electrical power that associated with the generation agent to supervise the generation capabilities from the RERs and transfer the energy according to the production.

2. The storage system and energy loads are considered for the consumption of the electrical energy and associated with the storage and load agents that supervise the electrical energy to store directly from the RERs or to transfer to the consumers considering the generation capabilities and consumer's energy demands.

3. Different control and supervision agents have been created that are linked in the MG arrangements and responsible for balancing of electrical energy, monitoring, and supervision. Such agents have the aptitude to accomplish responsibilities in possibly minimum time to direct the strategies efficiently and to improve the dependability of the grid.

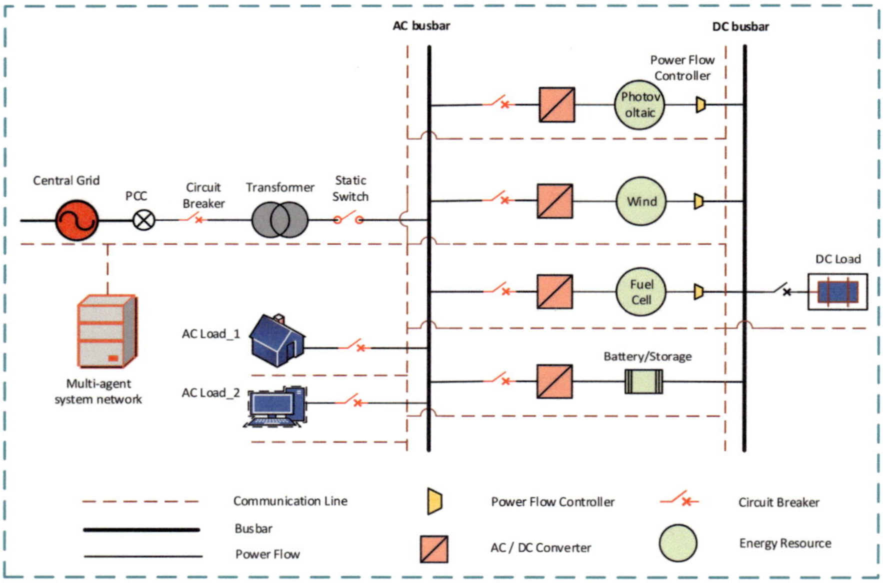

Figure 3.
Structure of the proposed supervision system at the DMG level.

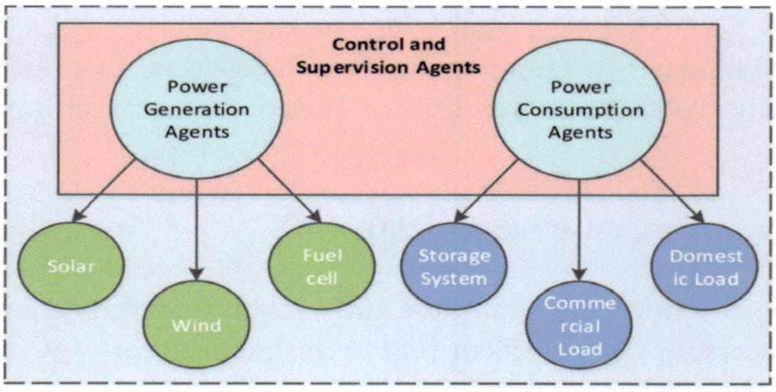

Figure 4.
Three levels of agent's communication technique [42].

4.3 Objectives of the smart energy system

The purpose of the smart energy management is to make the system more reliable and economical that is beneficial for both the electrical power generating companies and the consumers. Therefore, the main objectives of the smart energy management using MASs are given below:

1. Accomplish the best regulation and switching mechanism to extract the possible highest amount of power from the RERs considering the load petition.

2. Provide an environment where agents are inserted in different units to operate autonomously and perform tasks accordingly.

3. The podium where different agents communicate with their neighbor agents to make the synchronization job and operate the system optimally.

4. To create best monitoring strategies that applies in the MG network to enhance the trade-off between the technical and recital custodies.

5. To attain the finest operations considering the optimization of the units since the disparities occur in power generation from the RERs and consumers energy needs.

6. Transport reliable and clean energy to the consumers with less harmonics that leads to consumer satisfaction without creating any harm to the environment.

5. Conclusions

MGs are low-energy networks that are capable to increase the dependability and economy and offer clean generation of electrical energy and its supply to sustain the consumer's satisfaction. The incorporation of RESs in the MG system has developed to generate electrical power and distribute and supervise the arrangement optimally. Hence, many researchers have been involved in the designing procedures, controlling strategies, finest management of energy, and optimal operations of the MGs to deliver reliable, quality, and sustainable energy to their customers with low energy costs. Therefore, a DMG with optimal energy management strategies based on MAS technique has been focused in this chapter. A fully controlled architecture of a MG has been offered that associated with a combination of several RERs, which lead to generate clean energy without producing any harm to the environment. The concept of MAS has been employed in the MG network that supervises the entire arrangements in an efficient way. Similarly, MASs development platforms, its implementation, and operational procedures, along with some key features/drawbacks, have also been discussed in detail. In addition, agents have the ability to supervise their assigned duty competently; thus, operations and coordination of agents in the MG network have been provided by considering the supervision of the entire system autonomously. Lastly, optimal procedures of the MG energy supervision and power distribution system along with objectives of the smart energy managements system have been conferred considering the cost control and optimal operations of the entire MG at the distributed level.

Acknowledgements

This work was supported by the National Natural Science Foundation of China under Grant no. 61374155 and the Specialized Research Fund for the Doctoral Program of Higher Education PR China under Grant no. 20130073110030.

Conflict of interest

The authors declare no conflict of interest.

Dedication

I dedicate this chapter to my inspiring parents, brothers, and sisters, for being the role models, pillows, catapults, and cheerleading squad that I have needed throughout the completion of this research work!

Author details

Muhammad Waseem Khan*, Jie Wang*, Linyun Xiong and Sunhua Huang
Department of Electrical Engineering, Shanghai Jiao Tong University, Minhang, Shanghai, PR China

*Address all correspondence to: engr_waseem90@yahoo.com and jiewangxh@sjtu.edu.cn

References

[1] Khan MW, Wang J. The research on multi-agent system for microgrid control and optimization. Renewable and Sustainable Energy Reviews. 2017;**80**:1399-1411

[2] Khare V, Nema S, Baredar P. Solar–wind hybrid renewable energy system: A review. Renewable and Sustainable Energy Reviews. 2016;**58**:23-33

[3] Weldekidan H, Strezov V, Town G. Review of solar energy for biofuel extraction. Renewable and Sustainable Energy Reviews. 2018;**88**:184-192

[4] Elhadidy MA, Shaahid SM. Parametric study of hybrid (wind + solar + diesel) power generating systems. Renewable Energy. 2000;**21**(2):129-139

[5] Nowotny J, Dodson J, Fiechter S, Gür TM, Kennedy B, Macyk W, et al. Towards global sustainability: Education on environmentally clean energy technologies. Renewable and Sustainable Energy Reviews. 2018;**81**:2541-2551

[6] Lanzafame R, Mauro S, Messina M. Numerical and experimental analysis of micro HAWTs designed for wind tunnel applications. International Journal of Energy and Environmental Engineering. 2016;**7**(2):199-210

[7] Wissner M. ICT, growth and productivity in the German energy sector—On the way to a smart grid? Utilities Policy. 2011;**19**(1):14-19

[8] Khan MW, Wang J, Irfan M, Shiraz M, Khan AH. Design and implementation of Remote Digital Energy Meter (RDEM) based on GSM technology. In: Fifth International Conference on Wireless and Optical Communications. Vol. 10465. Bellingham WA, USA: International Society for Optics and Photonics; 2017. p. 104650B

[9] Guerriero P, Di Napoli F, Vallone G, d'Alessandro V, Daliento S. Monitoring and diagnostics of PV plants by a wireless self-powered sensor for individual panels. IEEE Journal of Photovoltaics. 2016;**6**(1):286-294

[10] Khan MW, Arif A. Automizing DC and induction motors based system through GSM technology. International Journal of Scientific and Engineering Research. 2013;**4**(2):865-869

[11] Khan MR, Jidin R, Pasupuleti J. Multi-agent based distributed control architecture for microgrid energy management and optimization. Energy Conversion and Management. 2016;**112**:288-307

[12] Xu Y, Liu CC, Schneider KP, Tuffner FK, Ton DT. Microgrids for service restoration to critical load in a resilient distribution system. IEEE Transactions on Smart Grid. 2018;**9**(1):426-437

[13] Rahman MS, Mahmud MA, Pota HR, Hossain MJ. Distributed multi-agent scheme for reactive power management with renewable energy. Energy Conversion and Management. 2014;**88**:573-581

[14] Mbodji AK, Ndiaye ML, Ndiaye PA. Decentralized control of the hybrid electrical system consumption: A multi-agent approach. Renewable and Sustainable Energy Reviews. 2016;**59**:972-978

[15] Borowy BS, Salameh ZM. Methodology for optimally sizing the combination of a battery bank and PV array in a wind/PV hybrid system. IEEE Transactions on Energy Conversion. 1996;**11**(2):367-375

[16] Tina G, Gagliano S, Raiti S. Hybrid solar/wind power system probabilistic modelling for long-term performance

assessment. Solar Energy. 2006;**80**(5):578-588

[17] Yang HX, Lu L, Burnett J. Weather data and probability analysis of hybrid photovoltaic–wind power generation systems in Hong Kong. Renewable Energy. 2003;**28**(11):1813-1824

[18] Yang H, Lu L, Zhou W. A novel optimization sizing model for hybrid solar-wind power generation system. Solar Energy. 2007;**81**(1):76-84

[19] Luderer G, Pietzcker RC, Carrara S, de Boer HS, Fujimori S, Johnson N, et al. Assessment of wind and solar power in global low-carbon energy scenarios: An introduction. Energy Economics. 2017;**64**:542-551

[20] Sathyamurthy R, El-Agouz SA, Nagarajan PK, Subramani J, Arunkumar T, Mageshbabu D, et al. A review of integrating solar collectors to solar still. Renewable and Sustainable Energy Reviews. 2017;77:1069-1097

[21] Yang H, Wei Z, Chengzhi L. Optimal design and techno-economic analysis of a hybrid solar–wind power generation system. Applied Energy. 2009;**86**(2):163-169

[22] Khan MW, Wang J, Ma M, Xiong L, Li P, Wu F. Optimal energy management and control aspects of distributed microgrid using multi-agent systems. Sustainable Cities and Society. 2019;**44**:855-870

[23] Ricordel PM, Demazeau Y. From analysis to deployment: A multi-agent platform survey. In: International Workshop on Engineering Societies in the Agents World. Berlin, Heidelberg: Springer; 2000. pp. 93-105

[24] Colson CM, Nehrir MH, Gunderson RW. Distributed multi-agent microgrids: A decentralized approach to resilient power system self-healing. In: 2011 4th International Symposium on Resilient Control Systems. IEEE; 2011. pp. 83-88

[25] Kantamneni A, Brown LE, Parker G, Weaver WW. Survey of multi-agent systems for microgrid control. Engineering Applications of Artificial Intelligence. 2015;**45**:192-203

[26] Hatziargyriou ND, Jenkins N, Strbac G, Lopes JA, Ruela J, Engler A, et al. Microgrids-large scale integration of microgeneration to low voltage grids. In: CIGRE 2006. Paris: MINES Paris Tech; 2006. p. 28

[27] Tan X, Li Q, Wang H. Advances and trends of energy storage technology in Microgrid. International Journal of Electrical Power & Energy Systems. 2013;**44**(1):179-191

[28] Levron Y, Guerrero JM, Beck Y. Optimal power flow in microgrids with energy storage. IEEE Transactions on Power Systems. 2013;**28**(3):3226-3234

[29] Zhang L, Gari N, Hmurcik LV. Energy management in a microgrid with distributed energy resources. Energy Conversion and Management. 2014;**78**:297-305

[30] Kyriakarakos G, Piromalis DD, Arvanitis KG, Dounis AI, Papadakis G. On battery-less autonomous polygeneration microgrids: Investigation of the combined hybrid capacitors/hydrogen alternative. Energy Conversion and Management. 2015;**91**:405-415

[31] Rigo-Mariani R, Sareni B, Roboam X, Turpin C. Optimal power dispatching strategies in smart-microgrids with storage. Renewable and Sustainable Energy Reviews. 2014;**40**:649-658

[32] Eddy YF, Gooi HB, Chen SX. Multi-agent system for distributed management of microgrids. IEEE Transactions on Power Systems. 2015;**30**(1):24-34

[33] Palizban O, Kauhaniemi K, Guerrero JM. Microgrids in active network management—Part I: Hierarchical control, energy storage, virtual power plants, and market participation. Renewable and Sustainable Energy Reviews. 2014;**36**:428-439

[34] Lopes JP, Moreira CL, Madureira AG. Defining control strategies for microgrids islanded operation. IEEE Transactions on Power Systems. 2006;**21**(2):916-924

[35] Mohamed YA, El-Saadany EF. Adaptive decentralized droop controller to preserve power sharing stability of paralleled inverters in distributed generation microgrids. IEEE Transactions on Power Electronics. 2008;**23**(6):2806-2816

[36] Gandomi AA, Saeidabadi S, Hosseini SH, Babaei E, Sabahi M. Transformer-based inverter with reduced number of switches for renewable energy applications. IET Power Electronics. 2015;**8**(10):1875-1884

[37] Xiao B, Hang L, Mei J, Riley C, Tolbert LM, Ozpineci B. Modular cascaded H-bridge multilevel PV inverter with distributed MPPT for grid-connected applications. IEEE Transactions on Industry Applications. 2015;**51**(2):1722-1731

[38] Shafiee Q, Guerrero JM, Vasquez JC. Distributed secondary control for islanded microgrids—A novel approach. IEEE Transactions on Power Electronics. 2014;**29**(2):1018-1031

[39] Khan MW, Wang J, Xiong L, Ma M. Fractional order sliding mode control of PMSG-wind turbine exploiting clean energy resource. International Journal of Renewable Energy Development. 2019;**8**(1):81-89

[40] Howell S, Rezgui Y, Hippolyte JL, Jayan B, Li H. Towards the next generation of smart grids: Semantic and holonic multi-agent management of distributed energy resources. Renewable and Sustainable Energy Reviews. 2017;**77**:193-214

[41] Netto R, Ramalho G, Bonatto B, Carpinteiro O, Zambroni de Souza A, Oliveira D, et al. Real-time framework for energy management system of a smart microgrid using multiagent systems. Energies. 2018;**11**(3):656

[42] Khan MW, Wang J, Xiong L, Ma M. Modelling and optimal management of distributed microgrid using multi-agent systems. Sustainable Cities and Society. 2018;**41**:154-169

Chapter 7

Multi-Agent Systems Based Advanced Energy Management of Smart Micro-grid

Leo Raju and Antony Amalraj Morais

Abstract

Microgrids play a major role in enabling the widespread adoption of renewable distributed energy resources. However, as the power generated from renewable resources is intermittent in nature, it impacts the dynamics and stability of the microgrid, and hence their integration needs new approaches to coordination and control. The existing systems lack run-time adaptive behavior. To face these constraints, the electric energy system must adapt by integrating Information and Communication Technologies (ICT). Multiagent system (MAS) is emerging as an integrated solution approach to distributed computing, communication, and data integration needs for smart grid application. Distributed and heterogeneous information can be efficiently processed locally, but utilized globally to coordinate distributed knowledge networks, resulting in reduction of information processing time and network bandwidth. Parallel operations, asynchronous communication, and autonomous actions of agents enable MAS to adapt to dynamic changes of the environment, thereby improving the reliability, responsiveness, fault tolerance, and stability of the microgrid. In this chapter, MAS is implemented with Java Agent DEvelopment (JADE) framework for advanced energy management of a microgrid. Also, MAS is linked with Arduino microcontroller for practical verification of agent operations. Three microgrids are interconnected to form a microgrid testbed, and smart grid features such as demand side management and plug and play are implemented, making it into a smart microgrid.

Keywords: multiagent system, microgrid, smart grid, Arduino, demand side management, plug and play

1. Introduction

The power sector is undergoing a profound change—depletion of fossil fuels and environmental considerations have made it to embrace renewable energy resources such as solar and wind. A microgrid is a building block of a smart grid and is poised to play a major role in enabling the widespread adoption of renewable distributed energy resources. However, as the power generated from renewable resources is intermittent in nature, it impacts the dynamics and stability of the microgrid, and hence their integration into the microgrid necessitates new approaches to coordination and control.

Power industry has vast experience in operating single, large, monolithic power systems, but little experience in the operation of the same grid with multiple renewable energy resources. However, there will be no single grid in the future, but only a large interconnection of virtual power plants, consisting of DERs, prosumers, and other energy resources. The high penetration of renewable energy resources requires new coordination and control approaches. The energy network has to be dynamically optimized for economic and environmental benefits. To meet these challenges, microgrid monitoring ought to incorporate communication and control in a distributive environment to achieve an optimal balance between generation, energy storage, and load demand.

Development in Information and Communication Technologies (ICT) has made a huge impact in the energy sector and the way energy is generated and distributed. We are moving toward more decentralized, more sustainable, and smarter power systems. The smart grid paradigm represents a transition toward intelligent two-way power delivery grids. Smart grid features such as self-healing, demand side management, plug and play, dynamic pricing, dynamic adaptation, and distributed optimization can be incorporated in the microgrid, turning it into a smart microgrid. A smart grid is a system of integrated smart microgrids.

2. Multiagent systems in microgrid

Agent-oriented programming is the latest paradigm of computer programming, used for complex and distributed systems. It has autonomic and proactive characteristics with higher level abstraction [1]. An agent is a computer program capable of flexible and autonomous action in a dynamic environment [2]. Multi agent system (MAS) has received a great deal of attention in the recent times due to its inherent ability to significantly improve the operational efficiency in a distributive environment [3]. A multiagent system (MAS) is a distributed system consisting of multiple software agents, forming a loosely coupled network and working together to solve problems that are beyond their individual capabilities [4]. MAS improves modularity, flexibility, adaptability, scalability, reconfigurability, and responsiveness with its inherent characteristics. MAS is run-time adaptive and distributes decisions to improve performance and stability.

Design and implementation of a MAS in a microgrid are discussed in [5]. MAS-based control in microgrid is explained in [6]. A real-time digital simulator used for real-time operation of MAS on microgrid is explained in [6]. MAS-based simulation of microgrid control is discussed in [7]. Ref. [8] gives a review of microgrids from MAS perspectives. Survey of MAS for microgrid control is given in [9]. MAS is promising heuristic techniques for solving problems whose domains are distributed, complex, and heterogeneous. Though MAS is widely recognized as the method of choice for realization of time-critical applications of smart grid, it has only been simulated for theoretical proof of concept [10]. There is a need for comprehensive real-time simulation considering all the options and practically verifying distributed energy management of microgrid using MAS, Arduino microcontroller through an experimental setup. MAS in JADE is linked with Arduino processor and the agent operations for environment dynamics are practically verified in [11, 12]. Verification and validation of MAS in microgrid have not been adequately addressed so far [13]. The recent development of control of microgrid using MAS is given in [14, 15]. Multiagent systems for grid outage management are discussed in [16]. Advanced energy management of microgrid using Arduino and multiagent system is discussed in detail in [17]. Here, only two microgrids are considered and transactive energy management is not adequately addressed.

To address the inadequacies, a smart microgrid testbed is implemented with interconnection of three microgrids, and the inherent features of MAS are leveraged for dynamic adaptation and distributed optimization to get the best of the service to the consumers, across the network, all the time, leading to economic and environmental optimization. Initially, two microgrids, one in the department and the other in the hostel building in the campus, each with solar unit, wind unit, load, battery, grid, and diesel unit, are considered. Then, the third microgrid in administration building is added to make a smart microgrid testbed. The characteristics of the smart grid are practically verified by linking MAS with Arduino microcontroller.

3. Environmental interaction in microgrid

The values from the environment such as the power required by the load, the power output of the solar PV, the state of charge of the battery, etc. are sensed and given as input to the JADE agent program through the Arduino microcontroller. Potentiometers are used to sense the environment values in Arduino. The communication with the Arduino microcontroller has to be in Java so that the sensed values can be directly given to the agents in the JADE environment.

3.1 Microcontrollers and communication methods

The microcontroller should have sufficient input pins for sensing the environment values. It should also be able to communicate with the agents using JADE framework. Various communication methods are discussed here.

3.1.1 Arduino as the microcontroller

There are numerous ways of sending the sensed values from the environment to the Java program using Arduino.

- Using Arduino plug-in in eclipse: Installation of the plug-in is simple and easy. However, the code is written in C++. This makes it difficult for the agents in the Java program to call the function accessing the microcontroller written in C++ language.

- Using J Arduino library: Using this library in the Java IDE, in our case Eclipse, we can access the microcontroller using a JAVA class itself. This library provides functions such as those in Arduino IDE `setup()`, `loop()`, etc. The main disadvantage of this method is the `loop()` function, without which the program is not allowed to run. When an agent calls this Java class containing the Arduino functions, to access the microcontroller, it goes into the `loop()` function and does not come out.

- Serial communication using RxTx library: This is the most suitable method for accessing Arduino from the Java code. A library called RxTx is used that facilitates serial communication with Arduino. Messages can be sent to and received from Arduino serially. However, since the communication is serial, only one agent can access the microcontroller at a time. In this case, the control agent is used for this communication.

The Arduino UNO board has limited number of analog input pins and hence Arduino MEGA is preferred to sense large number of environment variables in the microgrids.

3.2 Serial communication with Arduino

Potentiometers representing the environmental variables of the microgrid are connected to analog input pins of the Arduino board to input the environmental values. The potentiometers are range fixed with value of (0–1023) for all the environment variables. The environment variable values can be fixed such that the maximum value is fixed as 1024 and the variation is done accordingly. The agents receive the environmental values from the Arduino board through serial communication using RxTx library.

3.3 Actuators

The results of strategic operations of agents are reflected in the Arduino microcontroller, which can be given to the physical devices for actuation. This information is passed to the Arduino board through serial communication and given to its digital pins to which LEDs are connected. These LEDs indicate the action taken by the agents, and the status of the LEDs can be used for triggering the action of the actuators of solar power, load, battery, grid, etc. Each LED is fixed for a specific microgrid device and turning on the LED reflects the activation of corresponding device through actuators.

4. Advanced energy management of microgrid using MAS and Arduino

Two-grid connected microgrids, one in the department and the other in the hostel, each with solar unit, wind unit, load, battery, grid, and diesel unit, are considered. The model of the microgrid is shown in **Figure 1**.

Each component is considered as an agent and the agent communicates and coordinates for optimal energy management. The agents are decentralized and autonomous for local optimization and coordinate with other agents, distributed across the network for different levels of global optimization. Java agent programming is used to program the agents in JADE environment and executed in Eclipse Integrated Development Environment (IDE). The platform is multithreaded

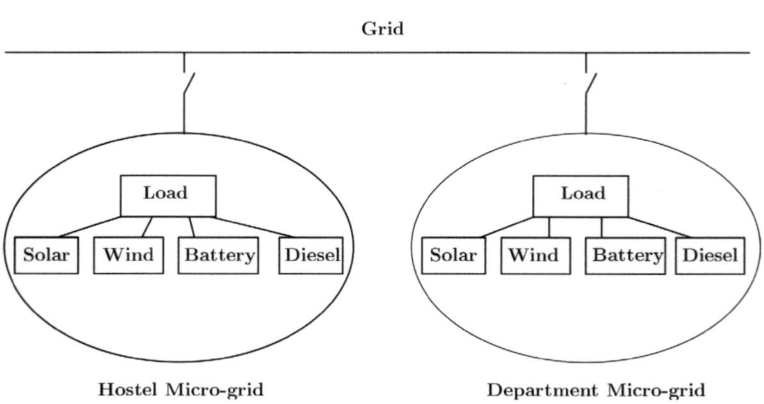

Figure 1.
Solar wind microgrid model.

allowing simultaneous decision-making capabilities for faster reaction and flexibility management. The agents communicate and coordinate with other agents for strategic decision and the resulting command signals are passed to the actuators for physical action. Arduino Mega board, which has more I/O pins to accommodate all the agents, is used for sensing the environment values. MAS is linked with Arduino Mega board for practical verification of operations of agents.

Initially, the department load receives power from the department solar. If it is not sufficient, it receives from the wind unit. If power is still required, it is received from the hostel solar and hostel wind units in the order. If the load requirement is more than the solar and wind power, it checks with the batteries and receives the available power from the batteries. If power is still required, it goes for noncritical load (NCL) shedding in department and hostel loads before going to the external power source of grid or diesel. Dynamic pricing is implemented and hence the choice of diesel or grid is made based on the unit price at that point of time. Similar procedure is followed for hostel load. Thus, the agents coordinate among themselves to take the best possible actions for optimal energy management of microgrid. The environment variables are sensed by using potentiometer where the maximum ranges are fixed for the value (0–1023). For example, if hostel solar power is 100 kW, then 1024 represents 100 kW. Similarly, all the environment variable values are fixed. By varying the potentiometer, these values can be varied within the fixed range. By varying these values, various scenarios are generated for validation and verification. A model for Arduino-based energy management of microgrid is shown in **Figure 2**. Here, the environment values are sensed by Arduino and given to the agents. The agents collaborate and coordinate for effective energy management, and after the operation, the resulting command signals are given to Arduino, which are observed through LED operations. Digital write of high or low is done on the agent when the ACL communication is active. An 8 bit number is considered with each bit representing a microgrid device action. Bit value 1 represents ON state and 0 represents OFF state. These 8 bit output is given through Arduino Mega microcontroller to the corresponding LEDs to show the physical action of the corresponding microgrid devices. In this case, all the LEDs glow, except the last two white LEDs that represent grid and diesel since the loads are not receiving any power from them. The console output of hostel and department units are shown in **Figures 3** and **4**. The sniffer diagram in **Figure 5** shows that the hostel load receives power from hostel solar, hostel wind, and hostel battery and that the department load receives power from department solar, department

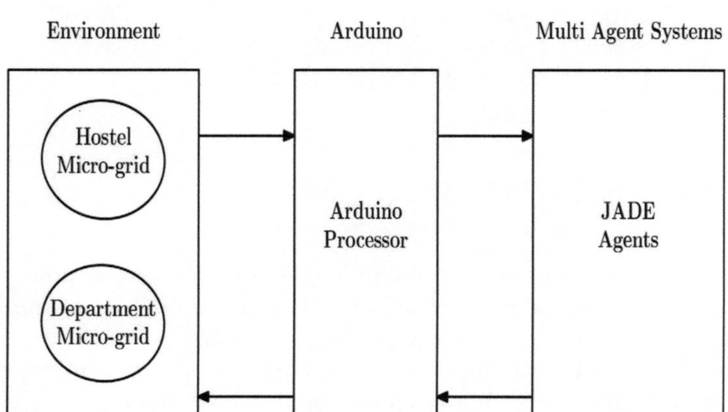

Figure 2.
MAS Arduino-based microgrid control model.

```
                    HOSTEL
Solar Power                            : 40kW
Wind Power                             : 18kW
Load                                   : 75kW
 WindSource  Price/kWh = Rs.5
Power Tapped from local Wind           : 18kW
 PowerSource Price/kwh = Rs.4
Power Tapped from local Solar          : 40kW
Power Tapped from Other Solar          : 0kW
Power Tapped from Other Wind           : 0kW
Power Tapped from local Battery        : 17kW
Power Tapped from Other Battery        : 0kW
Power Tapped by Local Battery          : 0kW
Power Remaining in Battery             : 2kW
Battery Charge in Percentage           : 4%
Power Remaining in local Solar         : 0kW
Power Needed                           : 0kW
```

Figure 3.
Console output of energy management of microgrid in hostel.

```
                  DEPARTMENT
Solar Power                            : 40kW
Wind Power                             : 21kW
Load                                   : 70kW
 WindSource1  Price/kWh = Rs.8
Power Tapped from local Wind           : 21KW
 PowerSource1 Price/kwh = Rs.7
Power Tapped from local Solar          : 40kW
Power Tapped from Other Solar          : 0kW
Power Tapped from Other Wind           : 0kW
Power Tapped from local Battery        : 9kW
Power Tapped from Other Battery        : 0kW
Power Tapped by Local Battery          : 0kW
Power Remaining in Battery             : 10kW
Battery Charge in Percentage           : 20%
Power Remaining in local Solar         : 0kW
Power Needed                           : 0kW
```

Figure 4.
Console output of energy management of microgrid in department.

wind, and department battery. Both the units are self-sufficient in power requirements and so there is no intercommunication between them. The execution of agents with the status of LEDs is shown in **Figures 6** and 7.

The department and hostel units are self sufficient and hence no power is received from the grid or diesel units as indicated in console outputs. The last two white LEDs that represent grid and diesel are OFF and the other LEDs are ON as shown in the pictures. Thus, the operations of the agents are verified using MAS-Arduino testbed. The inherent features of MAS increase the switching speed and

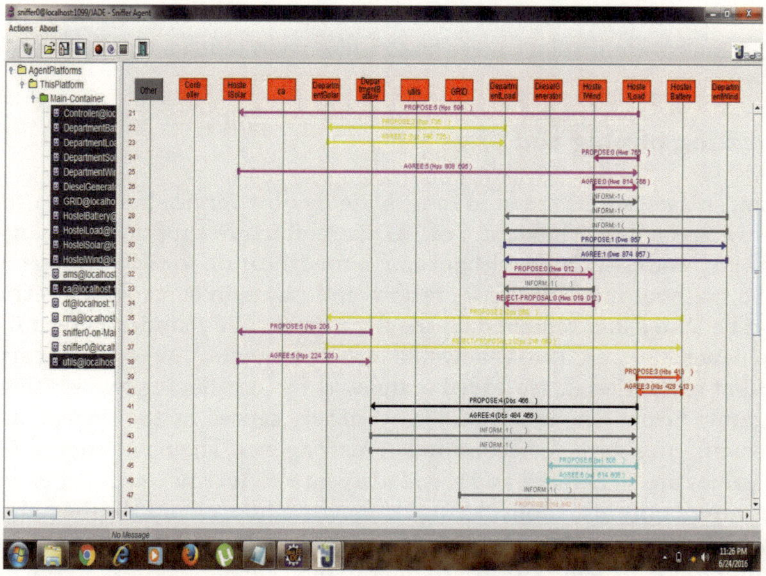

Figure 5.
JADE sniffer diagram of energy management of microgrid.

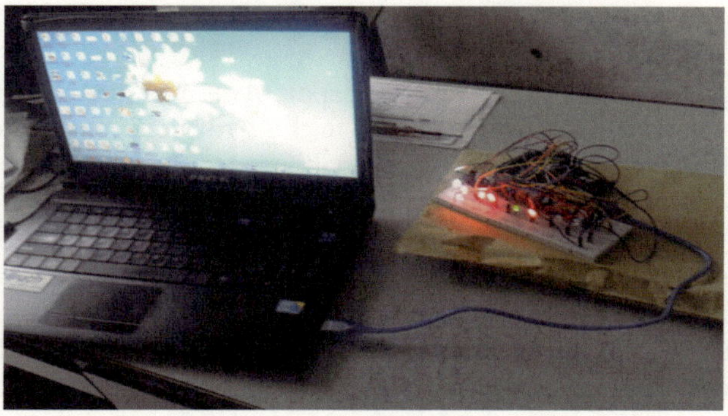

Figure 6.
Verification through Arduino output-1.

Figure 7.
Verification through Arduino output-2.

reduce the network load, which leads to better operational efficiency of microgrids even under intermittent solar power and randomness in load.

5. Verification of plug and play

Plug-and-play systems are used to provide flexible service based on a spontaneous networking facility. The nature of JADE architecture supports the plug-and-play capability and is scalable without much modification to the existing control scheme. So, without much reconfiguration on the system control architecture, agents can be added and removed on the fly. Microgrid dynamically reconfigures to adopt the new resources. Two renewable resource agents, one to the department and the other to the hostel, are added seamlessly by introducing two sensing devices in the Arduino board. The newly added agents are sensed by the system and the system reconfigures itself to accommodate new agents. The new renewable power resource values are accounted and the load agent receives power from external power resources only after considering the newly added agents. In the plug-out, the two agents are removed by removing the corresponding sensing devices connected to the Arduino board. The MAS-based energy management system in the microgrid reconfigures itself and manages the power deficit due to plug-out of agents by receiving power from grid or diesel unit based on their unit price at that point of time.

5.1 Verification of plug-in operation

A solar power resource is added to the department and hostel on the fly by introducing corresponding sensing devices in the Arduino board. The MAS senses the newly added agents and reconfigures itself to accommodate the new agents. In JADE, the plug-and-play operations are executed by walker and cyclic behaviors. When the new agents appear in environment, the walker behavior alerts the directory facilitator (DF). The new agent is given an agent ID by the agent management system (AMS) and it registers with AMS with its AID and also it registers its services with the DF. DF has the subscribe agent class, which will inform to all the agents registered to it about the new agent's arrival. Load agent is allowed to receive power from the new seamless solar agent through DF. The new solar power value is accounted and the load agent considers the seamlessly added solar power resource before going to grid.

The components of microgrid have their corresponding agents in MAS. Java agent programming is implemented in JADE environment and executed in Eclipse Integrated Development Environment (IDE). The input and output terminals of the Arduino Mega board is connected to potentiometers and LEDs, respectively. This Arduino Mega board is connected with computer serial port through Ethernet card. Arduino software is run on computer to upload the program into the board. The potentiometers are fixed with the environment variables of the microgrid. A bread board is fixed with eight LEDs representing two solar units, two wind units, two battery units, grid, and diesel units. The microgrid agents receive their environment variables from the sensing device through the Arduino microcontroller and take strategic decisions by communicating and coordinating with other agents. The resulting command signals are given to Arduino for showing the output through LEDs. The potentiometers' values are varied for various environment values and the ON/OFF operations of LED are verified with environmental dynamics. The console outputs and sniffer diagrams that represent the visual interaction of the agents are studied.

Solar power of 11 and 15 kW is seamlessly plugged in to hostel and department units of the microgrid by physically connecting the corresponding potentiometer pins to the Arduino input board. The microgrid reconfigures itself to account these newly added solar power resources. After receiving power from its internal resources, it receives power from seamless power resources. Then, the hostel load receives 15 kW from diesel unit, as it is cheaper, and the remaining power of 23 kW from grid. The capacity of the diesel unit is taken as 15 kW. The department load first receives power from its internal resources of solar and wind and then from seamless solar power resources. Since there is no diesel power, the department load receives the remaining power of 8 kW from grid irrespective of the price. The console and sniffer outputs of the hostel and department units are shown in **Figures 8–10**. In the sniffer diagram, the interactions of the agents are visually shown. In Arduino output, shown in **Figure 11**, when the two seamless resources are plugged in, all the LEDs go to ON state as all the components of microgrid are operational. Thus, the plug-in operation is implemented seamlessly by the behavior characteristics of JADE in MAS, leading to dynamically adding resources on the fly with autoreconfiguration.

5.2 Verification of plug-out operation

In this case, the two plugged in seamless solar power agents are removed from the microgrid by disconnecting the two sensing devices representing the two seamless solar powers from the Arduino board. The microgrid accounts the absence of the two seamless agents and reconfigures by itself. Then, it receives power from the other available resources to manage the power deficiency due to plug-out action. Here, the seamless power of hostel and department is removed. The DF deregisters the plugged out agents. The DF rejects power request proposal of load agents, which were earlier receiving power from the seamless agents. Now, the load agents do the

```
Solar Power                          : 19kW
Wind Power                           : 24kW
Load                                 : 120kW
Seamless Power1 Available            : 11kW
Seamless Power1 to Hostel Load       : 11kW
Seamless Power1 Remaining            : 0kW
Power Tapped from local Wind         : 24kW

Power Tapped from local Solar        : 19kW
Power Tapped from Other Solar        : 0kW
Power Tapped from Other Wind         : 0kW
Power Tapped from local Battery      : 19kW
Power Tapped from Other Battery      : 0kW
Power Tapped by Local Battery        : 0kW
Power Remaining in Battery           : 0kW
Battery Charge in Percentage         : 0%
Power Needed                         : 47kW
Non Critical Load Shed               : 9kW
Power Needed after Load shedding : 38kW
Preferred non-renewable power Source : Diesel Generator(DG)
Price/kWh = Rs.5
Power Tapped from DG                 : 15kW
Power Remaining in DG                : 0kW
Grid Price/kWh = Rs.6
Power Tapped from Grid               : 23kW
```

Figure 8.
Console output of plug and play of microgrid in hostel with seamless power.

```
Solar Power                          : 34kW
Wind Power                           : 21kW
Load                                 : 99kW
Seamless Power2 Available            : 15kW
Seamless Power2 to Dept Load         : 15kW
Seamless Power2 Remaining            : 0kW
Power Tapped from local Wind         : 21kW
Power Tapped from local Solar        : 34kW
Power Tapped from Other Solar        : 0kW
Power Tapped from Other Wind         : 0kW
Power Tapped from local Battery      : 15kW
Power Tapped from Other Battery      : 0kW
Power Tapped by Local Battery        : 0kW
Power Remaining in Battery           : 0kW
Battery Charge in Percentage         : 0%
Power Needed                         : 14kW
Non Critical Load Shed               : 6kW
Power Needed after Load shedding     : 8kW
Power Tapped from DG                 : 0kW
Power Tapped from Grid               : 8kW
```

Figure 9.
Console output of plug and play of microgrid in department with seamless power.

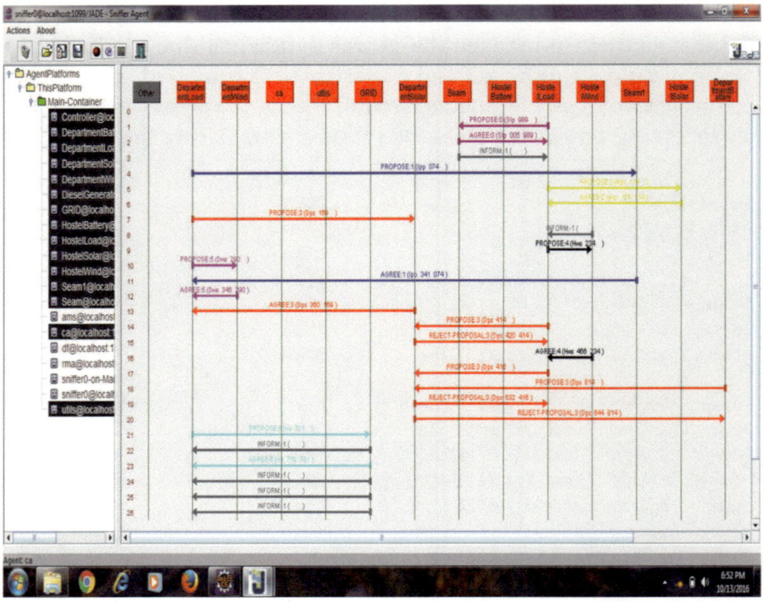

Figure 10.
JADE sniffer diagram of plug and play of microgrid with seamless power.

possible NCL shedding and get the remaining required power from grid or diesel to balance the microgrid after the plugged out event. The microgrid receives power from the grid irrespective of the price as full diesel power is exhausted. In this case, when the seamless solar power is plugged out from the department microgrid, the department load manages the event by receiving 12 kW power from the grid after noncritical load shedding of 6 kW. When the seamless power is plugged out in the hostel, the hostel load agent compensates by receiving 21 kW power from the grid

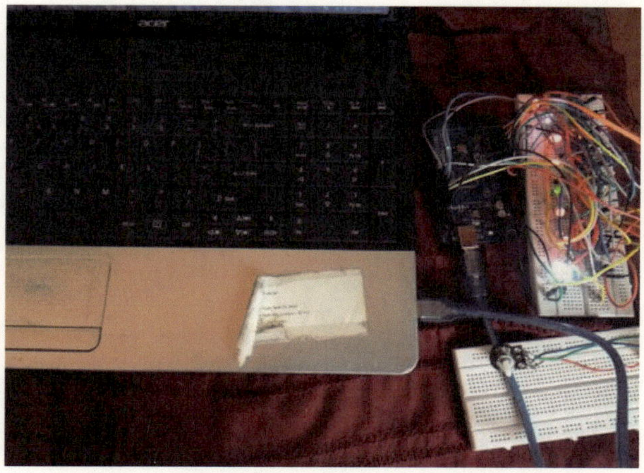

Figure 11.
Arduino output of microgrid with two seamless agents plugged in.

after NCL shedding of 9 kW. Thus, the plug out of the seamless power is managed by NCL shedding and receiving power from the grid. Since there is no diesel power available, all the external power requirement is received from the grid without considering the price. The console outputs of hostel and department units are shown in **Figures 12** and **13**.

The Arduino output is shown in **Figure 14**. In the sniffer diagram, shown in **Figure 15**, the power proposals to seamless power agents are rejected as they are disconnected. Here, the microgrid receives power from the grid to compensate the loss of power due to plug out event. Since all the microgrid devices are operational except the diesel unit, LED representing diesel unit is in OFF state and all the other

```
                 HOSTEL
Solar Power                      : 40kW
Wind Power                       : 30kW
Load                             : 120kW
 WindSource  Price/kWh = Rs.5
Power Tapped from local Wind     : 30kW
 PowerSource Price/kwh = Rs.4
Power Tapped from local Solar    : 40kW
Power Tapped from Other Solar    : 0kW
Power Tapped from Other Wind     : 0kW
Power Tapped from local Battery  : 20kW
Power Tapped from Other Battery  : 0kW
Power Tapped by Local Battery    : 0kW
Power Remaining in Battery       : 0kW
Battery Charge in Percentage     : 0%
Power Remaining in local Solar   : 0kW
Power Needed                     : 30kW
Non Critical Load Shed           : 9kW
Power Needed after Load shedding : 21kW
Power Remaining in DG            : 0kW
Power Tapped from DG             : 0kW
Grid Price/kWh = Rs.12
Power Tapped from Grid           : 21kW
```

Figure 12.
Console output of plug and play of microgrid in hostel without seamless power.

```
                    DEPARTMENT
Solar Power                               : 35kW
Wind Power                                : 22kW
Load                                      : 100kW
 WindSource1  Price/kWh = Rs.8
Power Tapped from local Wind              : 0kW
 PowerSource1 Price/kwh = Rs.7
Power Tapped from local Solar             : 35kW
Power Tapped from Other Solar             : 22kW
Power Tapped from Other Wind              : 0kW
Power Tapped from local Battery           : 25kW
Power Tapped from Other Battery           : 0kW
Power Tapped by Local Battery             : 0kW
Power Remaining in Battery                : 0kW
Battery Charge in Percentage              : 0%
Power Remaining in local Solar            : 0kW
Power Needed                              : 18kW
Non Critical Load Shed                    : 6kW
Power Needed after Load shedding          : 12kW
Power Tapped from DG                      : 0kW
Grid Price/kWh = Rs.12
Power Tapped from Grid                    : 12kW
Power Remaining in DG: 0kW
```

Figure 13.
Console output of plug and play of microgrid in department without seamless power.

Figure 14.
Arduino output of microgrid with two seamless agents plugged out.

LEDs are in ON state. Thus, the plug-out operation is implemented in the microgrid with behavior characteristics of JADE for autoreconfiguration.

6. Smart microgrid testbed using MAS and Arduino

In future, there may not be one single grid and there may be interconnection of multiple microgrids and prosumers to form virtual grid. The local flexibilities due to dynamic environment in the microgrid are addressed by decentralized multiagent approach for higher level distributed optimization to reduce overall cost in the

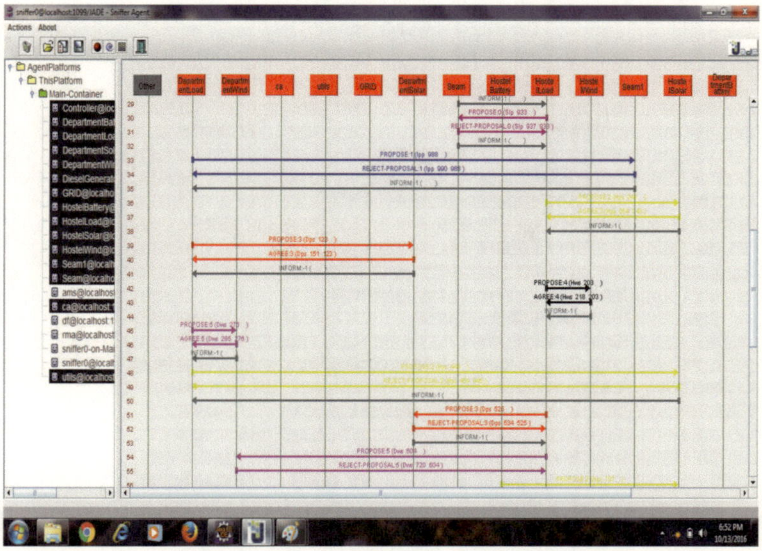

Figure 15.
JADE sniffer diagram of plug and play of microgrid without seamless power.

network. The consumer can choose the best resources available in the network for economical and environmental optimization. Also, the consumers can sell their power at best possible price. Effective demand side management can be implemented for optimal use of energy in a distributed environment. Here, a smart microgrid testbed is formed by MAS operations linked with Arduino for verifications of agent operations in supplement to visuals of sniffer diagram. The MAS-based dynamic management leads to economic use of resources in the network. MAS optimizes the use of flexibility provided by the local microgrids and prosumers. Thus, capacity management is implemented to diffuse the stress in the network. The optimization does not involve each end user only as an individual, but empowers them to participate in a larger community for global optimization. The scope of the optimization is to reduce the costs associated with the energy usage of end user. This can be effective in dealing with congestions at local level by optimal flexibility management and enhance performance, reliability, and resilience.

6.1 Simulation and verification of smart microgrid testbed

Three microgrids located in the hostel, department, and administration building are considered. Each microgrid has solar and wind and is grid connected. Each microgrid receives power from the local resources. The further power required is received from other sources of other microgrids by negotiating for better price and eventually getting the power from sources that offer lowest price. In this case, administration and department microgrids have their requirement satisfied by their own resources. In hostel microgrid, the local power is insufficient and so it receives the remaining required power from both administration and department power sources. The total power deficit is calculated and shared equally among the microgrids for maintaining balance in the network. In this case, the total power deficit is 27 kW. The microgrids share it equally and so each microgrid has to shed 9 kW. 3 kW is shed in each microgrid through NCL and the remaining 6 kW is received from the grid. The console output is shown in **Figure 16**. In the department microgrid, the load requires 36 kW. Out of this, the load shedding requirement

```
                          HOSTEL
Solar Power                           : 42kW
Solar Price                           : 2Rs.
Wind  Power                           : 18KW
Wind Price                            : 2Rs.
Load                                  : 152kW
Load Price                            : 5Rs.
Seamless Power 1 Available            : 18kW
Seamless 1 Price                      : 2Rs.
Seamless Power 1 to Hostel Load       : 18kW
Seamless Power1  Remaining            : 0kW
Seamless Power 2 Available            : 22kW
Seamless 2 Price                      : 2Rs.
Seamless Power 2 to Hostel Load       : 22kW
Seamless Power 2 Remaining            : 0kW
Battery  Power                        : 15KW
Power Tapped from Hostel Solar        : 42kW
Power Tapped from Dept  Solar         : 20kW
Power Tapped from Admin Solar         : 8kW
Power Tapped from Hostel Wind         : 18kW
Power Tapped from Dept  Wind          : 15kW
Power Tapped from  Admin Wind         : 0kW
Power Needed by the Hostel Load       : 9kW
Non Critical Load Shed                : 3kW
Power Needed after Load shedding      : 6kW
Power Tapped from Grid                : 6kW
Grid Price                            : 4Rs.
```

Figure 16.
MAS Arduino console output of hostel with three microgrids.

from control agent is 9 kW and so it requires 27 kW power. It receives 27 kW from local solar power source as the price of solar and wind is same. Then, out of 9 kW load shedding requirement from control agent, it sheds 3 kW of NCL and the remaining 6 kW is received from grid. In the administration microgrid, the load requires 52 kW. Out of this, the load shedding requirement is 9 kW and so it requires 43 kW power. It receives 30 kW from local wind and the remaining 13 kW from local solar. Then, out of 9 kW load shedding requirement from control agent, 3 kW is shed through NCL and the remaining 6 kW is received from grid. In the hostel microgrid, the load requires 152 kW. Out of this, the load shedding requirement is 9 kW and so it requires 143 kW of power. It receives 42 kW from local solar and 18 kW from local wind. Then, it receives the remaining available power from

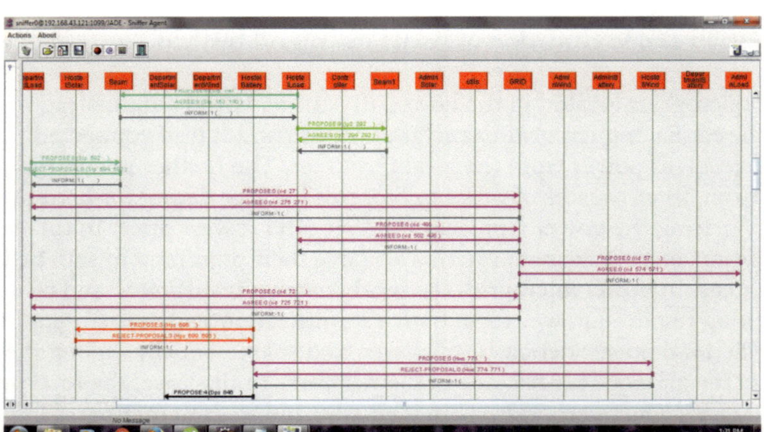

Figure 17.
JADE sniffer diagram 1 with three microgrids.

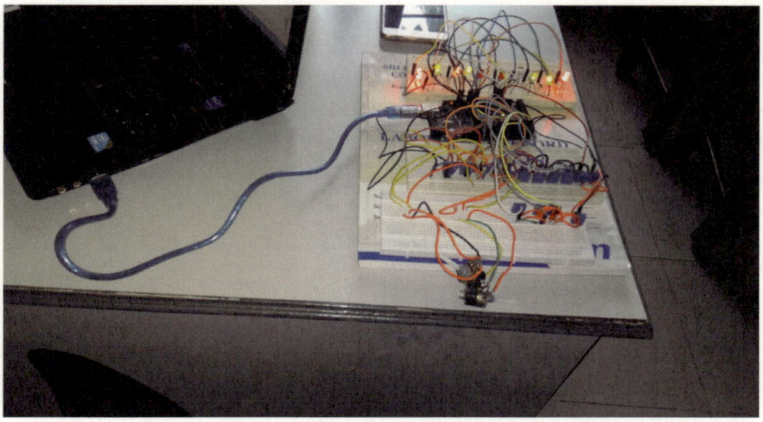

Figure 18.
Arduino output with three microgrids.

department and administration microgrids. It receives 20 kW from department solar, 8 kW from administration solar, and 15 kW from department wind. Also, it receives 18 kW from seamless source 1 and 22 kW from seamless source 2 through plug-and-play mechanism. Then, out of 9 kW load shedding requirement from control agent, it sheds 3 kW of NCL and the remaining 6 kW is received from grid. The sniffer diagrams are shown in **Figure 17**.

Sniffer diagrams show the complete communication between agents interconnecting all the three microgrids. The Arduino output is shown in **Figure 18**. In the Arduino output, except the three battery LEDs, the other LEDS are in ON state as all these devices are activated. Thus, dynamic energy management is implemented in smart microgrid testbed using MAS and Arduino. This work can be scaled up to large number of microgrids to form smart grid.

7. Conclusions

In this chapter, we have carried out a practical verification of multiagent operations in controlling the distributed energy management in a microgrid by linking MAS with Arduino microcontroller to form a smart microgrid testbed. This work forms a foundation for dynamic energy management in a distributed network of microgrids. The multiagent operation in plug and play, which is the significant feature of smart grid, is practically verified by adding and removing the renewable power resources in the smart microgrid testbed. Optimal flexibility management is implemented in smart microgrid testbed with a network of three microgrids, for best use of resources in a MAS-based distributed and dynamic environment. This method of using multiagent system to control the microgrid operation in a smart microgrid can be extended for effective energy management and demand side management across the networks so that the consumer can receive the best available resource, considering the dynamic nature of the environment. The prosumers can dynamically receive or sell the power at optimal price across the network. Also, the control unit can influence the customer by varying the price, leading to demand response management. This smart microgrid testbed can be scaled up to include large number of microgrids, and IoT (Internet of Things) can be incorporated in it to make smart grid a reality. After due diligence of experimental verification, real-time implementation of MAS-based autonomous distributed energy management of cyber physical microgrid can be implemented for economic and environmental optimization. Parallel and autonomous operation, asynchronous communication, faster computation, and flexibility management make MAS-based cyber physical system (CPS) a novel solution to large complex adaptive systems. This approach has its significance in the present energy Internet scenario as the energy industry is exploring distributed network through block chain for identifying opportunities for optimizing operations.

Abbreviations

ICT	information and communication technology
MAS	multiagent systems
DER	distributed energy resources
JADE	Java agent development environment
LED	light-emitting diode
ACL	agent communication language
NCL	noncritical load
DF	directory facilitator
IDE	integrated development environment
IOT	Internet of Things
CPS	cyber physical system

Author details

Leo Raju[1,2*†] and Antony Amalraj Morais[2]

1 SSN College of Engineering, Chennai, India

2 Tiger Analytics, Bangalore, India

*Address all correspondence to: leor@ssn.edu.in

†The authors contributed equally.

References

[1] Odell J. Objects and agents compared. Journal of Object Technology. 2015;**1**(1):41-53. DOI: 10.5381/jot.2002.1.1.c4

[2] Russell S, Norvig P. Artificial Intelligence. In: A Modern Approach. Pearson Education Inc; 2011. DOI: 10.1016/j.artint.2011.01.005

[3] Jennings NR, Bussmann S. Agent-based control systems. IEEE Control Systems. 2003;**23**(3):61-74. DOI: 10.1109/MCS.2003.1200249

[4] Wooldridge M. An Introduction to MultiAgent Systems. West Sussex, United Kingdom: John Wiley Press; 2010

[5] Pipattanasomporn M, Feroze H, Rahman S. Multi-agent systems in a distributed smart grid: Design and implementation. In: Proceedings of the IEEE Power Engineering Society Power Systems Conference (IEEE-PES)-2009; 15–18 March 2009; Seattle, WA, USA: IEEE. 2009. pp. 1-8. DOI: 10.1109/PSCE.2009.4840087

[6] Dimeas AL, Hatziargyriou ND. Agent based control of virtual power plants. In: Proceedings of the International Conference on Intelligent Systems Applications to Power Systems. 2007; 5–8 Nov. 2007; Toki Messe, Niigata, Japan: IEEE. 2007. pp. 1-6. DOI: 10.1109/ISAP.2007.4441671

[7] Logenthiran T, Srinivasan D, Khambadkone AM, Aung HN. Multiagent system for real-time operation of a microgrid in real-time digital simulator. IEEE Transactions on Smart Grid. 2011;**3**(2):925-933. DOI: 10.1109/TSG.2012.2189028

[8] Nunna HSVSK, Doolla S. Multiagent-based distributed-energy-resource management for intelligent microgrids. IEEE Transactions on Industrial Electronics. 2013;**60**(4):1678-1687. DOI: 10.1109/TIE.2012.2193857

[9] Gomez-Sanz J, Garcia-Rodriguez S, Cuartero-Soler N, Hernandez-Callejo L. Reviewing microgrids from a multi-agent systems perspective. Energies. 2014;**7**(5):3355-3382. DOI: 10.3390/en7053355

[10] Abhilash K, Laura EB, Gordon P, Wayne WW. Survey of multi-agent systems for microgrid control. Engineering Applications of Artificial Intelligence. 2015;**45**:192-203. DOI: 10.1016/j.engappai.2015.07.005

[11] Bellifemine F, Caire G, Greenwood D. Developing Multi-Agent Systems with JADE. West Sussex, United Kingdom: John Wiley Press; 2007. DOI: 10.1002/9780470058411

[12] Diwakar Purusothaman SRR, Rajesh R, Bajaj KK, Vijayaraghavan V. Implementation of Arduino-based multi-agent system for rural Indian microgrids. In: Proceedings of the IEEE Innovative Smart Grid Technologies (ISGT Asia, 2013); 10–13 November 2013; Bangalore, India. 2013. pp. 1-5. DOI: 10.1109/ISGT-Asia.2013.6698751

[13] Diwakar Purusothaman SRR, Rajesh R, Bajaj KK, Vijayaraghavan V. Design of Arduino-based communication agent for rural Indian microgrids. In: Proceedings of the IEEE Innovative Smart Grid Technologies (IGST-Asia, 2014); 20–23 May 2014; Kuala Lumpur, Malaysia. 2014. pp. 630-634. DOI: 10.1109/ISGT-Asia.2014.6873865

[14] Perkonigg F, Brujic D, Ristic M. Platform for multiagent application development incorporating accurate communications modeling. IEEE Transactions on Industrial Informatics. 2015;**11**(3):728-736. DOI: 10.1109/TII.2015.2428633

[15] Kumar Nunna HSVS, Srinivasan D. Multiagent-based transactive energy framework for distribution systems with smart microgrids. IEEE Transactions on Industrial Informatics. 2017;**13**(5):2241-2250. DOI: 10.1109/TII.2017.2679808

[16] Leo Raju MRS, Antony Amalraj M, Ramyaa R, Soundaryaa P, Thavam LD. Micro-grid outage management using multi agent system. Energy Procedia. 2017;**117**:112-119. DOI: 10.1016/j.egypro.2017.05.113

[17] Raju L, Antony Amalraj M, Milton RS. Advanced energy management of a micro-grid using Arduino and multi-agent system. Intelligent and Efficient Electrical Systems. 2018;**118**(10):65-76. DOI: 10.1007/978-981-10-4852-46

Section 3

Multi-Agent Systems Applied to Education

Chapter 8

Smart Learning Environment: Paradigm Shift for Online Learning

Punnarumol Temdee

Abstract

Online learning has always been influenced by advanced technology. The role of online learning is expected not only for delivering contents to massive learners anywhere and anytime but also for promoting successful learning for the learners. Consequently, this emerged role has introduced the concept of smart learning environment. More specifically, smart learning environment is developed to promote personalized learning for learners. Personalized learning focuses on individual learner and provides appropriate feedback individually. Currently, the advances of modern technologies and intelligence data analytics have brought the idea of smart learning environment into realization. Machine learning techniques are generally applied to analyze real-time dynamic learner behavior and provide the appropriate response to the right learner. In this chapter, the evolution of online learning environment from different points of technological overviews is first introduced. Next, the concepts of personalized learning and smart learning environment are explained. Then, the essential components of smart learning environment are presented including learner classification and intervention feedback. Learner classification is to understand different learners. Intervention feedback is to provide an individual response appropriately. Additionally, some machine learning techniques widely used in smart learning environment in order to perform smart classification and response are briefly explained.

Keywords: technology enhancing learning, smart learning environment, online learning, personalized learning, machine learning

1. Introduction

Generally, a face-to-face classroom environment is a traditional way of learning. For this learning, the teacher or the instructor can explicitly observe real-time interaction and participation of the learners. The advantage is that the instructor can provide the appropriate intervention immediately. However, face-to-face learning frequently faces some difficulties in challenging successful learning. For example, the instructor may find it difficult to gain attention from a large class. The adaptation of the teaching method can be challenging to fit in the large class size, such as flipped classroom, problem-based learning, active learning, etc. Generally speaking, time and space always affect learning management.

With the limitation of time and space, teaching and learning process has been transformed into many different forms for promoting effective and convenient learning. Pieces of evidence show that innovations of a system supporting learning usually employ the technologies emerging at different points of time [1]. Computer aided instruction (CAI) and instruction tutoring system (ITS) demonstrate the excellent examples of the system supporting learning with the advance of computer technology. They can provide convenient learning without the instructor as traditional learning through a stand-alone computer program. Both CAI and ITS are generally used for supplementing traditional face-to-face learning [2, 3].

Online learning has become the solution of time and space constraint explicitly. After the introduction of computer communication, electronic learning (e-learning) has been developed based on the basic requirement of delivering content in the digital form to the massive learners conveniently anywhere and anytime [4, 5]. Without time and space constraint, e-learning can be used not only for supplementing the face-to-face class but also the main class as an online course nowadays [6]. E-learning even becomes more popular after the high-speed Internet becomes commonly available and low cost. It is also customarily called web-based learning (WEB) [7, 8]. As shown by its name, web technology has influenced the presentation of e-learning. For WEB, interactive learning is also one of the main purposes besides convenient learning [9]. Web 2.0 has demonstrated how effectively web technology can promote interactive learning [10]. Interactive environment helps the online classroom to be more interactive overcoming the limitation of space as in the traditional classroom environment.

With mobile technology, mobile learning (m-learning) has been widely offered. The mobile phone becomes the smartphone having high-performance computing ability within portable size devices. It is evitable that mobile phone or portable devices have become necessary for the learner's daily life. M-learning explicitly promotes convenient learning which the learning process can happen anywhere and anytime, although the learning process on a small screen of the mobile phone might be easily distracted for some learners [11]. For m-learning, interactive learning is very challenging because of the small screen and the compatible ability of smartphone. However, it is easily integrated into the learner's daily life.

Currently, there has been the introduction of ubiquitous learning (u-learning) [12–15]. It employs the concept of ubiquitous computing [16] in which the computing can happen anywhere and anytime through the seamlessly connected small computing units. The users do not even realize about computations. For u-learning, learning can happen anywhere and anytime. Notably, the learning process of each learner happens unconsciously. The learners do not even realize those learning process. U-learning can be implemented as the physical learning environment [17]. For this environment, the contribution from different types of advanced technology such as sensors, sensor networks, embedded system, wireless communication, etc. is required. U-learning is commonly used for providing situation simulation for the learners. At the same time, u-learning is generally developed to guide the learners to achieve their learning goals or outcome individually with different learning paths and contents. It can be considered that u-learning has confirmed the concept of personalized learning, which the learning depends on individual context [18] such as needs, performances, goals, etc.

Online learning can also be considered with learning style points of view. Generally, online learning can promote both collaborative and individual learning. Collaborative learning believes that the learning process happens when the learners collaborate [19]. The learning outcome can be evaluated from the group product or even the consensus built within the group. Collaborative learning is important because this kind of skill is one of the marketable skills required in real-life situation. More specifically, collaborative learning aims to practice collaborative skills for the learners besides knowledge. It is essential for learners to learn how to encourage and engage team members to accomplish a common goal together.

On the other hand, individual learning aims to promote each learner individually. The assumption is made that all learners are unique and they require their learning path to achieve their individual learning goals. Personalized learning is one of the famous individual learning approaches. It can be implemented in many different forms and types of learners. It is popularly implemented as the curriculum for child learning [20] because of the expectation to enable the unique development of the child. Although, there are many different ways for the personalized learning pedagogy in child learning curriculum, the most critical processes are to assess an individual carefully and to provide the intervention appropriately. At the same time, personalized learning is widely found in online learning. Also, those two processes are essential for this environment. It has been claimed that personalized learning promotes flexibility and freedom for the learners as they are necessary not only for the twenty-first-century learning but also for lifelong learning.

2. Online learning environment

Generally, online learning is also called a virtual learning environment (VLE) [21–24]. After the emergence of the Internet in early 1990, VLE has been playing the leading role to support learning and teaching activities through Internet connection. Generally, VLE is used for distance learning as a complement to the traditional classroom. It provides convenient access to contents, tests, and virtual workspaces. It also provides communication tools and assessment for the instructor. Additionally, it is defined to cover the existing online learning environment including e-learning, m-learning, and u-learning.

In the recent past, VLE or online learning environment has successfully achieved a considerable interest from the learners worldwide. For example, massive open online course (MOOC) [6, 25], which is the largest online learning platform nowadays, provides massive online courses from all over the world for all learners. Although there are many provided online courses available, the learners are expected to be the active participants who know their own learning goal and can find their ways for achieving their goal. On the contrary, the concept of smart learning environment is that the learning system is smart enough to understand the learners individually both capability and personality so that it can provide the appropriate response or intervention appropriately. The learner may not even realize the happening learning process [14, 15].

2.1 Personalized online learning

As mentioned before, personalized learning is a significant characteristic of the smart learning environment, which expands the opportunities for lifelong learning and explores additional resources for individual according to personal interests [26]. Recently, personalized learning has become the most popular learning paradigm because it focuses on learners' interests. It is also tailored to promote online learning as personalized online learning [27]. Generally, personalized online learning can be described as the teaching and learning paradigm applying intelligent technology for matching the learners with the content or learning activities accordingly to their proficiency level, learning styles, and interests through different types of learning environments. Currently, personalized learning is extensively popular because it results in the awareness of learners' actual proficiency and needs. The instructors can design the course or give proper suggestions for the best results of learning.

In the early stage, the English instructional systems have been playing the primary role for personalized support for learners [28]. It makes the learners to be engaged with the learning system. The recommendation is given through the selection of lessons that can be matched with the learners' skills and abilities [29, 30]. Nowadays, personalized learning can easily simulate the situation for engaging the learners in a lesson, discussion, and any learning activities [31–33]. It can also provide online learning experience that professionals will need for professional learning. At the same time, web-based learning becomes a flexible way to promote personalized learning recently [10]. Currently, there is an increasing demand for personalized online learning to serve huge demands of learners with all ages [34, 35]. It is thus challenging to provide personalized online learning that can satisfy all current and future demands.

2.2 Personalized online learning and challenges

As mentioned before, personalized learning aims to promote successful learning individually. Understanding different learners are challenging since the learners are different in many aspects such as age, goal, need, etc. Personalized online learning is widely adopted for all learners of different ages. Different ages of learners imply different characteristics and require different intervention or recommendation. For child learning, the learners are still immature. The child might not know exactly their performances and their goals. There is the necessity to have the professional to estimate the potential performance and predict the learners' needs. For the teenager, some of them have explicitly shown their interests, goals, and demands. However, their goals can be changed dynamically due to many circumstances such as friends, family, school, etc. For professional learning, the learners know precisely about their goals. However, their different knowledge and backgrounds usually affect the ability to learn the same content. The content representation needs to be adjusted to fit different learners. For senior learning, their goals usually are clearly defined. However, the health condition may distract their ability to learn. Nowadays, implementing personalized online learning for learners of all ages is very challenging, as the learning environment is expected to cope with any differences dynamically. The environment needs to be smart enough to deal with and interpret any types of data. Consequently, smart learning environment is indeed required.

3. Smart learning environment

The concept of smart learning environment has been widely introduced [15, 36, 37] to satisfy the high demand for freedom in learning. Smart learning environment means that the learning environment can promote successful learning to the learners automatically. The concept of being smart can be implemented with both physical and online learning environments. The critical requirement is to make the environment to be smart. There have been many smart learning environments developed with a different degree of smart services or responses. For this chapter, smart learning environment focuses on only the online learning environment. More specifically, smart services or responses in an online learning environment mainly focus on promoting individual learning. It can be seen that smart learning environment in this context requires the implementation of personalized learning.

Generally, smart learning environment consists of two main components including learner classification and intervention feedback as shown in **Figure 1**.

In **Figure 1**, the learner classification is also called as learner modeling or learner assessment. For this component, the primary objective is to understand the different learners. There are different types of information which can be called as the contexts involved, such as individual context and interaction context, to classify the learner. Individual context includes any information relating the learner individually such as profile, preference, performance, goal, need, clinical data, etc. On the other hand, the interaction context means the context is generated from the interaction of any entities such as interactions among learners, interactions between learner and learning object, interactions among learning objects, etc. The combination of different types of contexts is expected to provide a better understanding of the learners. The classification can be done in many different ways.

In this chapter, machine learning-based data classification is the main focus. Machine learning is widely used for data classification. For learner classification, all involved contexts are classified into different types of learners. The machine learning technique learns the data and makes a decision based on the data. It can employ both supervised and unsupervised learning to perform data classification. Supervised learning technique requires the given answer for the classification process. On the contrary, the unsupervised learning technique can perform data clustering without any given answer during the training process. Selecting the right technique is challenging; the comparison between different techniques is generally performed. The knowledge-based system is usually required for determining different types of learners. Human experts generally do this process. At the same time, the intervention feedback provides the appropriate intervention to each learner. This process is to map the types of learners with a set of appropriate intervention obtained from the experts. Sometimes, the predictive model may be involved. Predicting what the learner wants and what they want to be after learning may help to provide the intervention more appropriate. Additionally, the predictive model frequently employs machine learning-based technique for analyzing historical data and predicting the right output based on any relationship among data. Generally, the contribution from different areas may be involved in the learner classification component to increase higher classification accuracy such as behavioral science, physiology, cognitive science, etc.

Along with the evolution of technology, supporting learning mentioned before, the concept of context-aware computing [38] has already illustrated implicitly and explicitly into the modern online learning environment nowadays. Generally, context-aware applications can be found with different forms of online learning

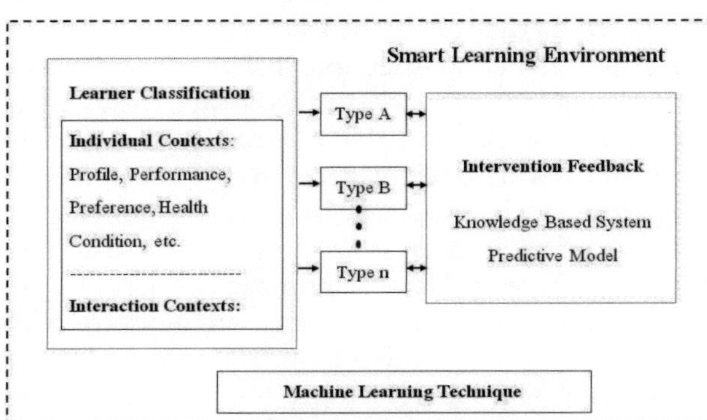

Figure 1.
Components of smart learning environment.

environment covering from stand-alone program and web-based, mobile, and ubiquitous learning environments. With the context-aware computing perspective, existing smart learning environments can be considered as a context-aware computing system. Any recommendation systems [39–41] frequently assess the learning's ability and employ it as the main factor for providing the appropriate response. The learner's ability can be considered as the primary context executing the smart intervention. The contexts used for smart learning environment can be any single context or the combination of many types of contexts [42]. It can be concluded that the vital element of context-aware computing is context awareness which is explicitly appropriate for smart learning environment so that all dynamic changes are observed, interpreted, and responded appropriately. It can be seen that developing a smart learning environment which can provide personalized learning for the learners requires the solution from multidisciplinary such as behavioral science, physiology, cognitive science, etc.

In conclusion, smart learning environment in this chapter mainly means the online learning environment with personalized learning implementation. This learning environment is expected to automatically respond to the learners appropriately for achieving their learning goal individually. For this instance, it is evitable to have advanced technology in many areas for satisfying smart ability of this learning environment. Machine learning-based techniques are the main aims of this chapter. Some techniques commonly used in the learning area are also briefly introduced in this chapter.

3.1 Machine learning for smart learning environment

Machine learning is a method of data analysis for building analytical model autonomously. It is a subset of artificial intelligence. As humans learn from experience, machine learning learns from data. It is widely used for identifying and classifying the pattern as well as making a decision on behalf of the human. Machine learning is popularly used in classifying problems in many different areas, such as manufacturing, finance and banking, and medical diagnosis [43]. For the learning environment, machine learning is generally used for supporting the learning and teaching process on behalf of a human instructor. As mentioned before, smart learning environment requires not only an automatic response but also an individual response. Machine learning technique applied in smart learning environment requires specific knowledge from different points of view to understand each learner correctly such as pedagogy, behavioral science, psychology, etc. For example, from the pedagogical point of view, different teaching approaches can engage different learners. From the behavioral science point of view, the individual learner acts differently when they are in the learning process. From the psychology point of view, the learner can be classified into different learning styles representing individual ways of gathering information and absorbing the knowledge. Machine learning needs to be trained with this different knowledge so that the classification of learner and intervention will be performed and given correctly.

Many machine learning techniques have been widely applying K-nearest neighbor (KNN) for different purposes such as learning analytics supporting instructor decision [44], predicting successful learning for the learners [45, 46], classifying learning patterns [27, 47], predicting the learning outcomes from historical learning behavior of each learner [45], etc. Another popular method for pattern classification problem is an artificial neural network (ANN). It usually is one of the comparative alternative techniques for learner classification [48]. Lastly, decision tree has also gained much attention for grouping or matching different types of learners to particular recommendation or feedback [27, 49].

In this chapter, a brief introduction of these machine learning techniques is introduced. The examples are shown in the next section to demonstrate the principle concept of applying K-nearest neighbor, artificial neural network, and decision tree for simple learner classification.

3.1.1 K-nearest neighbor

K-nearest neighbor algorithm is a type of lazy learning in pattern recognition. It is used to classify and perform a regression of the dataset. It can define whether target data matches with the specific classes by investigating the number of K in the nearest condition. It will assign the weight for any contributing data along with the distance of neighbor to classify the target. **Figure 2** shows the principle concept of KNN applied for classifying types of learners.

In **Figure 2**, KNN is applied for classifying two types of learners including learner requires assistant (learner with assistant) and learner does not require assistant (learner without assistant). The learning expert sets types of learners for the training process. The input of KNN can be any context relating to performance assessment of learners such as testing score, testing time duration, etc. It can be seen in **Figure 2** that the classification result changes accordingly to different K values. For K = 3, the new learner is classified as the learner does not require the assistant. For this case, two nearest neighbors of the new learner are learners without an assistant, and only one nearest neighbor is the learner with the assistant. However, when the nearest neighbor number has increased to 5 (K = 5), the classification of the new learner is the learner requires assistant because three out of five nearest neighbors are learners who require an assistant. Therefore, different K may cause a different decision. Generally, there are many considerations, such as K value, size of input data, etc., for obtaining the highest classification accuracy.

3.1.2 Artificial neural network

Having the inspiration by biological neuron networks, artificial neural network is widely applied in many application domains. An ANN consists of many neurons linked together with specific network architecture and learning algorithm. Those neurons usually are highly interconnected among each other. It can have many layers between the input and output layer so-called hidden layer. For learning algorithms, ANN learns from the examples and presents some degree of generalization

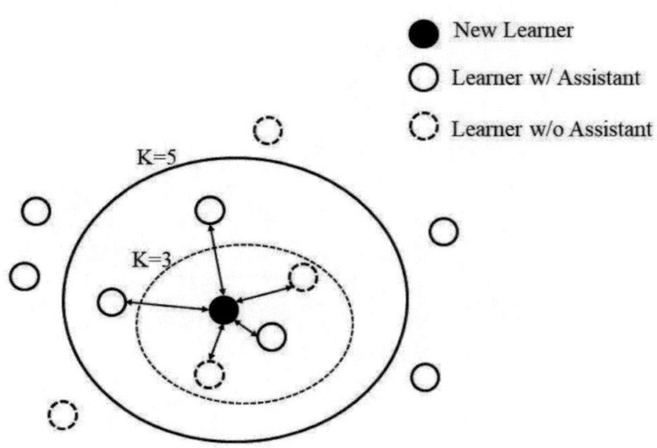

Figure 2.
Principle concept of KNN for learner classification.

from the training data later. Also, ANNs adapt itself by using some examples of similar problems with and without the desired solution during the training period. After sufficient training, the trained ANN can provide a solution relating to inputs and outputs. Moreover, it can offer an alternative solution to the new problem. The conceptual diagram of applying ANN for learner classification is shown in **Figure 3**.

Figure 3 shows that ANN is applied for classifying two types of learners including learner requires assistant (learner with assistant) and learner does not require assistant (learner without assistant). The learning expert sets types of learners. ANN learns from the examples or data during the process of the so-called training process. For the learning process, the corresponding type of learner together with its set of training data is required. The data can be any context, for example, the set of data representing the level of performance of the learners, time duration for content learning, etc. During the training process, the associated weights are adjusted so that the ANN can model two different types of learners correctly. The training process may require many times of iteration. Training parameters need to be set appropriately. Then, the trained ANN with updated weights is tested with testing data, which is the data from the new learner. ANN will finally classify the new learner into one of those two types. Selecting the type of ANN is challenging because different types of data fit with types of ANN differently. The comparison of classification accuracy among different types of ANN, different architecture, or even different configuration may need for achieving the highest classification accuracy.

3.1.3 Decision tree

The decision tree is another favorite machine learning technique for data classification. It is a predictive method having a tree structure which is built from a dataset for classifying data. More specifically, it has the leaf to represent a classification. The conjunction of features causing target classification is represented at each branch. The tree structure is constructed following the best attribute that can perform the best splitting set of data. The efficiency of this technique highly depends on the size of the training data. The conceptual diagram of the decision tree for learner classification is demonstrated in **Figure 4**.

In **Figure 4**, the decision tree is applied for learner classification problem which has two different target classes including learner requires assistant (learner with assistant) and learner does not require assistant (learner without assistant). The learning expert sets types of learners for training. As mentioned before, the training

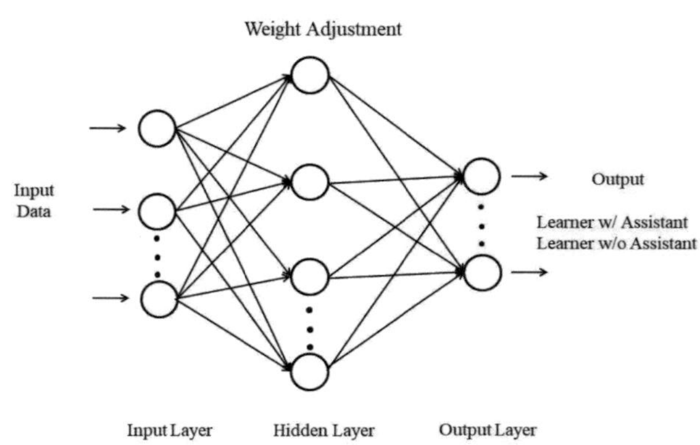

Figure 3.
Conceptual diagram of ANN for learner classification.

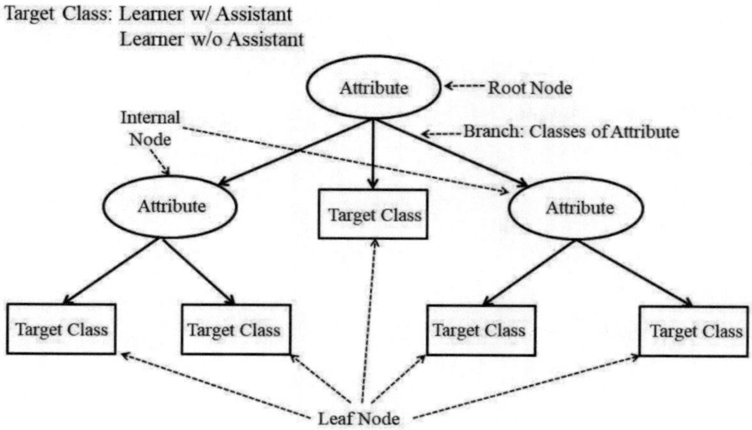

Figure 4.
Conceptual diagram of decision tree for learner classification.

data can be any context representing the performance level of each learner. After having the set of training data, the root node representing the best attribute can split the training data the most. Classes of the associated attribute are represented at each branch. For splitting data, all internal nodes represent all attributes involved in data separation. Target class is represented at the leaf node whether the learner requires or do not require the assistant. At the end of the process, all relevant rules are constructed based on all relevant attributes. The size of the training data always influences the separation of data. More specifically, different data sizes may obtain a different tree structure.

4. Conclusion

This chapter presents the concept of smart learning environment as the online learning that can promote personalized learning. For this instance, the smart learning environment consists of two main components including learner classification and intervention feedback. The objective of smart learning environment is to understand the different learners individually and provide each learner with the appropriate support or intervention for successful learning. Therefore, it is necessary to have smart data analytic method so-called machine learning technique involved particularly in dealing with a vast of dynamic change and real-time intervention. For this chapter, KNN, ANN, and decision tree are chosen to demonstrate for solving a simple learner classification problem. Although machine learning has been playing a critical role in a smart learning environment, supporting learning and teaching still require the knowledge from the multidisciplinary area such as pedagogy, behavioral science, psychology, etc. so that the leaner classification and intervention feedback in the smart learning environment can be performed correctly.

Acknowledgements

The author would like to thank all Ph.D. students who work collaboratively to determine the new findings in the smart learning environment area. Special thanks go to all participants for their valuable data for all studies.

Author details

Punnarumol Temdee
School of Information Technology, Mae Fah Luang University, Chiang Rai, Thailand

*Address all correspondence to: punnarumol@mfu.ac.th

References

[1] Cheng Z, Sun S, Kansen M et al. A personalized ubiquitous education support environment by comparing learning instructional requirement with learner's behavior. In: International Conference on Advanced Information Networking and Applications; 25 April 2005; Taipei, Taiwan: IEEE; 2005. pp. 567-573

[2] Arnold DN. Computer-Aided Instruction [Internet]. Online Encyclopedia; 2000. Available from: http://encarta.msn.com [Cited: 18 February 2019]

[3] Graesser AC, Chipman P, Haynes BC, et al. Autotutor: An intelligent tutoring system with mixed-initiative dialogue. IEEE Transactions on Education. 2005;**48**(4):612-618

[4] Rosenberg MJ, Foshay R. E-learning: Strategies for delivering knowledge in the digital age. Performance Improvement. 2002;**41**(5):50-51

[5] Zhang D, Zhao J, Zhou L, et al. Can e-learning replace classroom learning? Communications of the ACM. 2004;**47**(5):75-79

[6] Breslow L, Pritchard DE, DeBoer J, et al. Studying learning in the worldwide classroom research into edX's first MOOC. Research & Practice in Assessment. 2013;**8**:13-25

[7] Chumley-Jones HS, Dobbie A, Alford CL. Web-based learning: Sound educational method or hype? A review of the evaluation literature. Academic Medicine. 2002;**77**(10):S86-S93

[8] Zaiane O. Web Usage Mining for a Better Web-Based Learning Environment [Internet]. University of Alberta Library; 2001. Available from: https://era.library.ualberta.ca/items/0a182195-ce39-4b5d-a1c1-291ed91a0f36 [Cited: 26 February 2019]

[9] Johnson WL, Rickel JW, Lester JC. Animated pedagogical agents: Face-to-face interaction in interactive learning environments. International Journal of Artificial Intelligence in Education. 2000;**11**(1):47-78

[10] McLoughlin C, Lee M. Social software and participatory learning: Pedagogical choices with technology affordances in the Web 2.0 era. In: Proceedings ascilite Singapore 2007. Singapore: Centre for Educational Development, Nanyang Technology; 2007. pp. 664-675

[11] Gikas J, Grant MM. Mobile computing devices in higher education: Student perspectives on learning with cellphones, smartphones & social media. The Internet and Higher Education. 2013;**19**:18-26

[12] Barbosa J, Hahn R, Rabello S, et al. Local: A model geared towards ubiquitous learning. ACM SIGCSE Bulletin. 2008;**40**(1):432-436

[13] Hwang GJ, Tsai CC. Research trends in mobile and ubiquitous learning: A review of publications in selected journals from 2001 to 2010. British Journal of Educational Technology. 2011;**42**(4):E65-E70

[14] Hwang GJ. Criteria and strategies of ubiquitous learning. In: IEEE International Conference on Sensor Networks, Ubiquitous, and Trustworthy Computing (SUTC'06); 5-7 June 2006; Taichung, Taiwan: IEEE; 2006. pp. 72-77

[15] Temdee P. Ubiquitous learning environment: Smart learning platform with multi-agent architecture. Wireless Personal Communications. 2014;**76**(3):627-641

[16] Weiser M. The computer for the 21st century. Scientific American. 1991;**265**(3):94-104

[17] Chen CC, Huang TC. Learning in a u-Museum: Developing a context-aware ubiquitous learning environment. Computers & Education. 2012;**59**(3):873-883

[18] Hwang GJ, Kuo FR, Yin PY, et al. A heuristic algorithm for planning personalized learning paths for context-aware ubiquitous learning. Computers & Education. 2010;**54**(2):404-415

[19] Gokhale AA. Collaborative Learning and Critical Thinking. Encyclopedia of the Sciences of Learning. Boston: Springer; 2012. pp. 634-636. DOI: 10.1007/978-1-4419-1428-6_910

[20] Huang YM, Liang TH, Su YN, et al. Empowering personalized learning with an interactive e-book learning system for elementary school students. Educational Technology Research and Development. 2012;**60**(4):703-722

[21] Piccoli G, Ahmad R, Ives B. Web-based virtual learning environments: A research framework and a preliminary assessment of effectiveness in basic IT skills training. MIS Quarterly. 2001;**25**(4):401-426

[22] Van Raaij EM, Schepers JJ. The acceptance and use of a virtual learning environment in China. Computers & Education. 2008;**50**(3):838-852

[23] Chou SW, Liu CH. Learning effectiveness in a web-based virtual learning environment: A learner control perspective. Journal of Computer Assisted Learning. 2005;**21**(1):65-76

[24] Pan Z, Cheok AD, Yang H, et al. Virtual reality and mixed reality for virtual learning environments. Computers & Graphics. 2006;**30**(1):20-28

[25] Bruff DO, Fisher DH, McEwen KE, et al. Wrapping a MOOC: Student perceptions of an experiment in blended learning. Journal of Online Learning and Teaching. 2013;**9**(2):187

[26] Chen CM. Intelligent web-based learning system with personalized learning path guidance. Computers & Education. 2008;**51**(2):787-814

[27] Chaichumpa S, Temdee P. Assessment of student competency for personalised online learning using objective distance. International Journal of Innovation and Learning. 2018;**23**(1):19-36

[28] Hwang GJ, Sung HY, Hung CM, et al. A learning style perspective to investigate the necessity of developing adaptive learning systems. Educational Technology & Society. 2013;**16**(2):188-197

[29] Hsu CK, Hwang GJ, Chang CK. A personalized recommendation-based mobile learning approach to improving the reading performance of EFL students. Computers & Education. 2013;**63**:327-336

[30] Shahiri AM, Husain W. A review on predicting student's performance using data mining techniques. Procedia Computer Science. 2015;**72**:414-422

[31] Harun MH. Integrating e-learning into the workplace. The Internet and Higher Education. 2001;**4**(3-4):301-310

[32] Kabassi K, Virvou M. Personalised adult e-training on computer use based on multiple attribute decision making. Interacting with Computers. 2004;**16**(1):115-132

[33] Chen CJ, Liu PL. Personalized computer-assisted mathematics problem-solving program and its impact on Taiwanese students. Journal of Computers in Mathematics and Science Teaching. 2007;**26**(2):105-121

[34] Basuki A. Personalized learning path of a web-based learning system.

International Journal of Computer Applications. 2012;**53**(7):17-22

[35] Tan XH, Shen RM, Wang Y. Personalized course generation and evolution based on genetic algorithms. Journal of Zhejiang University-SCIENCE C. 2012;**13**(12):909-917

[36] Kim S, Song SM, Yoon YI. Smart learning services based on smart cloud computing. Sensors. 2011;**11**(8):7835-7850

[37] Huang R, Yang J, Hu Y. From digital to smart: The evolution and trends of learning environment. Open Education Research. 2012;**1**:75-84

[38] Temdee P, Prasad R. Context-Aware Communication and Computing: Applications for Smart Environment. Cham: Springer International Publishing; 2018. p. 151. DOI: 10.1007/978-3-319-59035-6

[39] Stone A. Online assessment: What influences students to engage with feedback? The Clinical Teacher. 2014;**11**(4):284-289

[40] Verbert K, Manouselis N, Ochoa X, et al. Context-aware recommender systems for learning: A survey and future challenges. IEEE Transactions on Learning Technologies. 2012;**5**(4):318-335

[41] Klašnja-Milićević A, Vesin B, Ivanović M, et al. E-learning personalization based on hybrid recommendation strategy and learning style identification. Computers & Education. 2011;**56**(3):885-899

[42] Das M, Bhaskar M, Chithralekha T, et al. Context aware e-learning system with dynamically composable learning objects. International Journal on Computer Science and Engineering. 2010;**2**(4):1245-1253

[43] Zhang GP. Neural networks for classification: A survey. IEEE Transactions on Systems, Man, and Cybernetics, Part C (Applications and Reviews). 2000;**30**(4):451-462

[44] Tanner T, Toivonen H. Predicting and preventing student failure—Using the k-nearest neighbour method to predict student performance in an online course environment. International Journal of Learning Technology. 2010;**5**(4):356-377

[45] Paliwal M, Kumar UA. A study of academic performance of business school graduates using neural network and statistical techniques. Expert Systems with Applications. 2009;**36**(4):7865-7872

[46] Rashid TA, Aziz NK. Student academic performance using artificial intelligence. ZANCO Journal of Pure and Applied Sciences. 2016;**28**(2):56-69. Available from: http://zancojournals.su.edu.krd/index.php/JPAS/article/view/544/351

[47] Yukselturk E, Ozekes S, Türel YK. Predicting dropout student: An application of data mining methods in an online education program. European Journal of Open, Distance and E-learning. 2014;**17**(1):118-133

[48] Tuparova D, Tuparov G. Automated real-live performance-based assessment of ICT skills. Procedia Social and Behavioral Sciences. 2010;**2**(2):4747-4751

[49] Lin CF, Yeh YC, Hung YH, et al. Data mining for providing a personalized learning path in creativity: An application of decision trees. Computers & Education. 2013;**68**:199-210

Chapter 9

ICT: Vehicle for Educational Development and Social Transformation

Adesegun B. Titus

Abstract

The world has become a global village as a result of the information tsunami and knowledge explosion being experienced as a result of Information Communication and Technology (ICT). The industrialized nations are miles ahead of the developing countries as a result of the information revolution. Education is a process by which society transmits its values, norms, mores, and ethos to generation yet unborn across time and space. The medium of transmission cuts across formal, non-formal and informal settings. This paper examines the impact/roles of ICT on education as an agent of social transformation and the hindrances of developing countries such as Nigeria in adopting ICT to aid their educational development and transformation of the society. The interconnection between information, ICT and social transformations is succinctly discussed in this paper. Furthermore, the paper examines the relationship between ICT and education and suggests measures that can be taken in adopting the use of ICT in Nigeria as well as the crucial role of government and the educational sector in this regard. The paper concludes that ICT make a significant contribution to the educational development and the social transformation of the Nigerian society.

Keywords: ICT, education, development, communication, social transformation

1. Introduction

The Integration of Information Communication and Technologies (ICT) into education takes the front burner in many developing countries of the world, more so with its potentiality of replacing the moribund and outmoded educational system of "chalk and talk" with modern technological tools that makes teaching and learning more meaningful to both the teacher and the taught. Active participation of private investors in driving the information revolution is necessary for the provision of an appropriate framework for social engineering and transformation, as the federal government must not be solely responsible for the provision of necessary wherewithal for ICT to cater for the needs of the entire citizenry. In this era of information boom driven advanced technology, accumulation of information is a major booster for social interactions and dynamics. ICT acts as a catalyst and at the same time a tool for inducing educational reforms thereby transforming our students from mere job seekers to employers of labor that are knowledge and technology driven. The focus on the use of ICT has been the needed impetus for

IntechOpen

the escalation of electronic transactions that transpired between the people and/or organizations in all facets of human endeavor, thereby turning the world into a universal community propelled by technology advancement. As a result of the foregoing, level of interaction of man with the computer, internet and other IT facilities has increased tremendously and this therefore makes it a major player in knowledge dissemination to human societies in the field of education. Based on paradigm shift in the global spectrum tilting towards ICT, stakeholders in the education sector of most developing countries in other to avoid being left behind are involved in the repackaging and redefining of their educational system by focusing on various approaches of integrating ICT into the delivery of instruction so as to improve the quality of both teachers and learners by emphasizing competencies in areas of cognitive disposition, decision making process, management of dynamic situations, teamwork and effective communication, and the development of necessary skills and knowledge required in this digital age [1]. To fully achieve the goal of integrating ICT into education, the federal government of Nigeria in the year 2001 established and published the national policy on Information Technology Development Agency (NITDA) to serve as a regulatory body for the implementation of the policy, nevertheless, this document falls short of tackling the issue of integrating ICT into the Nigerian education system, and without providing the panacea for local/homemade software to cater for the needs of its citizenry nor the method of infusing it into the school curriculum without causing a setback [2]. Further, most countries in the developing world are making concerted efforts aimed at improving their domestic programs for fusion into education curriculum. To avoid the abuse of ICT in education, policy planners must provide a detailed guideline for participants/actors in the education industry for proper fusion of the computer and other ICT features into the education system. As man is dependent on air, food and shelter for survival, such as the magnitude of the importance of information to man as information are no longer seen as a luxury but an indispensable factor for human survival and development. Information is considered today as one of the basic needs of people after air, food and shelter [3]. Due to the increase in level of awareness about ICT in every human facet, the Nigerian government in 2004 introduced a plan of infusing ICT into the educational system at the primary, secondary and post-secondary level of education. The reason for incorporating ICT into education is not far-fetched as its introduction is aimed at reinforcing the effectiveness and efficiency of the education sector to complement the responsibility of integrating IT educational practices into the school system.

2. The meaning of ICT

According to Abimbade et al. [4], they aver that from time immemorial, man has invented various machines for the survival and fulfillment of their needs, but with the emergence of computers the last millennium has witnessed a quantum leap through the level of impact of technological advancement in every sector. Information communication and technology (ICT) comprises of traditional and modern technologies used in the transmission or dissemination of information to a target audience. The traditional ICT products include; the printed pages (newspapers, journals, magazines) radio, and television, films and so on while the modern technologies comprise of email, voicemail, facsimile, internet, automated notice panels and mobile phones, among others.

The scope of ICT is broad and covers areas such as the internet service provision (ISP), mass media coverage, telecommunications equipment services and maintenance, information technology equipment and services, commercial information providers, and other related information and communication activities and international networking activities.

Michel's and van Crowder [5] summed up the meaning of ICT in their opinion as any electric device used for storing, acquisition, processing and, transmission of information by means of voice, sms, chat, text, data, graphics and video. In the words of Ejiaku [6], ICT doubles as a pivot for economic and technological growth through the means of modern scientific development and globalization. For the purpose of maximum efficiency and optimal effectiveness, ICT requires design, installation, configuration, training and maintenance of infrastructure. The emergence of ICT creates a level playing ground in the field of education by granting access to as many people as possible to generate and disseminate information for the end users, thus playing an active role in the education industry.

The concept of ICT in education is premised on four basic features viz

i. ICT as an object- meaning what is learnt about ICT

ii. ICT as a tool of assistance to both the teachers and the students to support learning

iii. ICT as an instrument of instruction

iv. ICT as a tool for organization of management in institutions [7].

2.1 Roles of ICT

Despite the slow response of integrating ICT into education in developing countries of the world, the benefits that accrue and the roles of ICT are numerous that it cannot be waved off. First, ICT being infrastructure-based led to a growing increase in information related activities germane for the socio-economic development of a nation and it lends its support as the fulcrum of complex societies, in the transmission and dissemination of information and guidelines between the various segments of such societies for efficient running of the system [8].

The gains derived from ICT spread across the various strata and this is noticeable in the areas of education (e-learning); job training, healthcare, food security, environmental management, government efficiency, e-commerce, e-banking etc. The influence of ICT on education is robust through the provision of enormous tools for enhancing teaching and learning. The positive effect of ICT on teaching and learning is achievable given the accurate atmosphere and conditions including the provision of appropriate facilities, adequate training and support. ICT also offers the potentials to cater for the learning needs of learners through individualized instruction in which the student learn at his own pace; promotion of equal opportunity to the learners, provision of learning materials (soft wares) and also promote interdependence of learning among learners. It is important to find out the scope of operation of ICTs use and its impact on our societies by concurrently examining its frame and extent of its outreach on a large scale.

Studies have shown numerous support ICT provides in the course of instruction delivery and this covers different fields viz creation of prospects for interaction between learners and knowledge acquisition. Equally some of the vital motives for teachers' use of technology in education include motivations, distinctive instructional abilities, and high throughput of teachers, which are critical skills germane for the information age which also lends credence for the emergence of new techniques.

Communication and access to information can be an empowering social process, therefore, ICT have the potential inbuilt capacity capable of creating a new information and communication models through its end-to-end information and communication flow at a relatively cost. The main role of the teacher is to act as an agent of change especially in the relationship that transpires between the student and technology. Integration of Information communication and technology in education has been the major focus of studies in the past two decades at local, national and international fora. These studies assessed the suitability, importance and application design of available ICT facilities; challenges confronting the use of ICT in the delivery of instruction; for instance social studies in schools and the effects of the computer on students' achievements. Studies conducted recently reveal that there is a strong correlation between teachers' attitude and behaviors towards the use of the computer as a medium of instruction [4].

The successful integration of ICT into education is hinged on the teachers' attitude towards knowledge gained outside of the traditional methods of teaching and their readiness to implement new knowledge acquired through technology. Teachers have the opportunity to modify their instructions and create better understanding with more emphasis now placed on students rather than the teachers and the students having more opportunity to interact with classmates and maximum use of the computer and internet to suit their learning needs. However, many teachers are more confident and comfortable with their traditional teaching methods in place of the modern method hence, ill-prepared, edgy and grossly inadequate using ICT gadgets in educational environments [9]. A study carried out by Anderson and Weert [1] revealed teachers desire to be computer-literate but not using ICT for the purpose of delivering instructions, rather, prefer computer-literacy to computer-application. However in a related study, it revealed the significant relationship that exists between social science teachers' computer level of awareness and computer application leading to a corresponding increase in the teacher's application of computer in their teachings. Further study reveals that emails, internet and other instructional software are packaged in CDs used as computer applications in the classroom by the teachers. ICT doubles as the driving force for growth and source of energy for the social and economic empowerment of developing nations such as Nigeria and as a result leading to a reduction in the level of unemployment could be attributed to the empowerment of the masses through ICT in the emerging Global Digital Network Information Economy.

2.2 Social transformation

Should society be embroiled in the cocoon of customs and tradition or flow with the tide of the information technology revolution that cuts across nations of the world in the last two and a half decades? In other to place this question in the right perspectives, there is an urgent need for social transformation.

Social transformation, therefore, can aptly be described as the tidal waves which brought about an alteration in the social patterns, cultures and values, political and economic relations, and impacted upon local communities and national experience. Going by this definition, the entire universe has become a global village through the means of technology and thus increasing the rate at which both humans and materials travel across countries. When this happens, the concerned sector or an aspect of the society can easily be influenced. Social transformation connotes social change; it is a change for a better quality of life and this implies progress, advancement or modernization. Social transformation can reflect on attitudes including values, beliefs and religion. It can also reflect on material practices, including technology, material customs (family, transportation), built environment (architecture, planning). ICT as an instrument for empowerment and social transformation is yet to be fully actualized as a result of the dislocation in the structural thinking that differs from the pursuit of the much sought change. This accounts for the set-back being experienced by developing countries in applying the theories of ICT as a tool for empowerment and social transformation. The place of education in transforming the society in developing countries is not in doubt and this is reflected in the way society and culture react to political, social and economic disorders. Social transformation has contributed to the development of our nation, Nigeria. Among the notable significant positive effect of social transformation is the reduction in the level of illiteracy in the countries educational facilities as a result of laudable private sector initiatives as well as limited contributions on the part of the government.

Distance learning centers also offer the opportunity of schooling to members of the populace who do not have the wherewithal for full-time program. An example is the Open University system introduced by the Nigerian government and run by various institutions of learning across the country as sandwich or external degree programs in satellite campuses and the open distance learning (ODL) in South Africa which eliminates the barrier of face-to-face classroom teaching and reduction in contact time. The dominance and central control of the internet as a driving force in the process of economic globalization is not a mirage but reality backed up by its intelligence and ability to reach out to the end-to-end users. The emergence of ICT as a game changer triggered major structural changes in almost every facet of human society, birthing a rapid and progressive social transformation.

2.3 Educational development

Education which is a life-long process commences from birth and ends at death i.e. from "cradle to grave." It is a process of continuous training and instructions transferred from the parent to the child; teacher to the learner and learner to learner and of course from the environment to the learner. The essence of education is skill development and knowledge acquisition. Education as a field of study deals with the process of instruction delivery and also acts as an instrument of social change and development that constitute an essential input in the development process itself. In other words, it is concerned with how an individual is integrated into his society; promotes his socio-cultural values and contributes to the development of his immediate environment with the ability to stand on his own and take decisions independently.

Education raises people's level of productivity, creativity and promotes entrepreneurship and technological advancement. Furthermore, it helps in securing economic and social progress for the improvement of the income distribution. Access to different employment opportunities as a result of education leads to the reduction of the poverty level in society. According to Chakraborty et al. [10], education is a precursor and acts as an instrument and an agent of change that prepares the society for a social, industrial and technological revolution. Drawing from the events in the field of education in India, most colleges lack the focus to create employable graduates as their curriculum is defective and only centered on preparing the students to pass exams and thereafter join the labor market seeking for employment. Therefore, there is an urgent need for an update on the current curriculum to meet up with the changing scenario of the world. An education system that does not bring about a change in the life of the recipients is, to say the least, dysfunctional and such should be discarded with without further delay as education is an agent of change in every society.

In recent times there is a shift from indigenous (traditional) education to a technology driven (modern) education all over the world and this could be attributed to the emergence of IT education that resulted in the tsunami in the education industry. This is informed by the determination to correct the anomalies identified in the education curriculum of some developing nations so that they can be at parity with the developed nations of the world.

2.4 Education, ICT and social transformation

Education is regarded as the backbone of national development. Education, therefore, is the key to social transformation. According to Lawal [11], self-realization is achievable through education if, there is proper and effective integration of the individual into the society through a well-tailored socialization process; developing economic, political, scientific, cultural and technological processes. In a world where the only thing constant is change, education acts as that change agent and must be embraced by all and sundry. Education plays a significant social role in this modern, complex and industrialized society acting as a catalyst for social change and transformation. Education initiates, prepares, directs, and determines the nature of social change or transformation that will take place in society. Anyaogu [12] is of the opinion that education is indispensable for human and societal development. It is both the engine of and catalyst to development. As a result of the realization of the importance of education to development, educators from all over the world gathered at Thailand in 1990 at a world conference tagged "Education for All," where a declaration for the eradication of illiteracy was pronounced with Nigeria as a signatory. The relationship between ICT and education are numerous and this has been clearly demonstrated in the developed countries of the world. ICT has been integrated into the various learning environments whether formal, non-formal or informal education. For instance, many people in developed societies have access to ICT gadgets through which they gather much information that affects them or influences their decision making. In formal education, ICT is used in developed countries to achieve a positive result. The use of microcomputers in the classroom in the United Kingdom (UK) has made it easier for teachers to emphasize the practical application of mathematics than ever before [4]. In non-formal education, distance education programs gained global recognition as an alternative form of education due to the introduction of Information communication and technologies (ICT) [13]. The introduction of ICT in the school curriculum resulted in an upsurge in the number of students been catered for and also improvement in the level of instructions. For instance the Saudi Arabian government in other to take learning to the doorsteps of its citizens introduced distance (mobile) learning. To achieve this objective, six sub-structures for higher and distance education were instituted with the following objectives: "(1) to link the electronic-learning educational gateway system; (2) to connect management in electronic-learning; (3) to launch an award of distinction for electronic-learning in university (4) the National repository for learning object Taiseer service for e-learning and (5) the establishment of Saudi national center for e-learning and distance education for e-learning and distance education for university education in the kingdom of Saudi Arabia and; (6) developing the academic and administrative skills and management system, e-learning and distance education, building electronic curriculum contents and forms of digital and print for a number of university courses and to build the educational portal for distance learning and e-learning and awareness program for electronic education and distance education [14]". The integration of ICT into education has become a process whose implications go far beyond rhetoric; it is a technological tool that brings an advancement in the educational milieu. Consolidation of worthwhile learning grew due to the introduction of teaching construction and method of a building based on technological use of education. The ICT revolution is enhanced by the use of educational tools that led to the improvement of the education quality of the students through the use of technological tools such as calculators, TV sets, and voice recorders, among others to facilitate learning.

In 2004, Nigeria took a step similar to that of Saudi Arabia in Abuja, at the conference for ministers in the sub-continent of Africa on "the Integration of ICT in education" and the following sectorial recommendations reached can be summarized as the integration of ICT to cover all strata of education from primary to tertiary education and other areas, such as e-libraries, and ICT in technical, vocational and professional training" [15]. ICT as a means of acquiring information has potentials for social transformation. According to IDRC's Gender and Information working group (GIWG) "Acquiring knowledge is the first step towards change, whether this change is technological, social economic, cultural, legal or political. Information is the catalyst, fuel and product of this process of transformation..." ICT has potentials for far-reaching changes towards development and it can ensure people-centered development that stems from the transformation process. Using ICT as a vehicle for educational development requires careful planning and implementation with the people as the benefactors. It is pertinent to ask at this juncture, of what relevance is ICT in the transformation of the society? What are the major determinants of social change actors? Inspite of different meanings ascribed to social transformation, in this context, it simply implies moving from a class society structure to a classless society structure where there is unbiased sharing of political, economic, social and cultural powers among the people.

2.5 ICT in developing countries towards the promotion of social causes

Concerted efforts are being made in developing countries to use ICT to address social issues or generate information targeted at ensuring an improvement in the quality of life of the people. Social transformation has contributed to the development of Nigeria as a nation. Among the notable possible effects of social transformation is in the area of education where facilities are made available by private organizations, individuals, missionaries, international organizations as well as the government at the federal, state and local government level which result in a tremendous reduction in the number of illiterate persons. The emergence of distance learning centers and satellite campuses of various institutions of higher learning also offer the opportunity of schooling to members of the public who do not have time for full-time university academic program. For example, the national open university (NOUN) introduced by the Nigerian government where course materials are packaged in compact disk (CD) for students to access and this affords the students concerned with the opportunity to learn at their own convenience. In the area of health and education, in Botswana, "Talkback and break the silence" is an educational television program aired on Tuesday 12 noon and it aims at teachers sensitizing their students about combating HIV/AIDS transmission and integration of control mechanisms into teaching and learning. It was reported that the program has a strong effect on the listeners. In Tanzania, Twende Na wakati ("let's go with time") a radio soap opera targeted at reducing the size of the population and fighting the scourge of HIV/AIDS Infection. According to Erwat [16], fifty-five percent of Tanzanians listened to it. The radio program that was aired consecutively for a period of time recorded appreciable success with about 23 % of the listeners reported to have adopted family control techniques and 82% reported a mechanism for preventing HIV. In Bida, Niger state north central of Nigeria, a multi-media campaign approach was used in combating the alarming rate of HIV/AIDS pandemic. The Center for Communications and Reproductive Health Service (CCRHS), Bida, executed the campaign which was funded by the U.S.A. The project sought to educate a target population of 50,000 men, women and youth about safe motherhood, human sexuality and reproductive health and sexually transmitted infections (STIs) in addition to HIV/AIDS. The multimedia facilities used includes- the TV, radio, music/drama outreach programs, radio tapes, visits and workshop/ seminars in secondary schools, posters, handbill and stickers. The result revealed that awareness of HIV/AIDS rose to a 100% against 83.3% on non-awareness in the baseline data. Majority of the population 85% could state birth control methods. Furthermore, 91.6% indicate blood and sex transfusion as a means of HIV/AIDS transmission as opposed to about 12% in the pre-intervention survey data [17] that was carried out.

In Peru, Video-based training has been used to reach rural farmers as part of government effort to bring about reform in the agriculture sector. The use of Audio-visual equipment helped to overcome high illiteracy in rural areas and also maximize the effectiveness of extension agents training activities. One hundred and forty (140) producers and one hundred and twenty thousand rural farmers have been trained and reached respectively by the program [17]. The impact of ICTs social structure on community-based relationship is expressed as a unit big enough (Meso-structure) to accommodate appreciable network effect and equally small enough to cater for local users to maintain their inter-personal relationships. There is equally a shift towards large scale operations but constrained by the availability of sufficient resources to sustain communication across its components.

The pace of development globally is massive especially for ICT-compliant society where big corporate organizations dominate the playing field resulting in a corporate-mediated social paradigm shift. The tempo is unmatched by the production systems put in place as ICT now dictates the policy and the social projects. The scope of their operation is global in outlook and monopolistic in operation, hence bringing about minimal state control. The social paradigm shift necessitated by the introduction of ICT resulted in the changes in the disposition of protagonists for social change and this reflected in roles played by corporate powers within our societies. What are the major roles of ICT in advancing corporate powers in our societies? Firstly, the central/national government has little or no regulatory control over ICT businesses across the globe, because it is mostly private sector driven. Secondly, the inter-connectivity of fundamental social processes of communication, information and association to ICT services empowers information communication and technology (ICT) business operators. Thirdly, pioneers of ICT business capitalized on the paucity of materials given the fact Information communication technology is in an embryonic stage thus outwitting the public sector and seeing it essentially as a private sector initiative. As a result the role of the public sector has been completely eroded. The normal checks and balances which is the prerogative of the government that is absent in the ICT space between public and private actors created a leeway and this shaped the new social information process in an evolving society.

The emergence of ICTs created an enabling environment for conducting business with ease with the outside world and at a cheaper rate as a result of the interconnectivity between communities at a global level. It created a platform to connect with the outside world with access to international markets and various kinds of economic benefits such as banking, employment, commerce etc. Communities' earlier cut-off due to distance are now relieved as a result of ICT which has made the world to become a global village by removing the distance barrier. Such official connections involve a fitting set of new community at the intermediate level to be developed for the moral good of the public. The reason for this is not only to guarantee equal access within the community but to ensure that, the emerging power play in the new dispensation with the outside bodies is not at the detriment of the community. This factor should be consciously borne in mind at the inception of any project before the community begins to utilize ICTs rather than a later date with the hope that things will take shape as utilization of the facilities commence. In the last two decades, ICT has made landmark achievement in the social and economic life of the people, but, this impact is yet to be fully felt in developing countries especially in the area of ICT and ICT4D nations despite its dynamism.

2.6 Hindrances to the adoption of ICT in developing countries

There have been some concerted efforts by developing countries to adopt the use of ICT. Ezeliora [18] listed "computer literacy, inadequate infrastructures, uncertainty, lack and inconsistency of state policy" as some of the problems affecting the effective use of IT. Further works in consonance with the above were carried out to buttress the point raised. UNESCO according to Osokoya [19] reported that schools in developing countries in 1992 registered only 39% girls and 50% boys while in Nigeria UNICEF [20] cited by Osokoya [19] reported that there was a reduction in the general literacy level from 57% in 1990 to 49% in 2001 while that of women reduced from 44% to 41% during the same period. According to current statistics released by the federal ministry of education in Nigeria in 2018, the national literacy level stands at 65.1%; female 59.3% while male stands at 70.9% [21] The problem of illiteracy needs to be tackled in order to break through in the application of ICT in accelerating development without any hindrance. For ICT to be successfully adopted in Nigeria or any developing country, there has to be the full backing of the government in terms of entrenching IT policies. In 2004, agencies of the federal government of Nigeria under the auspices of the federal ministry of education introduced diverse ICT programs namely; library automation project and the Nigerian universities management information (NUMIS) among others but to mention a few.

Anyaogu [12] stated that the availability of ICT resources in developing countries is dependent on the level of effectiveness of government agencies. Nigeria's 90th position according to world IT ranking (The Punch 2006) indicate a level of progress as regards computer integration, while Global information technology report of 2016 ranked the network readiness of Nigeria as 3.2 occupying 119th position among the countries of the world.

According to Abimbade et al. [4] computer education has already been included in the national policy on education, but the detailed curriculum for the primary and pre-primary levels has been prepared but largely inadequate. At the secondary school level, the curriculum recommended has not been fully implemented in many schools due to various obstacles, such as lack of computer facilities, incessant power failure, security requirements, conducive environment and inadequate trained and qualified computer teachers.

Infrastructure is another major problem that needs to be addressed in developing countries so that ICT can easily be used. A recent study on ICT barriers in developing nations revealed that an aggregate of forty-three ICT barriers are common in developing countries [22] and these barriers are classified broadly as economic and socio-cultural; infrastructural, political and leadership, legal and regulatory, educational and skills, technical, security and safety. Other critical barriers identified are lack of internet exchange points (IXPs), invisible hands and micromanaging. In many of the developing countries, the power supply is poor and facilities for internet connectivity are yet to be fully installed. Adomi [23] revealed that Nigeria is at the embryonic stage of connectivity mainly as a result of basic problems with infrastructure; epileptic supply of electricity and the overbearing cost of the internet through a service provider. ICT depends on efficient communication systems and these are lacking. For example in Africa, South Africa accounts for over ninety % of the internet link of the whole African region [24].

Another problem that developing nations need to address is the provision of IT professionals to implement ICT projects. According to Ogunseye [25], the professionals in Nigeria need to be trained to put in place infrastructure to meet the varying needs at the local, national and international levels. In a research carried out by Oladimeji and Folayan [26] on the practicability of teaching and evaluating STM with ICT in Nigeria, the result showed that eighty percent of the samples (Teachers and students) used in the research were willing to be trained in the use of ICT.

3. Suggested roles of government, private sector and educational institutions

There is a need for Nigeria to wake up from her "deep slumber' to meet up with the "information revolution." The adoption of ICT in developing countries such as Nigeria is highly imperative in order to kick start our socio-economic development.

Nigeria's government must ensure that illiteracy is eradicated to meet up with the vision 2015 which is less than a decade from now through the full implementation of Universal Basic Education (UBE) program. There should be proper monitoring and regular evaluation of this Program web and other IT programs to ensure maximum success.

More funds should be released for the building of infrastructure and supply of facilities to equip secondary schools for the proper take-off of the computer education at the post-primary level. Also at the tertiary level, each postgraduate student should be provided with one laptop, similar to a Program on "one laptop per child" in which two junior secondary schools situated in Abuja, were beneficiaries in March 2007 (NTA Nationwide News, 24th Jan, 2008). The government should endeavor to provide stable power supply to nooks and cranny of the nation for effective and efficient performance of ICT gadgets, while training in the use of computer should be accorded its rightful position in our education system, due to its relevance in the development of the system. The training of IT professionals to implement ICT projects should be taken as a priority by the government. IT professionals are needed to make ICT relevant to local and national information and information technology needs. The government should seek the collaboration of private sectors and the assistance of international donors to donate ICT facilities and also reduce the import duties charged on ICT facilities. The education sector and educational institutions should adopt measures for capacity building of the populace to be able to use ICT and also develop ICT culture. ICT should be adopted in the extra-mural to reach more learners through distance education. Mobile learning, (M-learning) could also be introduced and adopted mainly for better outreach and an improvement in the learning experiences of the students through sandwich and external degree programs, a method already in use and with a high success rate in Saudi Arabia. Programmed software relevant to local needs should be developed and packaged for use of students from pre-primary to the post-graduate level of our education system.

4. Conclusion

The place of education as a basic tool for social transformation and modernization cannot be underestimated. A society's level of development is determined by the quality of its education, therefore, for a nation to be on the same pedestal with others it must pay serious attention to the education of its citizenry. People need to be literate in order to take full advantage of the benefits of ICT. It is the backbone of national development and the engine of, and a catalyst for development. ICT is a powerful tool for social transformation with the potential to empower people to affect peoples' lives positively for the purpose of effecting to social change. In other to avoid the risk of being marginalized from the rest of the world, the onus rest on government of developing countries to ensure the growth of ICT so that they can be in the mainstream of information flow. ICT and information are now regarded as major factors in the socio-economic development of every nation. However, for ICT to be a powerful tool to promote social causes, ICT application needs to be packaged to meet the needs of the people and this must be backed up with programs of training and system development for IT professionals who can adopt ICT to suit local needs. The adoption of ICT in a developing country such as Nigeria is an enormous and capital-intensive task that needs the Nigerian government to collaborate with the private sector, the educational sector and assistance of international donor bodies/agencies.

Acknowledgement

I appreciate the Govan Mbeki Research Development Center (GMRDC) of the University of Fort Hare, South Africa for the award of supervisory-linked bursary during my PhD program and also all authors whose work were used and adequately referenced in this chapter for their contributions to knowledge in the area of Information and Communication Technologies. I also extend my immense gratitude to Dr Olugbenga Ige of the department of educational studies at the University of the Free State, Bloemfontein South Africa for his useful comments on the structure of the paper. Last but not least, I would thank the language editor Mrs Seun Amusa who took time to read through this paper and offer useful suggestions to enrich the quality of this work.

Conflict of interest

There is no conflict of interest whatsoever as regards this work.

Abbreviations

CCRHS	Center for Communications and Reproductive Health Service
EFA	Education for All
GIWG	Gender and Information Working Group
NOUN	National Open University of Nigeria
NUMIS	Nigerian Universities Management Information
ODL	Open Distance Learning
OLPC	One Laptop per Child
VIHEAP	Virtual Institute for Higher Education in Africa

Author details

Adesegun B. Titus
Faculty of Education, School of General and Continuing Education,
University of Fort Hare, East London, South Africa

*Address all correspondence to: seguntitus09@gmail.com

References

[1] Anderson J, Weerts VT. A curriculum for schools and program for teachers' development. In: Information and Communication Technology in Education. UNESCO: Division of Higher Education; 2002

[2] Adeyemi TO, Olaoye FO. Information communication and technology for the effective management of secondary schools in Ekiti state, Nigeria. American-Eurasian Journal of Scientific Research. 2010;**52**:106-113

[3] Cambie E-Access to and utilization of quality information in rural development programmes in BAMAO zone of Borno state [thesis]. Ibadan: University of Ibadan; 1992

[4] Abimbade AA, Aremu A, Adedoja GO. Providing information communication technology (ICT). Environment for teaching and learning in the Nigerian education system. In: Ayodele-Bamisaye O, Nwazuoke IA, Okediran EA, editors. Education This Millennium: Innovations in Theory and Practice. Ibadan: MacMillan Nigeria Publishers, Ltd; 2003. pp. 172-188

[5] Michiele BI, Van Crowder L. Discovering the "Magic Box". Local appropriation of information and communication technologies (ICTs). In: Sustainable Development Department. Food and Agricultural Organisation of the United Nations. 2001

[6] Ejiaku SA. Technology adoption: Issues and Challenges in Information Technology adoption in emerging economies. Journal of Information Management and Educational Technology. 2014;**232**(5):59-68

[7] Jager AK, Lookman AH. Lahti: Impact of ICT in education. The role of teacher and teacher training. European Conference on Educational Research 22-25 September 1999. Finland

[8] Sandro MR. Role of ICT in sustainable development. Our experience, Aeronomy and radio propagation laboratory [Internet]. 2009. Available from: http://wireless.ict.it./school-2005 lectures/radicella/G11 and Radio [Accessed: 15 June 2009]

[9] Garba SA. Towards the effective integration of ICT in educational practices; a review of the situation in Nigeria. American Journal of Science and Technology. 2014;**13**:116-121

[10] Chakraborty S, Chakraborty B, Dahiya VS, Timajo L. Education as an instrument of social change and enhancing teaching-learning process with the help of technological development [Internet]. 2018. pp.1-17. Available from: https://www.researchgate.net/publication/325143953 [Accessed: 14 January 2019]

[11] Lawal BO. Comparative Education. Osogbo: Swift Publishers Nig; 2004. p. 35

[12] Anyaogu U. The place of library services in the success of the UBE programme. African Journal of Educational Planning and Policy Studies. 2002;**251**:109-120

[13] Ojokheta KO, Adepoju T. Two-way communication concept and implication for interaction and collaborative learning in distance education. Ibadan Journal of Educational Studies. 2002;**21**:487-494

[14] Fahad A-FN. Saudi-Arabia: Student attitude and perceptions towards the effectiveness of mobile learning at King Saud University. Turkish Online Journal of Educational Technology. 2009;**8**(2):10

[15] Oyelekan OS. An Overview of the status of Information and Communication Technology (ICT) in the Nigerian Education System. African Symposium. 2008;**8**(2):8-14

[16] Erwat EA. Information and communication technology (ICT) and social transformation. In: Nwazuoke LA, Okediran PA, Moronkola OA, editors. Education for Social Transformation. Ibadan: The faculty of Education, University of Ibadan; 2007. pp. 375-390

[17] Yahaya MK. Development Communication: Lessons from Change and Social Engineering Projects. Vol. 44. Ikeja: Corporate Graphics Ltd; 2003. pp. 64-65. 152-160p

[18] Ezeliora B. A comparative analysis of the effect of improvised achievement and interest in chemistry. Journal of the Science Teachers Association of Nigeria. 2003;**3412**:51-56

[19] Osokoya IO. Renovation and renewal of basic education in Nigeria since Independence. In: Proceedings of the International Conference for the History of Education (ISCHE XXVI'04); 13-17 July 2004. University of Geneva; 2004

[20] UNICEF. Literacy education in Nigeria [Internet]. 2003. Available from: http://www.google.com.ng [Accessed: 30 June 2017]

[21] Young adult literacy rate in Nigeria. (state by state) [Internet]. 2018. Digest of Education statistics in Nigeria. Federal Ministry of Education (FME). Available from: http://educeleb.com [Accessed: 01 March 2019]

[22] Touray A, Salimien A, Mursu A. ICT Barriers and critical success factors in developing countries. The Electronic Journal of Information Systems in Developing Countries (EJISDC). 2013;**56**(7):1-17

[23] Adomi EE. Internet Development and Connectivity in Nigeria. Abraka: Department of library and information science. Delta state university; 2005. pp. 45-47

[24] Seye KCM, Sylla F. Rethinking education for production, use and management of ICT. In: Rathgeber EO, Adera EO, editors. Gender and the Information Revolution in Africa. Ottawa, ON, Canada: International Development Research Centre; 2000. pp. 169-186

[25] Ogunseye FA. Prospects for knowledge and information transfer managers in Nigeria in the new millennium. In: Oyedele-Bamisaiye O, Nwazuoke IA, Okediran A, editors. Education this Millennium: Innovations in Theory and Practice. Ibadan: Macmillian Nigerian Publishers, Ltd; 2003. pp. 124-143

[26] Oladimeji TT, Folayan GB. ICT and its impact on National Development in Nigeria: An overview. Research and Reviews: Journal of Engineering and Technology. 2018;**7**(1):5-10